GOD'S NATURE and the END OF THE AGE

"Tell us, when will these things will happen, and what will be the sign of Your coming, and of the end of the age?" Matthew 24:3 NASB

BOB PALUMBO

Copyright © 2019 by **Bob Palumbo**

All rights reserved. No part of this publication may be reproduced, distributed or transmitted in any form or by any means, without prior written permission.

Bob Palumbo/Plumbob Press
Avon Lake Ohio
www.bobpalumbo.com
God's Nature and the End of the Age/Plumbob Press.

Scripture quotations are taken from an online source, Bible Gateway (www.biblegateway.com), from the New American Standard Bible (NASB) Copyright 1960, 1962, 1963, 1968, 1971, 1972, 1973, 1975, 1977, 1995 by The Lockman Foundation. Used by permission.

All rights reserved.

FOR HIS BELOVED BRIDE

"It has been my earnest endeavor ever since I have preached the Word, never to keep back a single doctrine which I believe to be taught of God. It is time that we had done away with the old and rusty systems that have so long curbed the freeness of religious speech. The Arminian trembles to go an inch beyond Arminius or Wesley, and many a Calvinist refers to John Gill or John Calvin as any ultimate authority. It is time that the systems were broken up and that there was sufficient grace in all our hearts to believe everything taught in God's Word, whether it was taught by either of these men or not...If God teaches it, it is enough. If it is not in the Word, away with it! Away with it! But if it be in the Word, agreeable or disagreeable, systematic or disorderly, I believe it."

Charles Haddon Spurgeon

THE COVER PHOTO

The background for the cover of this book is a picture of a half-painted wall, of course.

When I first saw it, it instantly captured (at least in my mind) the separation of the two extremes I am attempting to portray in this book...chaos vs order...darkness and light, and the contrast between the fallen state of mankind....and the future glory of our new and eternal condition, which is our blessed hope in Jesus Christ. As you can tell, the grey wall is being painted over with a crisp, clean covering of white, not unlike a fresh falling of the winter snow that completely hides whatever is hidden beneath it. Is that not what our glorious redemption reveals, a fresh and clean covering for whatever lies beneath it?

Is that not what the Lord did when He provided a better and more suitable covering for Adam and Eve after they had sinned? I believe that was, not unlike the cover photo for this book, a perfect picture of God's divine nature and His perfect love for us. As the Scriptures tell us...He makes all things new. And I, for one, am very grateful for that.

Bob Palumbo

Table of Contents

FOR HIS BELOVED BRIDE iii
THE COVER PHOTO iv
PREFACE vii
INTRODUCTION xiii

PART ONE:
GOD'S NATURE IN THE HISTORIC

1. ORDER OUT OF CHAOS 2
2. THE UNCHANGING GOD 8
3. THE SUBSTITUTION FACTOR 16
4. A CATCHING AWAY? 25
5. A GOD OF PROMISES 33
6. THE SPECIALNESS OF TWO-NESS 42
7. TRIED BUT NOT FORSAKEN 50
8. I'LL TELL YOU WHAT I'LL DO 59

PARENTHETICAL PAUSE #1
A GATHERING OF THE SUMMONED 65

PART TWO:
GOD'S NATURE IN PROPHETIC PATTERNS

9. "TEST THE SPIRITS…" 76
10. GRECO-ROMAN WRESTLING 84
11. "NOW I LAY ME DOWN TO SLEEP" 93
12. THINGS SEEN, YET UNSEEN 103
13. DO NUMBERS REALLY MATTER? 113

14. THE IMPORTANCE OF SEVENS 119

15. "RAPTURO" IS A LATIN WORD 127

16. "AN ENEMY HAS DONE THIS…" 137

PARENTHETICAL PAUSE #2
LOST IN TRANSLATION 144

PART THREE:
GOD'S NATURE IN FUTURE EVENTS

17. THE WEEK IN REVIEW 166

18. "SUMMER IS NEAR…" 176

19. "AS IN THE DAYS OF NOAH…" 183

20. "TELL US WHEN…" 192

21. THE FORK IN THE ROAD 206

22. THE MAN OF SIN REVEALED 219

23. THE GREATEST TRIBULATION 234

24. "AFTER THE TRIBULATION…" 242

FINAL THOUGHTS
NOT WHEN YOU THINK… 263

ABOUT THE AUTHOR 273

PREFACE

"Awake, Sleeper..."

But all things become visible when they are exposed by the light, for everything that becomes visible is light. For this reason, it says, "Awake, sleeper, and arise from the dead, and Christ will shine on you." [Ephesians 5:13-14 NASB]

On the morning of November 5th, 1979, I arose from my bed on a rather normal morning, a workday seemingly like so many others before, yet this one would be different. I stumbled to the coffee pot and with sleepy eyes, made a fresh pot and wandered to the door to get the morning paper. The first thing I noticed was the headline on the front page (usually I bypassed that and went straight for the sports page), "Fifty-Two Americans Taken Hostage in Iran." That was my first clue that this was not going to be just another day, but I had no way of knowing how different it would be.

At this point in my life, I was twenty-five years old, married for just a little over a year with two daughters, one from my wife's first marriage and one of our own who was just five months old. I had a good job as an Ironworker, just like my father before me. He had been elected as head of the Ironworker's Union a year before I graduated from high school, so I immediately went into the apprenticeship and had been doing that type of work for about seven years. Back then, it seemed to be more of an honor to follow in your father's footsteps than it is today. But maybe that is just my view of it. I know it was an honor for me. My father was of Italian descent. My mother's maiden name was Jones, and her mother's maiden name was Kennedy, so I am roughly half Italian, mixed with a combination of English, Irish,

Scottish, and German ("a Heinz mixture," as they used to say).

As a child, I was christened in the Catholic Church, made my first communion and confirmation as a Catholic, and my wife and I were married in June of 1978 in the Catholic Church. If someone were to ask me if I believed in God or if I believed that Jesus died for my sins, I would say, "Absolutely." But that was about as far as I went with it. My wife, Lauri Lee (who grew up a Lutheran), and I went to church regularly, and our daughter, Jessica, was christened in the Catholic Church, as well. But I will also tell you that from about the time I was around sixteen, I was beginning to have questions about many of the things the Catholic Church taught as doctrine.

[Before I go any farther, I want to make sure you all understand. I have no intention, in this book, to throw stones at the Catholic faith, or any other religion. I have many wonderful family members and friends who are still Catholic, and that is fine by me. They are great people and I believe their faith in God is sincere. I am just talking about my experiences and the questions that were surfacing in my mind. It is not my desire to knock anyone else's faith. The Bible says in Romans 14, "The faith that you have is your own with God," and I believe that. I respect people of all faiths, even though my beliefs may be different. It is not for me to judge, and I will do my best not to, so help me God.]

So, it was around that time that I started going steady with a girl who was Presbyterian, and I would go with her to their church, occasionally, and found that I enjoyed it. It was fresh and different, and it seemed to not have as many rituals attached. I was also surprised to see that people took their Bibles with them to church and were even encouraged to read it. That was certainly not my experience in the Catholic Church. The Catholics believed that only the priests were spiritually equipped enough to understand the Holy Scriptures. Needless to say, a spark of curiosity ignited in my soul and I began to explore other ways of interacting with God Almighty.

Apparently, I was not the only one searching for answers in those days. I had read a book called, "Chariots of the Gods" by Erich von Daniken and another called, "The Late, Great Planet Earth" by Hal

Lindsey. I stumbled upon all of this around the time of the Viet Nam War. It was a byproduct, I believe, of all the war protests, that many young people became part of what we now call "The Jesus movement." I had read about this and was quite intrigued. So yes, I was beginning to be open to the idea that there was more to the concept of God than I had learned in church or my catechism classes and I was becoming hungry for answers.

But, let me go back to the 5th of November 1979, before I wander too far off the subject, here (as if I haven't already). Later that same evening, a good friend of mine showed up at my house quite incidentally (so I thought), in response to an ad I had in the newspaper to sell some musical equipment. He and I had been in a rock band together in high school, and he had come over to look at the gear I was selling. He did not know it was my house, nor did I know it was him that was coming. We had not seen each other in about seven years, and I was shocked to find out that he was now a pastor of an evangelical church. It was at this point that I began to think this chance meeting was not all that coincidental. Thank you, Lord!!

After we had looked at the equipment, we sat down to catch up a bit before he shoved off and I asked him how in the world he had ended up becoming a pastor of a church. He explained that while in college, he had accepted Christ and became involved with some of the campus ministries and that after graduating, one thing just led to another. That caused me to bring up some of my own questions about my Catholic upbringing, the Bible, and what his church believed. He told me that they believed the whole Bible, from cover to cover, and embraced the full Gospel of Jesus Christ. What stuck out, for me, was that he kept saying God was more interested in having a relationship with us, than He was in religion. I honestly had never heard anything like that before. Was that true? I had to find out.

As you may have guessed, every one of his answers checked off boxes on my "questions list" and over the next hour or so, Lauri Lee and I became convinced that we wanted to have a deeper relationship with God, so we prayed and received Jesus Christ as our Lord and Savior. From that moment on, nothing was quite the same. For months after that, whenever I saw news reports on TV regarding the hostages in Iran, they would say, "This is Day 185 of the hostage situation in Iran," I would respond, "And this is Day 184 of my freedom in Christ, who sets the captives free!!"What a great way to remind myself of how profound that change in my heart, and in my life, would become.

Over the next few years, I probably read more books including the Bible, of course, and heard more preaching based on the totality and reliability of the Holy Scriptures than I had read or heard in my entire life. I was learning so much and the more I learned, the hungrier I became for spiritual wisdom. It was truly incredible, especially for me. Before that, I was not much of a "book reader." But, out of everything that I was learning, there was one subject that not only caught my attention but seemed to have all the other Christians I knew buzzing, too. That subject was, of course, the End Times and the Second Coming of Jesus Christ.

I guess you could say, as I became more and more exposed to the light, the sleeper inside me was awakened. Dawn was breaking on a new and glorious day. And for someone like me, who loved to dig deep into the details of such things, this subject was (and still is) very fascinating to me. There were countless books and theories out there, and believers seemed to be "all over the map" as to which one was right (or maybe I should say...which one they believed). There was pre-tribulation, mid-tribulation, post-tribulation, pre-millennial, post-millennial and even some minor variations of all the above, depending on who you talked to or whose book you were reading at the time.

I was soaking it all up. I wanted to know as much as I could about all the theories so that as I read my Bible and matured in my faith, I could figure things out for myself. Years later, I am still learning and still trying to put all the puzzle pieces in place. The Bible says in 1 Corinthians 13, "For we know in part...but when the perfect comes, the partial will be done away with." So, maybe we will never get it all figured out, at least not during our time here on Earth. Nevertheless, it sure is fun trying to connect all the dots. I wanted to make sure my family and I were ready, should these things happen in my lifetime. Don't you? Not only that, even if I were to die before these things happened, what I was learning was readying me for entering the kingdom of God, when my time here was finished. I saw that as a "win/win situation."

So, why did I decide to write this book? And, why do I feel qualified to write a book like this? Good questions. For starters, I have never been a pastor or called into full-time ministry. And, no, I do not have a degree in Divinity or Theology from a Bible college or Seminary. So, what are my credentials, and more importantly, why do I believe God has led me to do this and why should anyone listen to anything I have to say on the subject?

I would like to answer that in two parts:

1) I have been studying this subject intently for thirty-eight years. I have studied all the different theories and timelines thoroughly, and I feel I have a pretty good grasp of the differences and similarities. That's important because there are a lot of similarities and those are usually a good place to start. Then you can take more time and carefully sift through the differences. I believe I have done so, and I do see clear differences. I am going to try to highlight those differences in this study, so you can decide for yourself.

2) My goal here is not to favor one theory over another, and I will try hard to avoid using second-hand information or the opinions of men (or women) to fill in the gaps in order to make my conclusions more believable. For me, there is only one criterion to meet, is it biblical? What does the Bible say? I believe the Bible tells us everything we need to know to get from this life to the next. God does not want us to have to guess. He was very clear about this stuff, I'd say.

So, this is meant to be a book that is not about Bob's opinions, or anyone else's, for that matter. It is not a book that is going to endorse one man's theory over another. As I said, I am not into labels or tags. I only want to know what God intends for us to know, plus or minus nothing. Also, as we will see, I believe if we truly understand God's nature and how He handled things in the past, it makes it easier to decode the signs and prophecies pointing to future events.

My goal is to present a simple, clear case for what the Bible teaches about the End Times and the return of Christ. I refer to my view of these matters is, "The Natural Order Theory." I call it that because I believe God's Divine Nature is unchanging and what He has done in the past is how he will interact with us in the future. So, you won't hear me quoting bible scholars, theologians or translators, not because I don't think they have anything important to offer, but because I believe God's Word says it all.

So, whether you are a new believer, have been a Christian for many years, or just someone searching for answers, I believe the answers are right in your Bible, and they are not that hard to understand if you look at the big picture.

After all, this is His story. He said it all. I am just passing it on, as so many others did for me. And may I say, I truly hope you enjoy this study, and that the light of God's grace may lead you accordingly.

INTRODUCTION

"The Bible Tells Us So…"

Moving on from my story and how I got to where I was itching to write a book on this incredibly fascinating subject, let's talk a little bit about the book itself. What is it about this book, that makes it different than the hundreds or thousands of others written on this subject?

From the very first time I thought about taking on this monumental task, I had one overriding thought. I had no desire to write a book that simply parroted what others, on all sides of this debate, had written or taught before. I was only interested in doing my very best to ascertain what God's intentions might have been, from Day One, for bringing about the culmination of His earthly endeavors. "Thy kingdom come, Lord, thy will be done on Earth as it is in Heaven." May it ever be so!!

Let me also be very clear. I had no desire to write a book that merely supported a pre-tribulation argument or a post-tribulation one, or any of the other popular views, for that matter, because my heart tells me that God is neither "post-trib or pre-trib." His ways are higher than that. These theories are all interpretations conceived by man, all with good and sincere intentions mind you, but I certainly did not want to put my name on a book that would seem to elevate the concepts of man to the level of the heart of God. That is not to say, however, that I think I know God's heart better than anyone else. I am sure I do not.

NOTE TO THE READER: Since it is not my intention to slight those who believe in one theory over the other, I will affectionately refer to those who believe the rapture will come before the tribulation period as those who favor an "early departure," and those who believe it will come after the seven years of trouble as those who lean towards a "late check-out." I think it is okay to have a little fun with this since it can be such a heavy and controversial issue at times. After all, these are not "salvation issues" or "core Christian beliefs" we are talking about. These are secondary matters of Christian doctrine, and certainly not worthy of causing division between the people of God (which is a nice way of saying, "I hope you don't "unfriend" me after reading this book").

My goal is to dig deeper, beyond the usual verses and connecting dots so often used to confirm one view or another, to see if there are other factors to be considered since it is such an important subject. I felt there had to be more to all of this than just what we have heard so far. However, was I qualified to be the one to discover the missing pieces? I honestly was not sure, but I had it in my heart to try my best to do so.

So, I prayed and thought and thought and prayed some more. It took a while, but I finally stumbled on what I thought was a line of thinking that was not only worth digging in to, but one that could also uncover some key elements that had previously not been part of these discussions. And once these new elements are added to the mix, I began to believe they could potentially clear up many of our questions and make our conclusions more in line with Scripture, as a whole. Now, I was getting excited.

For starters, two important things occurred to me:

To truly understand the Master's Plan, we first must get to know the Master and His divine nature. The Bible teaches us that He does not change. So, how God has interacted with His children before, especially in times of trouble, is most likely how He will involve Himself with us in the future, So, that is the first underlying premise for this study.

Jesus Christ is the same yesterday and today and forever. [Hebrews 13:8 NASB]

This book you hold in your hands is my third book, by the way, but the first one on this subject. However, I only recently noticed as I started doing the research and pre-planning for this one, that there is one common thread running through all three of my books...discovering God's true nature. The first book was called, "Unlocking Creation: God's True Nature Revealed." The second one was called, "The Red Letter Parables: Introducing Jesus As Master Storyteller." So, the focus of the first one was to discover God's divine nature through all that He has created. The second one pointed to how God's divine nature was revealed through His Son, Jesus Christ, and the memorable stories He told. I guess I should not have been surprised, then, that maybe the way I was going to find the missing pieces to the end time puzzle, was by doing another deep dive into a study of God's divine nature.

So, hang in here with me, if at times you feel like I am taking the long way around the block only to end up at the same place others have. One of the "men of God" I greatly esteem (and the man who led me to Christ) did me a tremendous favor by reading and reviewing my first draft of this book. He said, "I think you might have two separate books here, not one." While I certainly do understand his point, for me, I think it is impossible to fully grasp my conclusions without understanding how God has revealed Himself in the past, especially in times of trial and tribulation. So, I believe (or, at least, hope) it will be worth it in the end. After all, God Himself took the time to patiently unfold four thousand years of human history (what we call the Old Testament) before revealing a new and better covenant in His beloved Son, Jesus Christ.

I think it is safe to say that it is impossible to fully understand the wonder and beauty of the redemption that Christ provided for all who call on His name without a clear understanding of just what it was He redeemed us from, the power of sin and death. The laws that God gave to Moses may have provided some prudent guidelines for human behavior, but those same laws, in and of themselves, had no power to save.

He has revealed His plans to us not only through His holy prophets but through His Holy Word. I am sure that God has not told us everything, but He has revealed everything we need to know to get us from "Point A to Point Z."

> ***I testify to everyone who hears the words of the prophecy of this book: if anyone adds to them, God will add to him the plagues which are written in this book; and if anyone takes away from the words of the book of this prophecy, God will take away his part from the tree of life and from the holy city, which are written in this book. [Revelation 22:18-19 NASB]***

These were the words of the Apostle John, the same John who wrote the fourth Gospel and revealed so many new key elements about the "Good News of Jesus Christ." He taught us that Jesus was the living Word of God who became flesh and dwelt among us and that He was also with God in the very beginning. Jesus was also the one who taught Nicodemus, a high priest of the Jewish faith, that he needed to be "born again," if he hoped to see the Kingdom of God.

So, I guess if he tells us to be careful not to add anything to this book, or take anything away from it, we should probably take heed. We shouldn't think that we need to be Greek or Hebrew scholars to figure it all out, either. It's all there, from Genesis 1 to Revelation 22. One ongoing and unchanging story in which God has been putting His divine nature on display for all to see, if we choose to do so (isn't that the beauty of it all…Jesus implied that if we choose not to…we wouldn't be able to see it anyway…I love that).

In a nutshell, then, those were my goals for writing this book. First, by looking at how the Lord chose to interact with mankind in the past, to reveal the aspects of God's nature that are relevant to understanding "the end of the age" and explain, with the help of Scripture, why they are so important. Then, I will begin to plug in these new elements, one by one, and see how they might help us to understand the "end time order of events," as I believe God chose to reveal them. He even spoke through the prophet Isaiah regarding the value of understanding the past as a way to help us understand the things yet to come:

> ***"Remember the former things long past, for I am God, and there is no other; I am God, and there is no one like Me, declaring the end from the beginning…saying, 'My purpose will be established, and I will accomplish all My good pleasure';" [Isaiah 46:9-10 NASB]***

To do this, and do it well, I felt I had to set some guidelines about what I would include in my reasoning and what I would not include. And it was here that I felt that I might "step on a few toes," because all the modern end-time scenarios I have read and heard about have relied upon, to some degree, interpretations, and views of godly men and women who have gone before us. Some were preachers. Some were authors. And others were Bible scholars who worked on various translations and included their opinions on these things in their study notes.

Now, again, I have no desire to discredit or criticize them, personally. I do not doubt that what they did was bathed in prayer and carefully pursued with the best of intentions. But for me, and for the scope of this book, I only want to rely on God's Word. I believe it is enough. Nothing needs to be added to arrive at the right conclusions. In fact, if we add or subtract from it, we may be veering away from the path that leads to truth. That is not something I was willing to risk.

From time to time, however, I will include some historical information that will help us clarify some things. History is not "man's opinions," it's history. So, I felt justified in doing that for our purposes here.

After all, it has been two thousand years since Jesus was born, died and was resurrected. The sacred writings and traditions of the faith have gone through many changes, even though God has not changed. So, I think some of these things are important to this discussion, as well. But again, when I do bring up various religions or belief systems, I will not be doing so to besmirch what others believe. I will only be pointing to the stepping stones that have led us to where we are as the body of Jesus Christ, today, and how that might affect what we believe regarding the final days leading up to the return of our King and beyond.

So, let me thank you up front, for taking the time to read this book. I greatly appreciate it. And if you can, try to resist the temptation to flip to the back of the book and jump right into my conclusions (I know that is what I would be thinking, I confess).

My hope is here, that not only will the signs and prophecies we have all struggled with over the years begin to come into better focus, as we look at them through the lenses of God's divine nature. But, I also pray that you might acquire a greater understanding of God Almighty, Himself, in the process. And that, I believe, would hopefully enhance every part of your Christian walk, as it has mine.

Like the song says, *"To know, know, know Him...is to love, love, love Him."*

May we all only grow to know Him better, as the day of redemption approaches.

Part One

GOD'S NATURE

IN THE HISTORIC

"The things which you have seen..."

(Revelation 1:19)

CHAPTER ONE

ORDER OUT OF CHAOS

Whenever I think about the Bible in its entirety, I am constantly amazed by the cohesiveness of these miraculous writings. Sixty-six books penned by around forty authors (the exact number has been debated for years), most of whom never had the opportunity to meet or even speak to each other, at least to compare notes. And one thing that sticks out to me, as I think about Bible prophecy, the end of the story seems to point to the beginning and the beginning most certainly points not only to the end of this world, as we know it, but it also clearly points to another new beginning of a much more permanent nature.

So, before I start digging into the specifics of how this world will end, I felt we should take a fresh look at how this incredible story began. I think it is vitally important to have a firm grip on where we have been, or maybe I should say where we have come from, to be able to fully understand where we are headed. Let's start out with some verses from the first few chapters of Genesis, as I believe they set the stage for everything that was to follow:

> *In the beginning, God created the heavens and the earth. The earth was formless and void, and darkness was over the surface of the deep, and the Spirit of God was moving over the surface of the waters. [Genesis 1:1-2 NASB]*

It says that in the beginning, the earth was "formless and void." I take "formless" to mean that the world was "without order," like a lump of clay that had not yet been shaped into anything useful or creative. And I would think of "void" as meaning "empty" or "without purpose." That leads me to think of the "pre-creation world" as one of chaos. In fact, if you look up the word "chaos" at Dictionary.com, you will see they define it as "complete disorder and confusion" and "the infinity of space or formless matter supposed to have preceded the existence of the ordered universe." When I saw that, I almost fell out of my chair. I was surprised that they would refer to the creation of the universe in their definition, in particular, describe it as a state of chaos. Very interesting, indeed.

But that is what chaos is, a lack of order, form, and purpose. Why would you bother to create something out of nothing, if not for a distinct purpose? So, we can safely assume that it is part of God's divine nature to create order out of chaos, to take that which has no form or purpose and change into something both orderly and purposeful. It is sort of like writing this book. I am hoping to turn all these random thoughts and observations into something purposeful and enlightening. After all, God did make us in His own image. I would like to think I am "a chip off the ol' block" in that way. But, this "chip" needs a lot of help from the "chip-maker," trust me.

Why take on such a monumental task, just to create something useful and then just let it go like pulling the string of a top, not knowing where or how it would all end, with sort of a "let's see what happens" attitude? That is not the God I have come to know. His thoughts and ways are not only thorough and complete, but I believe they are also predictable (not because we are so smart, but because He has chosen to reveal them to us). He is, indeed, a "revealer," is He not? From Genesis 1 to Revelation 22, he has done nothing but reveal who He is and His attributes, that we might know Him.

> *Then God said, "Let there be lights in the expanse of the heavens to separate the day from the night and let them be for signs and for seasons and for days and years; and let them be for lights in the expanse of the heavens to give light on the earth"; and it was so. God made the two great lights, the greater light to govern the day, and the lesser light to govern the night; He made the stars also. [Genesis 1:14-16 NASB]*

In this excerpt from Genesis 1, the creation story, God is again "revealing" something very important to our study, here, and it is quite prophetic, as well. The lights in our sky are multi-purpose. Yes, they provide light for our daytime hours and less light (which is quite beautiful, too) for our nights. But they were also designed to be "signs" by which we could mark and measure intervals of time. And now, of course, we rely heavily on those "time signatures" (I am a musician, so it just sounded right) to mark our days, our months and even our years.

In my first book, "Unlocking Creation," I went into great detail as to how God revealed aspects of His nature and character through the things He created. I won't go into it that as deeply, here, but we should keep the premise in mind. God intentionally gives us ways to measure the passing of time and to help us learn when certain things are likely to occur, all by these same heavenly markers. We should make good use of them. In this book, it is my hope and prayer to do so.

Lately, we have been treated to all sorts of "heavenly light shows." Blood moons, tetrads (four blood moons in short succession), solar and lunar eclipses and even things like solar flares seem to be popping up quite regularly. These events, of course, were studied and talked about in a physical sense for the pure beauty and scientific value of such things, no doubt. But, those who have a fondness for God, as the Creator (and a curiosity for the prophetic relevance that they might hold), they were having their own conversations about what they might mean in a spiritual sense, as well, regarding what lies ahead on the biblical timeline.

> *Then God said, "Let Us make man in Our image, according to Our likeness; and let them rule over the fish of the sea and over the birds of the sky and over the cattle and over all the earth, and over every creeping thing that creeps on the earth." God created man in His own image, in the image of God He created him; male and female He created them. God blessed them; and God said to them, "Be fruitful and multiply, and fill the earth, and subdue it; and rule over the fish of the sea and over the birds of the sky and over every living thing that moves on the earth." [Genesis 1:26-28 NASB]*

The crowning achievement, most would agree, was God's making of mankind in their own image. I am saying "their" because in the passage above it says, "in Our likeness." It is plural. No, I am not saying there is more than one god. May it never be!! The Bible is clear that God is made up of three distinct persons; the Father, the Son, and the Holy Spirit. Each one of them has a unique function and role within the Godhead. But, collectively, they are One God. Even the Hebrew word used for God in Genesis 1:1, Elohim, is a plural word. In Hebrew, the suffix "him" at the end of a word denotes plurality. And this aspect of God being three persons, one God, also has a prophetic significance because each of the three persons would play a role in the coming of a Messiah, a Savior and, of course, end time scenarios, as well.

This biblical truth, stating that God created man in His own image, has another important prophetic factor, I believe. God has great plans for mankind, eternal plans. Did God ever make any of the other creatures, including Lucifer and the angels, in His image? He did not. Could that have been a little bit of "salt in the wound" for the devil? Do you think that when he found out that God created these new creatures in His own image, maybe he felt a bit slighted? Oh yes, I suspect that was somewhat of a "bone of contention" for the prideful one. And he has not gotten over it to this day.

I believe that is why he went after Adam and Eve and tempted them. And I believe that is why, to this day, he is working so hard, going after each of us to try to keep us from receiving God's promises. Let's just call it what it is, good old-fashioned jealousy. He is basically saying to God, "If I cannot inherit Your kingdom, I am going to do my best to see that none of your kids do, either."

Last, but not least, let's talk about a little time off. I think God earned it:

> ***God saw all that He had made, and behold, it was very good. And there was evening and there was morning, the sixth day... Thus the heavens and the earth were completed, and all their hosts. By the seventh day, God completed His work which He had done, and He rested on the seventh day from all His work which He had done. Then God***

blessed the seventh day and sanctified it because in it He rested from all His work which God had created and made. [Genesis 1:31; 2:1-3 NASB]

For those of us who are students of biblical prophecy and for those who are interested in learning more about such things, there are a few widely accepted "attention-grabbers" that the Lord revealed right from the beginning and they appear over and over again, all through Scripture. And since one very important key was revealed in the first few chapters of Genesis, I thought I should talk about why it is so important and how it might be used going forward, all the way through the Old Testament, the New Testament and, not surprisingly, all through the Book of Revelation.

Of course, I am referring to the number seven and, as we will see, even multiples of the number seven. We will be talking about the significance of certain numbers many times, in this book. So, I wanted to do a little explaining, here, so later we can better understand how these things are all connected, prophetically.

God revealed this "principle of sevens" very early in the biblical narrative by simply creating everything in the universe in six days, stepping back and saying, "It is good," and then giving Himself a "day of rest" on Day Seven. Now mind, you, I do not believe God required six days to do His amazingly creative work. I believe He chose to allow it to take six days, specifically, so He could reveal this principle as a pattern for us to follow. Most Bible experts believe the number seven is God's perfect number regarding temporal things, matters of importance in this world. They would also point to the number twelve as God's perfect number regarding eternal things, as we will see.

And so then, we are told that "God blessed the seventh day and sanctified it" (the word "sanctify" means to "set apart" or to deem something as "holy"). So, I'm suggesting that we need to take special notice of anything God reveals that has a connection to the number seven…seven days in a week…the Sabbath…the seven feasts…the seven churches…the seven lampstands…the seven trumpets and of course, the seven years of great tribulation which we will be talking about a lot in this book. The number seven is sort of like God saying, "Pay attention…this is important!!" Yes, even the use of numbers has order and purpose to it. If God does something, you can count on it to have meaning and be purposeful. It is who He is at His core...orderly and purposeful.

So, in this chapter, we have pointed to four examples of how God displayed his "orderly nature" in the things He has made:

1) He created all things and turned a formless and purposeless void into something beautiful and orderly.

2) He gave us lights in the heavens as signs by which we could mark our days, seasons and years.

3) He created mankind in His own image, that they might also be creatures of order and purpose.

4) He gave us a pattern of six days of work and one day of rest. And I do not think that is something we should glaze over or take lightly, especially when we talk about the end times, as we will see.

So...do I think that things will be any different when the end of this age comes? I do not. And the reason is, not only is He a God of order, He changes not.

THERE IS A TIME FOR EVERY EVENT UNDER HEAVEN
[ECCLESIASTES 3:1]

CHAPTER TWO

THE UNCHANGING GOD

Next, I would like to dig a little deeper into the story of Adam and Eve and see what else we can uncover regarding the things yet to come and how God's nature might play into it all. I know I touched briefly on the subject of God's unchanging nature earlier. But, if we are truly going to gain a fuller understanding of who God is, and be able to understand why it is so important in helping us understand how things will unfold as we approach "the great and terrible day of the Lord" (as it is described in Scripture), I think we need to expand our investigation a little more. Don't you?

If I were pressed to make an educated guess as to what is one of the main tripping points people have in understanding God, I would have to say it is this idea of a person, a thing, or an entity having no beginning, no end and never changing, not one iota. That goes against everything we have seen and experienced in this life, here on Earth. We tend to think that everything has a start and has to end somewhere, right? So, the idea of God not having a start and not having an end is quite hard to swallow.

Hey, I am right there with you, folks. It boggles the mind. And, if you add to that, the fact that we are led to believe that this eternal being, the One with no beginning and no end, chose to create a universe that had a distinct beginning and is apparently not without an end as He is, well my goodness, it is no wonder that the fuses of our minds are blowing.

But, before we veer too far off the path, past the creation story and on to juicier fruit, I believe there is a lot more to learn from the story of the world's first two humans and their fall from grace. Let me say, I believe there was more happening here than just God creating the first "lovebirds," who then chose to pick and eat fruit from the wrong tree.

BTW...did you know that Moses, when writing this story (whether he realized it or not), was giving us a sneak peek into the Gospel? If not, you are not alone. I didn't have a clue, either.

So, if I may, I would like to point to five words that we will be talking about a lot in this book because for me, they are the five governing principles of God's divine nature and His intended purposes, as they relate to both creation and the things yet to come. These five little nuggets are found right at the beginning of God's earthly endeavors, in Genesis 2 and 3, which should not be all that surprising. After all, they set the tone for what was to come. And they not only point to the Good News revealed during the Lord's first appearance on Earth, but I believe they also point to the culmination of all earthly things, as we know them, when He returns a second time and establishes His eternal kingdom.

Without any further ado, then, may I present to you, "The Gospel According to Moses." It is a series of five "C" words that clearly lay out the progression from a place of blessing and providence to a fall from grace and ultimately to a plan of redemption and restoration. Isn't that just like our God? He is not making things up as He goes, is He? No, He is a God of order who plans things well in advance, as we shall see. Step One...set the ground rules:

- Commandment: ***Then the Lord God took the man and put him into the garden of Eden to cultivate it and keep it. The Lord God commanded the man, saying, "From any tree of the garden you may eat freely; but from the tree of the knowledge of good and evil you shall not eat, for in the day that you eat from it you will surely die." [Genesis 2:15-17 NASB]***

Here we see that the Lord clearly and specifically gave Adam one rule to follow regarding the trees from which they may and may not eat. This was the first commandment from God to His new creations.

Step Two...provide some help:

- Companionship: ***Then the Lord God said, "It is not good for the man to be alone; I will make him a helper suitable for him." [Genesis 2:18 NASB]***

Immediately after the commandment was given, God decides that being human should not be a solo experience. He chose to have a relationship with us, and He saw fit that we should desire to have relationships with others, as well.

Step Three...define the failure:

- Conviction: ***They heard the sound of the Lord God walking in the garden in the cool of the day, and the man and his wife hid themselves from the presence of the Lord God among the trees of the garden. Then the Lord God called to the man, and said to him, "Where are you?" [Genesis 3:8-9 NASB]***

So, the commandment was given, and a suitable mate was provided for the man. But then, they fell into temptation and disobeyed God. The serpent convinced Eve it was alright for them to eat the forbidden fruit and she did so and then, shared some with her husband, as well. Both had done exactly what God commanded them not to do. Sin had officially entered the world. But I do not want to move on without taking notice of how God confronted them about their sin. Of course, God knew where they were, but they were hiding from Him because they realized they had done wrong. Sound familiar? Don't we sometimes hide from God when we realize we have sinned against Him? Some things never change.

Step Four...make clear the cost of non-compliance:

- Consequence: ***To the woman, He said, "I will greatly multiply your pain in childbirth, In pain you will bring forth children; Yet your desire will be for your husband and he will rule over you." Then to Adam He said, "Because you have listened to the voice of your wife, and*** *have eaten from the tree about which I commanded you, saying, 'You shall not eat from it'; Cursed is the ground because of you; In toil you will eat of it all the days of your life. By the sweat of your face You will eat bread, Till you return to the ground, Because from it you were taken; For you are dust, And to dust you shall return." [Genesis 3:16-17,19 NASB]*

It is important to point out here that before there was forgiveness for our two apple-eaters, there was a consequence. The serpent was judged and penalized. Eve was given a harsh sentence, too, as was Adam. Sin had changed everything. Before they had disobeyed God, they were designed to live forever in the Garden of Eden, and everything they needed would be provided. Not anymore. Sin has consequences…period.

Step Five…provide a way of healing and restoration to, once and for all, make things right again.

- Covering: *The Lord God made garments of skin for Adam and his wife and clothed them. [Genesis 3:21 NASB]*

God, then, did provide a covering (or forgiveness) for their sins, so to speak. He provided them with clothes to hide their nakedness. But if we look back at verse 7, before God called to Adam, they realized they were naked and tried to provide their own covering (they sewed fig leaves together) and tried to hide from God. The fact that the Lord provided more suitable clothing for them says, "Our efforts to cover our own sin will never be sufficient. Only God's grace is sufficient, and only He can provide the type of covering we truly need."

But what does all of this have to do with the end times and the return of Christ? I would say it has everything to do with it. Without Adam and Eve falling into sin, Jesus would not have had to come the first time and become the "Lamb of God who takes away the sin of the world." And He certainly would not have to come to Earth a second time to redeem His children out of this wicked and perverse world we now live in, right?

Keep in mind, our God is a "revealer." He reveals who He is through His prophets and His Word. And He clearly revealed from the beginning, that Christ would come a second time to restore all things, so that we may receive what was promised long ago. In other words, He intends to provide a more enduring "covering" for His children, a permanent dwelling place where sin will reign no more, just as He provided a better covering for Adam and Eve.

Those coverings God made from animal skins were quite symbolic (or should I say prophetic) of what was to come, as well. Even when we read about the Third Temple that is going to be built (Revelation 11), will they not again begin to offer animal sacrifices to provide the Jewish people covering for their sin? And will the Antichrist not come along and discontinue those sacrifices (Daniel 9:27)? The Bible says those things will happen. So, a covering provided by animals is pretty important, both then and in the future, too. But we know that a better covering was to come through Jesus Christ, for all who put their trust in Him…and Him alone.

God made sure we knew that sin and death will be conquered in the end, make no mistake about that, but it was not going to be easy or quick. God chose to give mankind "free will" and because of that, things will have to run their course. God cannot just step in and bring things to a sudden finish before the appropriate time and before evil has a chance to fully manifest itself. If He did, then it truly would not have been "free will" at all. It is important to understand that, especially in light of all the suffering in the world around us these days. The fullness of time has not come yet. Oh, but it will…and quite suddenly, my friends.

But bear with me a moment, if you will. This next portion of Scripture is also an important key and one that is many times overlooked when people talk about Bible prophecy:

"And I will put enmity between you and the woman, and between your seed and her seed; He shall bruise you on the head, and you shall bruise him on the heel." [Genesis 3:15 NASB]

After Adam and Eve disobeyed God and ate of the forbidden fruit, God came to them for an explanation of what happened. Adam was quick to blame his wife and Eve, of course, blamed the serpent. Sound familiar? Six thousand years have passed, but not much has changed. Blame-shifting is still a "go-to strategy" when dealing with other people…and if we are honest…sometimes even in dealing with God.

But what I want to highlight, here, is the first judgement that God decreed in the entire Bible. It was a prophetic promise of punishment to the serpent (who we learn in the Book of Revelation was the devil, Satan himself). He is telling the serpent that, going forward, there is going to be "bad blood" between the woman and him…between her seed and his seed (which I interpret as the children of God and the children of the devil). What is interesting is that God says her seed will bruise him on the head (which sounds fatal) and he will bruise her on her heel (which does not sound fatal). God is telling the serpent there would be an ongoing battle, of sorts, between the powers good and the evil. But, in the end, there would be a winner, a survivor, if you will, and it would not be the devil or his offspring.

We need to keep that in mind as we move forward, because so often when people talk about Adam and Eve and the fall of man into sin, the underlying "seed war" gets swept under the rug. But, I cannot suggest strongly enough that to do so is a mistake. When we talk about the trials and tribulations we endure as humans, I believe it has a lot more to do with the ongoing "seed war" than just sneaking a piece of forbidden fruit. But more on that a little later.

As a reminder, then, let me just say that God is not surprised by anything. Things will happen just as God said they would happen. We will not be able to say we were not warned. I think the Apostle Peter summed it up best, in Acts 3, when He spoke of the return of Christ:

> ***But the things which God announced beforehand by the mouth of all the prophets, that His Christ would suffer, He has thus fulfilled. Therefore, repent and return, so that your sins may be wiped away, in order that times of refreshing may come from the presence of the Lord; and that He may send Jesus, the Christ appointed for you, whom heaven must receive until the period of restoration of all things about which God spoke by the mouth of His holy prophets from ancient time. [Acts 3:18-21 NASB]***

Notice the words, "that He may send Jesus, the Christ...whom heaven must receive until the period of restoration of all things" and "that times of refreshing may come from the presence of the Lord." Think of that as sort of a "revival of the Garden of Eden." Things will be as they were before the fall of man. You see, "until the period of restoration of all things" sounds quite different from "until a time of great tribulation." So, I take that to mean that Jesus will remain in heaven until it is time to set things right, to defeat His enemies and once again establish His Kingdom. It is by His arrival and His presence that the "times of refreshing" will come. It does not say we will be whisked off to where the refreshing is, until some years later when His enemies are defeated. Big difference. But, again, I am just looking at what the Bible says, at face value...not the theories of men. I think we have gotten some skewed information over the centuries, as many well-intended people have tried to "read between the lines."

The moral of the story, in this chapter is...He is not One to change and He was looking for a people who, once they have accepted His invitation to be joined to Him, would stay the course and, to the best of their ability, resist all temptations to be unfaithful until the very end, no matter what.

And that is going to be another important key as we move forward. God is looking for people who are willing to endure to the end. As Jesus said in Matthew 24, "the one who endures to the end will be saved." No one said following Christ would be easy. Jesus certainly did not suggest that.

Our take away from the failings of Adam and Eve, I believe, is that God is righteous, and He desires for His children to be righteous. And when they are not, there are consequences for sure, but there is also a plan to preserve, redeem and restore those that are His. Satan's works of corruption are not permanent. They will be negated, and things will be put back as God intended them to be from the beginning and that plan, like the Lord, Himself, has not changed.

In the next chapter, I want to take a good look at what happened when God's first two children had children of their own. And, of course, since sin and death had now entered the picture, need I say,

"It was not a pretty family portrait." Yet, it does paint a picture of something that I think will play a big part in how things will play out in those final days.

YOUR WORKS MAY PERISH, LORD, BUT YOU WILL ENDURE
[PSALM 102:25-26]

CHAPTER THREE

THE SUBSTITUTION FACTOR

In the last chapter, we dove into the story of Adam and Eve and discovered how that story was used to lay the groundwork for the Gospel of Jesus Christ and even set the stage for what is yet to come. I would imagine you would not be surprised to learn that when they decided to have children of their own, the plot continued further down that path, and yet another key aspect of the divine nature and character of God was about to be revealed. Say hello to Cain and Abel:

> *Now the man had relations with his wife Eve, and she conceived and gave birth to Cain, and she said, "I have gotten a manchild with the help of the LORD." AGAIN, SHE GAVE BIRTH TO HIS BROTHER ABEL. AND ABEL WAS A KEEPER OF FLOCKS, BUT CAIN WAS A TILLER OF THE GROUND. [GENESIS 4:1-2 NASB]*

So, it seems that in a relatively short time, the first loving couple decided to create others "in their own image," too. That is also a key, as we will see. God often does His work, just as with creation, as an example for us to follow or emulate. Just as he worked six days, creating the universe, and rested on the seventh (a pattern for us to follow), Adam and Eve also followed a pattern God established by choosing to have children of their own who, not surprisingly, were a lot like them physically and otherwise. I have always gotten a kick out of the fact that our children resemble us, not only in physical appearance but often, in our quirks and mannerisms too. And, they say God does not have a sense of humor. Yeah, right. But, unfortunately, this happy family did not stay that way for long:

> *So, it came about in the course of time that Cain brought an offering to the LORD OF THE FRUIT OF THE GROUND. Abel, on his part also brought of the firstlings of his flock and of their fat portions. And the LORD HAD REGARD FOR ABEL AND for his offering; but for Cain and for his offering He had no regard. So Cain became very angry and his countenance fell. [Genesis 4:3-5 NASB]*

As the story goes, God was pleased with Abel's offering, but not Cain's (most point to the fact that Abel's gift was from the firstlings, or first fruits, and Cain's was not), so Cain became distraught to the point that he eventually killed his brother, Abel.

Another interesting part of this story is that in Hebrew, Cain's name means "spear" or "possessed." When I read the verse that says Cain's countenance fell because God did not regard his offering, one could say he was "possessed" or "overcome" by hatred for his brother, and that led to him giving in to the temptation to take Abel out of the picture. Meanwhile, Abel's name means "breath" or "son" and isn't that exactly what Cain decided to do away with, Abel's breath, to eliminate any further competition between them? We should also note that to take someone's breath from them, as Cain did to Abel, is synonymous with "taking their life." Remember, God "breathed life into Adam." Breath and life are not independent, and I believe as we shall see a bit later, a key factor in understanding what happens when our time on Earth is finished. So, hold on to that thought.

And, if we look at this story and compare it to the life of Christ, what did the enemy try to do with Jesus? He tried to negate the threat to his kingdom. Rather than make peace with God, himself, he decided that preventing the Lamb of God from becoming the One who would pay the price for the sin of mankind was a good plan. Of course, he failed to realize that it would not solve his problem with God. While he might be able to cause mankind to not receive the promise of forgiveness and redemption through Jesus Christ, Satan would still be at odds with his maker.

But, there was yet another problem that needed to be addressed. The Lord was looking at the bigger picture, the one where eventually a plan of redemption would have to come to light, and there was this matter of bloodlines that was now in jeopardy. Cain had become the first murderer and now, the "only son," while Abel had become his first victim. Surely, since Cain would not be a good candidate for a "blameless lamb of God" to come through, there needed to be another option at this point. Again, God was not surprised. He had it covered.

Adam had relations with his wife again; and she gave birth to a son, and named him Seth, for, she said, "God has appointed me another offspring in place of Abel, for Cain killed him." [Genesis 4:25 NASB]

Well, wouldn't you know it, Seth's name means "anointed" or "compensation." So, then, God was providing a substitute for Abel, one who would be worthy of preserving the bloodline of the Messiah. And what was Jesus? Was He not a substitute who took our place and our punishment on the Cross? Isn't it amazing how early in Scripture we see these patterns and precursors developing? The whole Gospel is contingent upon God providing a worthy substitute. And it turns out that he did the same thing with Abel and Seth, as well. As I said before, He is truly an "unchanging God," and one who knew the end from the very beginning.

But, before we go any further, this concept of providing a "substitute" needs to be examined a little further in light of the entirety of Scripture and, of course, the End Times. There is the question of "first-born sons" to handle. We read about "first fruits" and many times we hear about a promise to "first-born sons." But, if we look throughout the biblical narrative, it did not always hold water.

To show you what I mean, I would like to ask a few probing questions:

1) Who found favor with God, Cain or Abel?

2) Who inherited the paternal blessing of Abraham and his descendants, Ishmael or Isaac?

3) Who received the birthright and paternal blessing of Isaac, Esau or Jacob?

4) From which of Jacob's twelve sons did the Messiah descend? Was it the first-born son, Reuben or the fourth son, Judah?

5) Which son of Jesse became God's chosen one to replace Saul? Was it any of his first seven boys, or the eighth son, David?

6) Which son of David inherited his throne, his first son, Absalom, or one who came later, Solomon?

7) And to take this one step further, which covenant will eventually bring about the salvation of God's people, the first one made with Moses and the Law, or the new covenant established with God's beloved Son, in whom He was well-pleased?

Do we see a pattern developing, here? It seems God has used "substitutes" many times to bring about His ultimate will. Do I think those were mistakes that God made and later, chose to correct? I do not. I believe just as with the number seven, the Sabbath, and with Adam and Eve having children of their own, God was setting forth patterns for us to "keep an eye on" as the Day of the Lord draws near.

So, is there another "substitute" we need to be looking for in the days ahead? I would say, "Yes there is." I would say there are two more, to be truthful. But I want to be careful how I explain the first one because this is one of those things that I believe has been misunderstood and used to advance end time philosophies that I believe are not completely biblical. So, bear with me here, if you will.

Abraham was the father of Isaac. Isaac was to be sacrificed by Abraham, but God spared him and provided a substitute sacrifice. Then, Isaac fathered Jacob, who was the twin brother of Esau. We are taught that when Esau and Jacob were born, Jacob was holding onto Esau's heel, some have even speculated that Jacob was trying to be the first-born, even from the womb. His name means "supplanter" or "holder of the heel" and wouldn't you know it, Jacob colluded with his mother, Rachel, to trick Isaac into giving him Esau's blessing. And that was after Jacob talked Esau into trading his birthright to Jacob for a bowl of stew. And it was Jacob, who eventually "wrestled with God and prevailed." Hence, his name was changed to Israel, which means, "one who wrestles with God."

So, we see Israel as being the nation named after the one who tried to get his father's blessing by conniving and through deception... and someone who "wrestled with God" to get a blessing of his own. Interesting, isn't it? Are we to invoke God's favor by trickery or by our own strength or cunning? Of course not. Could it be that there would have to be another "substitute" who would arise and receive God's inheritance and promises in a way more in line with what the Bible teaches about the nature of God? Well, yes, I would say so.

But this is where it gets tricky. Nowadays, there is this teaching called "dispensationalism." It means that there will be different manifestations of God's nature interacting with various people or groups at various times. To boil it down a bit, many believe that God will deal differently with the nation of Israel and the Jews than He will with the church, by that I mean those who accepted Christ's work on the Cross (not a particular denomination, religion or faith). Let me just say, up front, I agree with that (somewhat), but not in the way that some dispensationalists understand it.

Yes, I believe that God will treat those who have accepted Christ, God's only-begotten Son, as their Lord and Savior, differently than those who reject Him (as the Jews did when He came the first time). But it will not be because Christians are loved more or more highly favored by God. The only reason anyone will not be welcomed into God's kingdom with open arms will be because they refused to accept the selfless sacrifice of His Son on the Cross. Nothing else matters, eternally. Like Jesus said, "You are either for Me or against Me." There is no middle ground. Therefore, if a Jew (either by birth or religion) comes to accept Christ as his Savior and Messiah (as many Jews have), he or she will be saved, as well.

So yes, I do believe God is again raising up a people who will go about seeking the Lord the right way, by accepting the "free gift" of eternal life" that the Apostle Paul talked about in the Romans 6, which was the forgiveness we have in the blood of Jesus. And no, I do not believe the Kingdom of God can be earned or entered by trickery or even human effort as the namesake of the nation of Israel tried to do. It can only be received by grace, through faith in the blood and work of Jesus Christ on the Cross.

And, I also want to make this perfectly clear, the Apostle Paul was a "Jew among Jews." Before encountering Christ, he was a champion of the Jews and an enemy of the followers of Jesus. Yet, he thought it was important enough to say two different times in Scripture that there is no longer any difference between the Jew and the Greek, or Jew and Gentile…they are made one through Christ who is Lord of all. BOOM…go the dispensationalists!! Here are the two passages:

> ***For the Scripture says, "Whoever believes in Him will not be disappointed." For there is no distinction between Jew and Greek; for the same Lord is Lord of all, abounding in riches for all who call on Him; for "Whoever will call on the name of the Lord will be saved." [Romans 10:11-13 NASB]***

"WHOEVER BELIEVES IN HIM WILL NOT BE DISAPPOINTED." Again, this was a man who was highly regarded as a defender of the Jewish faith saying this. He is now saying, "There is no distinction between Jew and Greek." That is a big deal. He eventually died for his boldness in proclaiming this message. But he believed it to the point of being willing to do so. Then, he adds another statement worthy of all caps (by the Bible translators…not me), "WHOEVER WILL CALL ON THE NAME OF THE LORD WILL BE SAVED." It sounds like he is adding a little insult to injury to those who are still clinging to the laws and the traditions of the Jewish faith by saying, "You must call on Jesus, our Messiah if you are to be saved and forgiven of your sins." It does not sound like he is keeping the Jews separate from anyone else. No, quite the opposite. He is saying it does not matter if you are a Jew or a Greek. Only Christ and His blood that was shed on behalf of all mankind can save you from your sins.

> ***But before faith came, we were kept in custody under the law, being shut up to the faith which was later to be revealed. Therefore, the Law has become our tutor to lead us to Christ, so that we may be justified by faith. But now that faith has come, we are no longer under a tutor. For you are all sons of God through faith in Christ Jesus. For all of you who were baptized into Christ have clothed***

yourselves with Christ. There is neither Jew nor Greek, there is neither slave nor free man, there is neither male nor female; for you are all one in Christ Jesus. And if you belong to Christ, then you are Abraham's descendants, heirs according to promise. [Galatians 3:23-29 NASB]

Here again, we have Paul saying, "faith was shut up" (or had not been revealed through Christ yet), so "the Law was our tutor," not our salvation. But now, that Christ has come, "we are no longer under a tutor," we have become sons through Christ. He goes even farther here, destroying dividing lines by saying, no Jew and no Greek, no slave or free man and neither male or female. Those distinctions have all been torn down. We are either "in Christ," or we are not. That is now the only distinction that remains. Nothing else matters.

There will be tribulation and distress for every soul of man who does evil, of the Jew first, and also of the Greek, but glory and honor and peace to everyone who does good, to the Jew first and also to the Greek. For there is no partiality with God. For it is not the hearers of the Law who are just before God, but the doers of the Law will be justified. [Romans 2:9-11;13 NASB]

And lastly, here Paul says, "there will be tribulation and distress for every soul," first the Jew and also the Greek...and peace to everyone who does good "for there is no partiality with God." I wanted to talk about all of this because it is going to be extremely important when I get into the specifics of what I believe regarding the End Times.

No, I do not believe some will go through the Great Tribulation and others will be spared. I believe people of all nations and faiths, of those who are yet alive at the time, will go through those terrible years and see great tribulation, as Paul taught. But, I also believe those who are "in Christ," those who have "applied the blood of Christ to the doorposts of their hearts" (as we saw with the Passover when the angel of death "passed over" the homes who applied the blood) will be preserved and protected through the storm, like Noah, not removed from the Earth prior to it.

Up next, then, I want to take a good look at the story of Noah and the Ark. I cannot think of a better one to illustrate God's righteous ways and how He chooses to relate to those of us who seek His righteousness, faithfully in our hearts, and those who do not. It also is a great example of how God chooses to preserve those who are faithful, even in times of trouble, rather than plucking them out of the way altogether. Hmmm…this ought to be interesting.

Oh yes, as I suggested, there is yet one more "substitute" we should talk about briefly, and it is one we all (no matter which end-time scenario we embrace) should be looking very much forward to:

Then I saw a new heaven and a new earth; for the first heaven and the first earth passed away, and there is no longer any sea. And I saw the holy city, new Jerusalem, coming down out of heaven from God, made ready as a bride adorned for her husband… and He will wipe away every tear from their eyes; and there will no longer be any death; there will no longer be any mourning, or crying, or pain; the first things have passed away." And He who sits on the throne said, "Behold, I am making all things new." [Revelation 21:1-2;4-5 NASB]

Yes, no matter how we think "the end of this world as we know it" may unfold, what is going to be revealed after those things will be glorious, to say the least. And again, I do not see whatever end-time theory a believer in Christ embraces as being a "salvation issue.' All that matters, truly, is if we have put our hope and our trust in Jesus, the Messiah, and our Lord and Savior.

But I did want to touch on the new heaven, new earth, and new Jerusalem briefly. It is very important. As we mentioned, Abraham was asked to sacrifice the son who he loved, Isaac. And it happened to be on the same mountain where the Temple Mount now sits. After God provided the substitute sacrifice, Abraham named the place "God will see," and the words "will see" can be translated into "yireh" in Hebrew. That is the first half of what became the word Jerusalem. The second half of it, of course, comes from the word "Shalem" or "Shalom," which means "peace.'

So, the final substitute (or maybe I should say "upgrade") will be, if I have connected the dots properly, God bringing about His ultimate peace in the very place that Abraham said God would see it revealed, "Yireh Shalem," or in English, "God Will See His Peace." New Jerusalem will not only be the place where God's peace is finally revealed. Scripture says, it will be the Bride of the Lamb in Revelation 21:9 and I feel very confident in my heart that this glorious new city, the Bride of the Lamb if you will, will not be a divided one with one section for Jews, another for Christians, and another for Muslims (as Jerusalem is now). No, I firmly believe "all things will be made new," and the city will be united under the banner of Christ, Jew and Gentile alike, the name by which all of the redeemed shall be saved.

THERE IS NO OTHER NAME BY WHICH WE MUST BE SAVED
[ACTS 4:12]

CHAPTER FOUR

A CATCHING AWAY?

In the first few chapters, we have established that God, by nature, is one who creates order out of chaos and that He is a God who is stable, consistent and changes not. We have also discovered that God very often provided a substitute to bring about His perfect will. And that is all fine and good, providing of course, His intentions towards us are loving and kind and merciful. Let's face it, His adversary, Satan, is consistent and unchanging, as well. But his intentions are not good... they are evil.

The Scriptures are full of references to God's nature, at its core, being "for our good and not our harm." The most well-known verse on the subject is, of course, from the Apostle Paul:

"And we know that God causes all things to work together for good to those who love God..." [Romans 8:28 NASB]

Therefore, we can hitch our wagon to the promise that God is good and only wants what is best for us. That is a great place to start, is it not? Paul tells us that "all things" are for our good, even the things that are unpleasant or even painful. I know that might seem a little odd, but God knows what is best in the long run, that which will achieve the fulfillment of His ultimate will. So yes, we are permitted to endure (and by His grace overcome) some difficult things in life that, if we were to choose, we would most likely prefer to avoid. But, rest assured, our struggles never are without a good and godly purpose.

Like the song says, "He's got the whole world, in His hands," and that includes you and me, no matter what we may be facing.

So, keep this thought in the back of your mind, as well. Just as with the weightlifter or the sprinter, we are often reminded that life is not often easy. If we are to achieve something great, there is often resistance. "No pain, no gain," as they say. God designed us that way. And, so it is with our relationship with Him and His will. The greatest victories are often the result of our greatest struggles, are they not? Did I mention David and Goliath...talk about a mismatch? It looked like David had no chance of survival. But God was with David, and that changes everything.

When we think about the hardships of life, not even as they may apply to the end of the age, just life in general, we should take comfort in three words often used in the Bible to describe God. He is righteous, fair and just. That is good to know, is it not? I mean, if you are going to put your physical life into someone's hands, let's say a doctor or a surgeon, for instance, you want to make sure they are good at what they do, and you would want to know that they truly want you to be well, right? So, it was with a man named Noah.

The story of Noah and his Ark is a great one when looking for examples of how God dealt with people in the past for a couple of reasons. One reason is that God chose to deal differently with Noah than He did with all the rest of the people who were alive at the time, except for the seven members of his family (there is that number again) who were spared along with him. I believe God was showing us that He is more than able to judge certain people harshly (if they deserve it), while at the same time, sparing others from judgment. He is the original and the ultimate "multi-tasker."

> **Remember the words of Peter who said, "then the Lord knows how to rescue the godly from temptation, and to keep the unrighteous under punishment for the day of judgment, and especially those who indulge the flesh in its corrupt desires and despise authority." [2 Peter 2:9-10 NASB]**

After all, we learn in the Bible that God sometimes uses others to execute judgement, which is why He allowed the devil to stick around as our tempter and tormenter (the rod of correction, if you will), while He remains as ths single source of all blessing. However, we do see many times in Scripture that God is quite capable of allowing both to occur at the same time. He may bless and protect those that are His, while simultaneously judging those who are not. The story of Noah and his family certainly is a great example of that.

Speaking of God and His orderly ways, have you ever read through the instructions for building the Ark that were given to Noah? Not exactly, "There is going to be a great flood, so go ahead and build a great big boat. You are smart. You'll figure it out." Or how the Lord specified that Noah should gather all the animals by twos (one male and one female…so they could repopulate the earth.). Pretty darn orderly was it not, and with a very distinct purpose in mind…repopulating the earth with both man and beast. Ummm…hold on a second. If the earth was going to need repopulating, that sounds like God was planning to un-populate it. Cha-ching…you got it!!

God also did not vary from the original plan, as it was coming together. Even though it took over a hundred years for Noah to make it all a reality, God never changed His mind. And, of course, the point of building the Ark in the first place was that judgment was coming upon the earth, upon the wicked ones who had strayed from His path, just as Adam and Eve did. But…He was also showing us that He was quite serious about righteousness and obedience. After all, He is holy, and He desires that His children be holy, as well. And let us not forget what we saw with "the five Cs." Sin has consequences, and death is one of them.

What I would like to do now is comment on some of the key verses from this story, in the order in which they appear in the Bible. I suspect, as always with God, order is important. Then, I will highlight a few often overlooked, or intentionally skipped aspects you don't usually hear much about, whenever the story of Noah is taught or discussed.

Have you ever asked yourself, "Why was the world so wicked before and during the days of Noah?" Could it be true that the entire human race, except for one family of eight, became exceedingly wicked just because one man and one woman ate the forbidden fruit from a tree that God said not to eat from? Or, were there other factors that contributed to the corruption of mankind, as well? In my opinion, Genesis Six is quite clear about that.

> ***Now it came about when men began to multiply on the face of the land, and daughters were born to them, that the sons of God saw that the daughters of men were beautiful; and they took wives for themselves, whomever they chose... The Nephilim were on the earth in those days, and also afterward, when the sons of God came into the daughters of men, and they bore children to them. Those were the mighty men who were of old, men of renown. [Genesis 6:1-2, 4 NASB]***

Well, now that is a strange kettle of fish. It seems that there were fallen angels (called sons of God there) who found the daughters of men beautiful, took them as wives and had children with them. So, apparently, there were many who were infected by the seed of these fallen angels. And then, it spread to nearly all the people of those days when they reproduced, getting to the point where God finally said, "they only do evil continually."

I do, also, want to pause and talk about one peculiar word from this passage because it would be easy to glaze over it as if it were just another nation or tribe back then. Who were these Nephilim spoken of here? In the King James Version, the word is translated as "giants." And, as it says, they were sometimes referred to as "the mighty men of old" or "men of renown." Clearly, they were special, most likely in size or physical stature and strength. But, because they were born of fallen angels, the resulting descendants were corrupted. A strong case could be made that after a few generations, these "demon seed" beings could have been quite great in number, if not by far, the majority.

Talk about taking the "seed war" to another level. If the seed of the serpent was now breeding with the seed of the woman in large numbers, we can easily see that the chances of there ever being a "sinless one" worthy of being the Messiah or Savior of the world would quickly evaporate, hence leaving mankind saddled with their sin and separated from God forever. Game, set, and match for Satan and his minions.

Now, before you toss this whole thought-process aside as "fringe theology," remember that Abraham encountered tribes of giants (Rephaim...Genesis 14:5). And so did Joshua and Caleb (Anakim... Deuteronomy 2:10). And, we also know that young David faced off with maybe the most famous of these overgrown offspring, Goliath, the Philistine champion.

Keep in mind, in each of these instances, God caused His chosen ones to prevail. That is hugely important. One of God's other attributes is to cause His children to stand victorious whenever they step out in faith, even when it appears that they are greatly outnumbered or at a sizeable disadvantage. He always has, and He always will.

> ***Then the Lord saw that the wickedness of man was great on the earth, and that every intent of the thoughts of his heart was only evil continually. The Lord was sorry that He had made man on the earth, and He was grieved in His heart. The Lord said, "I will blot out man whom I have created from the face of the land, from man to animals to creeping things and to birds of the sky; for I am sorry that I have made them." But Noah found favor in the eyes of the Lord. Noah was a righteous man, blameless in his time; Noah walked with God. [Genesis 6:5-9 NASB]***

From what the Scriptures tell us, only Noah and his family's bloodline had not been infected. In the New King James Version, it says Noah was "perfect in his generations," which I believe means that his family's bloodline had not been corrupted. It seems God found Noah to be more righteous, not necessarily sinless, than the rest of the folks walking the earth at that time. So, He chose to start civilization over again, wiping out the wicked ones and using Noah and his family as good soil and good seed to repopulate the earth.

Numerous times, when Jesus walked among us, He spoke of good seed and bad seed. The Parable of the Sower and the Parable of the Wheat and the Tares are good examples of this. And I do not believe it was just a coincidence that Jesus used to make his stories more interesting. I believe He was fully aware of the ongoing "seed war" and its implications going forward.

Remember, it was through Noah's bloodline that the Messiah would eventually come, so God supernaturally protected them even though the enemy was trying to corrupt all flesh so that Jesus could not come and redeem us. No wonder the world had become evil to the point where God had to step in and neutralize the spread of the infection by eliminating all those except Noah and his family, eight people in all.

All the rest were corrupt and had to be destroyed. Isn't that interesting, it is right there in our Bibles, yet it is seldom talked about. I would think it should be considered a major biblical plot point and one that we should all be aware of, since the Bible implies it will likely happen again right before Jesus returns to take us home.

And that leads me to the second reason why the story of Noah is so important to our main topic of discussion in this book. Jesus, Himself, pointed to the story of Noah as something to consider when looking for signs that His return is fast approaching. Here is what He told His disciples when they asked about the signs of His return:

"For the coming of the Son of Man will be just like the days of Noah. For as in those days before the flood they were eating and drinking, marrying and giving in marriage, until the day that Noah entered the ark, and they did not understand until the flood came and took them all away; so will the coming of the Son of Man be. Then there will be two men in the field; one will be taken, and one will be left. Two women will be grinding at the mill; one will be taken, and one will be left. [Matthew 24:37-41 NASB]

Yes, the earth had become exceedingly wicked and was filled with violence, and now we know why. So, I believe in Matthew 24, Jesus was telling His disciples (and generations to come) that the world would be a very wicked and violent place, again, right before He returns to redeem us, as well. It doesn't sound like Jesus was telling them, "Don't worry, I'll be back to get you before things really get bad." Before the flood came, things had already gotten extremely bad, and I believe Jesus was saying that is how it will be again before He returns to claim His Bride.

But the good news is that God made a covenant with Noah. He made him a promise that He would save him and his family from the coming flood by providing them safe passage through the storm. Now, while we do not know exactly how long it took for Noah to build the Ark, it was about 120 years from when God first told Noah of the coming flood until it began raining (see Genesis 6:3) and God never wavered or changed His mind. What He said He would do, He certainly did. And Noah believed God and trusted that "He changes not" every step of the way, even when everyone around him was laughing and mocking and calling him a silly fool.

Before moving on, I would like to zoom in on the last two sentences of the passage from Matthew 24. Isn't it interesting that these two verses are lumped together with the ones where Jesus is talking about how the world will be "as the days of Noah," right before He returns in the latter days? He says this:

Then there will be two men in the field; one will be taken, and one will be left. Two women will be grinding at the mill; one will be taken, and one will be left. [Matthew 24:40-41 NASB]

God sent a great flood upon the earth. The unjust were punished (or should I say removed), while at the same time, the godly ones were preserved (or should I say remained) throughout God's time of judgment. The Lord provided them "safe passage." Some people refer to the flood and Noah's Ark as the "first rapture," and I can understand their reasoning. But it raises a question, "Who was taken, and who remained on the earth?"

Maybe we have jumped to a wrong conclusion, there. We have always been taught that these two sentences are a picture of the "good ones" being taken away and the "bad ones" being "left behind." Jesus talked about the days of Noah as being a sign of His impending return. And in those days, it was the "bad ones" who were removed and the "good ones" were "left behind" to repopulate the earth. Something to think about, is it not?

If we have misinterpreted what Jesus was saying there, wouldn't it change our view, to some degree, of what the end times might look like? I say, "Absolutely, yes." What if He was implying that when He returns, the evil ones will be removed, as with the great flood, and the redeemed ones will remain here with Him, to establish His Kingdom here on Earth? Well, my goodness, that would certainly change everything, wouldn't it?

So, what can we take away from the story of Noah and the flood, in addition to the attributes we have already learned about in the previous chapters? I would say that God is deadly serious about righteousness. He is righteous, through and through, and He desires that His children be righteous, as well. But, of course, there is a serious problem now that Adam and Eve fell to temptation and the "seed war" seems to have taken the battle to another level.

Righteousness matters. It is something we need to seek, to desire. As with everything else concerning God and man, He is always ready and available to help, to strengthen and even forgive us because at His very core, He loves us, and He is a redemptive God. Jesus, Himself, made it very clear in His famous Sermon on the Mount that our help and our healing begins when we seek Him, it all starts with us. Here is how Jesus explained it:

But seek first His kingdom and His righteousness, and all these things will be added to you. [Matthew 6:33 NASB]

So how, then, do we become righteous? How do we, who are sinners, become pleasing in God's sight again? By seeking Him and then trusting Him, by faith, to do what He said He would do. He saves us from the consequences of sin not because of our good works, but because the sacrifice of the blood of Jesus was sufficient to save all of mankind from their sin. We only need to accept His gracious gift and trust Him with all our hearts.

Noah trusted God. He sought God's help, and God provided it. Noah learned that, no matter what may come, God will do what He promised to do. Even during a time of great judgment, God saved Noah and his family by providing safe passage through the storm. Not by taking them out of it.

BUT THE RIGHTEOUS WILL LIVE BY HIS FAITH
[HABAKKUK 2:4]

CHAPTER FIVE

A GOD OF PROMISES

It has been said, "To do something well, you have to truly love it." That makes sense to me. I know that to be good at anything, it is going to take time, patience, dedication, persistence and something called "tunnel vision." And those are principles that apply to just about anything you might desire to do. They are somewhat universal unless you are the Creator of the Universe, that is.

Since God is God and we are not, of course, He does not have to keep trying or practicing until He gets it right. No sir, whatever He does, it is done right the first time, no need for a v2.0 or v3.0. The Psalmist wrote, "As for God, His ways are perfect." And to do perfect things, you guessed it, perfect love is required. So then, it is safe to make some assumptions, I'd say:

1) When God first conceived creating the universe and all that is in it, it was motivated by love.

2) When God decided to create Adam out of the dust of the earth and breathe life into his nostrils, it was motivated by love.

3) When God created Eve out of Adam's rib and provided him with a suitable mate, so he would not be alone, it was motivated by love.

4) When God sent His Son to become the ransom for our sins, to die that we might live forever, it was motivated by love.

5) And when He sends the risen Lord to us a second time, this time to redeem us out of this evil and wicked world, that we may be risen with Him and live with Him forever, it will most certainly be motivated by love, His perfect love towards us.

So, as we move forward in this study of what the Bible teaches regarding future events here on Earth and the kingdom yet to come, we must always keep fixed in our minds and in our hearts that God loves us. Everything He has done and will do in the future is motivated by His great and perfect love for us.

But, the words "perfect love" also imply that God's love for the world is not just your everyday, garden variety-type of love. In John 3:16, the apostle did not write, "For God loved the world..." No, he went a step further. He wrote, "SO LOVED," and continued with "that He gave His only-begotten Son." I am sure that you would agree with me that it takes a special kind of love to sacrifice a child of your own, willingly, to save others.

So, while we are on the subject of "sacrificial love," I wanted to touch on another amazing story from the Book of Genesis...the story of a man named Abram, who later became known as Abraham and was called "the father of many nations." Let's look at a passage from Genesis Chapter 22 that I find utterly amazing, one that I believe has much to do with the central theme of this book, our eternal destiny, and how things may unfold before the Lord returns.

> *Now it came about after these things, that God tested Abraham, and said to him, "Abraham!" And he said, "Here I am." He said, "Take now your son, your only son, whom you love, Isaac, and go to the land of Moriah, and offer him there as a burnt offering on one of the mountains of which I will tell you." So, Abraham rose early in the morning and saddled his donkey and took two of his young men with him and Isaac his son; and he split wood for the burnt offering and arose and went to the place of which God had told him. [Genesis 22:1-3 NASB]*

Have you ever taken notice of the fact that it is in this passage of Scripture, twenty-two chapters into the Book of Genesis, that the word "love" appears for this first time in the Bible? It did not come up regarding Adam and Eve (romantic love) or during God's six days of creation (which I would call "a labor of love"), nor did it come up during the story of Noah and his family. And it was never mentioned that God's decision to spare them, while judging the evil ones among them, was motivated by love (although I have no doubt that it was).

I believe it is a huge revelation, and not something to be overlooked, that God chose the story of Abraham and Isaac to be the point where He introduces the concept of love. Imagine, if you can, a Valentine's Day card depicting the love that Abraham had for Isaac (even though he was willing to sacrifice him out of obedience to God) as the real "true love?" I don't think it would sell very well, do you? But I think that goes a long way to show us how far removed our concept of love is, these days, from the genuine article, the love of God.

Two key points can be taken away from this incredible story that has major ramifications on how all things will eventually be resolved and made right again. First, I would say, is this idea of "redemption through sacrifice." Abraham proved to be willing to obey God, even if it meant sacrificing his only son, trusting that He would never ask such a difficult thing of him were it not for a godly purpose. And in the end, his faith was rewarded. God provided the sacrifice, a substitute if you will so that Isaac could be spared. If there is a better picture of the Gospel in the Old Testament, I do not know of it. Isaac had done nothing wrong, nothing to deserve this fate, just as Jesus had done nothing wrong.

And secondly, Abraham's story hinges on this whole matter of faith. That is why I love the Book of Hebrews. It does a great job of highlighting the role of faith and obedience in the lives of so many of the great saints who came before us. Let's look at a couple of key verses, before moving forward:

> *For when God made the promise to Abraham, since He could swear by no one greater, He swore by Himself, saying, "I will surely bless you and I will surely multiply you." And so, having patiently waited, he obtained the promise. [Hebrews 6:13-15 NASB]*

Yes. God is, as the title of this chapter implies, "A God of Promises." That is how Abraham became the father of many nations. Through God's promise and Abraham's obedience and faith in God, he obtained the fulfillment of God's promise to him. And that is still how we obtain the promises of God, through faith. God promised that because of Abraham's faith and obedience, his descendants would be a great nation and those that bless them would be blessed, and those that cursed them would be cursed. That nation, of course, is Israel. And how important are they in the big picture of things yet to come?

We should also note that it has been anything but a four thousand-year honeymoon between Israel and God. The Jews, of course, rebelled many times and ignored many stern warnings to repent, yet God kept His promise, and Abraham's descendants will see all His promises fulfilled at the appropriate time and according to God's abundant grace and mercy. Even though they did endure times of judgment and great suffering for many years, because of their disobedience, the promises of God were never revoked.

Recently, I learned an interesting fact, and I thought I should share it. According to Jewish tradition, Abram was born in the city of Ur in Babylonia in the year 1948 (measuring forward from the time of creation). And, in what year was Israel reborn as a nation, following their two-thousand-year exile? That became official about seventy years ago, in 1948 AD. How cool is that? It is like God saying, "If you had any doubts about all the forethought and planning that went into all this stuff, think again. I have loved you from before the foundations of the earth were formed." But the writer of Hebrews was not done:

Now faith is the assurance of things hoped for, the conviction of things not seen. For by it the men of old gained approval. [Hebrews 11:1-2 NASB]

I certainly think that Abraham "gained approval" for his display of faith and love for God. Don't you? Being willing to sacrifice your only son, a son whom you greatly love and waited 100 years to receive? Yeah, that type of faith is quite special. But that was not the only time Abraham was asked by God to display great faith:

> *By faith Abraham, when he was called, obeyed by going out to a place which he was to receive for an inheritance; and he went out, not knowing where he was going. By faith he lived as an alien in the land of promise, as in a foreign land, dwelling in tents with Isaac and Jacob, fellow heirs of the same promise; for he was looking for the city which has foundations, whose architect and builder is God. [Hebrews 11:8-10 NASB]*

Abraham was a man of faith. He proved it time and time again. He loved God, and so He believed God had his best interest at heart. He never doubted that God's intentions for him were ultimately good, even though it might have seemed, at times, that God had some peculiar ways of going about things. Am I right? The writer of Hebrews also wrote this amazing statement:

> *And without faith it is impossible to please Him, for he who comes to God must believe that He is and that He is a rewarder of those who seek Him. [Hebrews 11:6 NASB]*

So, we cannot please God without faith and faith is hard to display without trust. And trust is hard to show without love. Abraham not only had faith in God, but he also trusted God. And he trusted God because he loved God and believed He wanted to bless him. Let's go back to the beginning of Abraham's story if we can. It all started with a promise:

> *Abram said, "O Lord God, what will You give me, since I am childless...And He took him outside and said, "Now look toward the heavens, and count the stars, if you are able to count them." And He said to him, "So shall your descendants be."Then he believed in the Lord; and He reckoned it to him as righteousness. [Genesis 15:2, 5-6 NASB]*

God gave Abraham a promise, one which He most definitely has fulfilled. He was promised that he would have many, many descendants, that they would become a great nation (even a favored nation) and that they would eventually inherit a land of promise, physically and spiritually speaking, as we know now, of course, they did.

So, I started out this chapter talking about love and ended up spending a lot of time talking about faith and trust. Is there yet a deeper connection between these things, as to how they relate to the days when Christ will return and the events leading up to that glorious revealing? I am so glad you asked!!

> *We have come to know and have believed the love which God has for us. God is love, and the one who abides in love abides in God, and God abides in him. By this, love is perfected with us, so that we may have confidence in the day of judgment; because as He is, so also are we in this world. There is no fear in love; but perfect love casts out fear, because fear involves punishment, and the one who fears is not perfected in love. [1 John 4:16-18 NASB]*

These words written by John, who not only wrote the Gospel of John and the three letters or epistles of John (which these verses came from), it is the same John who years later recorded the Book of Revelation. I say "recorded," because he was faithfully writing down what Jesus, Himself, revealed in a series of visions regarding the things that must happen in the future.

So, I want to make sure that when we talk about the various theories or interpretations regarding the end times, we must keep in mind that whenever Jesus comes for us, and He will, it will be motivated by the same perfect love that sent Him to Earth the first time. That must be central to whatever end-time scenario we embrace. God's love for us will not be greater or somehow less if we are caught up to meet Him in the air before the seven years of tribulation, or after them. His love is perfect, come what may.

Remember what we talked about earlier. Can God bring judgment on some while protecting others at the same time? Of course, He can. So then, times of great trouble should be a time of great confidence for believers in Christ, as well. I would say. Jesus taught us to pray, "Thy kingdom come, Thy will be done…" Are you willing to pray that… even as the storm clouds are approaching? Good question, right?

I want to clarify one central point, right now, if I may. I believe in a physical rapture (a catching away if you will) of those who belong to Christ and only those who belong to Christ. Yes, Scripture is clear that we shall "meet Him in the air." My only point of contention is, "When will this gathering of believers occur?" And that is something believers have debated for centuries. Even the first-century church was consumed with this desire to know when these things would happen. They thought Jesus was coming back in their day. And almost every generation since has said, "The day of His return is near." Sooner or later, one generation is going to be correct. He said that He would, one day, come back to claim His bride and I believe He always keeps His word, especially about something as important as a wedding day. I cannot even think for a second that Christ would leave His bride standing at the altar. No way.

The verses above also talked about "perfect love" casting out all fear and how "fear involves punishment." Again, I would say that should the Lord intend for His chosen ones to remain here during the Great Tribulation and not be taken up before it, His grace is sufficient. We should have nothing to fear either way. Let's remember the words of Paul:

Who will separate us from the love of Christ? Will tribulation, or distress, or persecution, or famine, or nakedness, or peril, or sword? Just as it is written,

"For Your sake, we are being put to death all day long; We were considered as sheep to be slaughtered."

But in all these things, we overwhelmingly conquer through Him who loved us. For I am convinced that neither death, nor life, nor angels, nor principalities, nor things present, nor things to come, nor powers,[39] nor height, nor depth, nor any other created thing, will be able to separate us from the love of God, which is in Christ Jesus our Lord. [Romans 8:35-39 NASB]

These verses could apply to any of the scenarios. If God the Father chooses to call us home before the tribulation, fine with me. There most certainly are tribulations, persecutions, famines and other perils going on in the world right now. So, this could be implying that nothing happening in the world today, before the Great Tribulation, can separate us from the love of God. And I would say, "Amen, to that."

But, I would not think it should apply any less to the scenario that suggests we will remain here until the Great and Terrible Day of the Lord when Christ returns to pour out His wrath on His enemies. I would say that if, as believers, we are still present on the earth when things get much worse, God's grace will not be any less sufficient. In fact, the Bible teaches that where evil abounds, the grace of God abounds even more. So, my guess is, we will be just fine. He will not leave us or forsake us, no matter what.

Have you ever had to do something difficult, even scary to the point that you sweated it for weeks and weeks beforehand, worrying if you would be up to the test or maybe even worse, chicken out? But, you hung in there and when the time came, by God's grace, you got through it just fine. You probably even found yourself saying, "That was not that bad. To be honest, it was quite exciting. I'm glad I went through with it. Silly me, what was I so worried about?"

Could it be that if God were to decide to take us home before the tribulation period starts, we could be missing out on the most glorious and exciting days to be a Christian, ever? How amazing would it be to be able to stand firm in our faith against the threats of the Antichrist, to reject the mark of the beast and even to face death for Christ's sake, should it come to that, knowing that God is going to be right there with us and that nothing can happen to us outside of His will?

Yes, I believe some Christians will be persecuted and even die during those seven years, just as Christians are being persecuted and martyred for their faith, right now, all around the world today. Jesus said, "If they persecute Me, they will also persecute you because of Me." The Book of Revelation tells us about the martyrs who came out of "great tribulation." If God so wills me to be one of them, so be it. I would be honored to die for the One who died for me.

So, if we are honest, the only real question is, "Who are these Christians who will be alive during the tribulation?" Are they those who were Christians before the seven years of great trouble started and remained firm in their faith, intent on enduring to the end? Or, will it be new Christians, ones who will come to Christ after the rapture? More on that a little later. Either way, this much I know to be true, just as the words of the well-known hymn teach us:

The steadfast love of the LORD NEVER CEASES; *His mercies never come to an end; They are new every morning, new every morning Great is your faithfulness, O Lord Great is your faithfulness*

WE LOVE, BECAUSE HE FIRST LOVED US
[1 JOHN 4:19]

CHAPTER SIX

THE SPECIALNESS OF TWO-NESS

While we are talking about Abraham, God's promises and this "crazy little thing called love," I do want to highlight one more example of Jewish traditions and practices that I believe should be an important part of any discussion of future biblical events. These traditions surely seem to point, symbolically, to the culmination of everything that must happen, leading up to our eternal destiny, the Marriage Feast of the Lamb.

> ***Then he said to me, "Write, 'Blessed are those who are invited to the marriage supper of the Lamb.'" And he said to me, "These are true words of God." Then, I fell at his feet to worship him. [Revelation 19:9-10 NASB]***

As I have alluded to a few times, when we look at the Bible and how God chose to reveal Himself to us, looking at the beginning gives us an accurate picture of how things may be at the end because, as we discussed earlier, God changes not. And of course, in the beginning, the Lord saw that it was not good for the first man, Adam, to be alone, so He created and blessed him with a helpmate and partner, Eve.

Our God is a God of relationship and wasted little time in establishing a pattern of "two-ness" for human relationships. But, in addition to that, the pattern also included "exclusivity" and "permanence" as parts of the arrangement. And in the Gospel of Mark, we see Jesus confirming these things, so let it be noted, these were not just Old Testament principles."

But from the beginning of creation, God made them male and female. For this reason, a man shall leave his father and mother, and the two shall become one flesh; so they are no longer two, but one flesh. What therefore God has joined together, let no man separate." [Mark 10:6-9 NASB]

As you might guess, when I see something like this that is set as a pattern in the Old Testament and then confirmed as something meant to continue by Christ, in the New Testament, my mind immediately expects to see a correlation in how things will be in the end (and beyond). But, since we are also taught that marriage (meaning human matrimony) will not continue beyond our earthly existence (Matthew 22:30), I found myself looking for something more spiritual and eternal to be part of the restoration and redemption picture. I believe the Marriage Feast of the Lamb is that culmination.

But, just as with the Sabbath (the seventh day), the Shemitah (the seventh year), and the Jubilee (the fiftieth year), I was sure there would be Old Testament examples that would give us an indication as to how things will manifest, leading up to that final marriage feast. That seems to be God's "modus operandi." He likes to establish a principle or pattern early on the story that may seem a little unusual or strange, at first glance. But, He fully plans to use it again, as things draw closer to the final stages, with even an added level of weight and significance. Like I said numerous times, here, "If you want to know how things will unfold, later on, look at what happened in the past." A wise man once said of the Bible, "Nothin' is in there for nothin'."

Isaac, of course, was Abraham's son. He was spared from being sacrificed as a child. But God had big plans for him. Let's examine how the joining of Isaac and his beloved, Rebekah, came about:

Now Abraham was old, advanced in age; and the Lord had blessed Abraham in every way. Abraham said to his servant, the oldest of his household, who had charge of all that he owned, "Please place your hand under my thigh, and I will make you swear by the Lord, the God of heaven and the God of earth, that you shall not take a wife for my son from the daughters of the Canaanites, among whom I live, but you will go to my country and to my relatives, and take a wife for my son Isaac." The servant said to him, "Suppose the woman is not willing to follow me to this land; should I take your son back to the land from where you came?" Then Abraham said to him, "Beware that you do not take my son back there! [Genesis 24:1-6]

The verses above point to two very key elements of how the joining of Isaac and Rebekah eventually came to be. First, Abraham made a point of telling his servant to find a suitable wife for his son, but not a daughter of Canaan (remember the seed war we talked about?). He wanted his offspring to remain untainted.

And secondly, if the woman was not willing to come back to where Isaac was, the servant was not to take Isaac to where she was. Here we see a precedent for what Jesus said much later, "That where I am, you may be also." The bride was to go and be with the groom where he was, not the other way around.

Behold, I am standing by the spring, and the daughters of the men of the city are coming out to draw water; now may it be that the girl to whom I say, 'Please let down your jar so that I may drink,' and who answers, 'Drink, and I will water your camels also' – may she be the one appointed for Your servant Isaac; and by this I will know that You have shown lovingkindness to my master." Before he had finished speaking, behold, Rebekah who was born to Bethuel the son of Milcah, the wife of Abraham's brother Nahor, came out with her jar on her shoulder. [Genesis 24:13-15 NASB]

The servant prayed and asked the Lord to point out the woman He had chosen for Isaac. If the Lord did not, the servant would be relieved of the responsibility of bringing back a bride at this time. I just love how the servant blanketed this mission in prayer. So yes, it would be an "arranged marriage," but it would be the Lord doing the arranging…as it should be.

Then Laban and Bethuel replied, "The matter comes from the Lord; so we cannot speak to you bad or good. Here is Rebekah before you, take her and go, and let her be the wife of your master's son, as the Lord has spoken." [Genesis 24:50-51 NASB]

It became clear not only to Abraham's servant but to Laban (her brother) and Bethuel, her father (two witnesses) that God had chosen Rebekah to be joined with Isaac. Proper permission had been received, and an agreement was reached, yet there was one more approval that needed be granted…Rebekah's:

And they said, "We will call the girl and consult her wishes." Then, they called Rebekah and said to her, "Will you go with this man?" And she said, "I will go." [Genesis 24:57-58 NASB]

So, we can clearly see that Jewish wedding traditions were based purely on what God had spoken and revealed. We see that it was important for the bride to be suitable (in modern times that means not necessarily Jewish by birth, but at least willing to convert). That also points to the fact that the bride was supposed to go and join the groom. The groom was not to go and be with the bride. But, here we see that the bride-to-be was given a choice, as well, just as we are through the Gospel of Christ. She could accept or reject the proposal. And, as we apply these things to the end time scenarios, this will all become very important. We, too, are given a choice. But, more on that later.

Then, as we look ahead a bit, to the story of Jacob (Isaac's son… and God changed his name to Israel), we learn that he (Israel) was tricked into marrying the older sister, Leah, first by Rachael's father, Laban (yes, this is the same Laban who was Rebekah's brother in the first story). Rachel was "the apple of his eye," but Laban made him work two seven-year periods, one for Leah and one for Rachel. I think we will discover something quite amazing about this, especially since we talked at length about the number seven, and we are now talking about "two-ness.".

Then Laban said to Jacob, "Because you are my relative, should you therefore serve me for nothing? Tell me, what shall your wages be?" Now Laban had two daughters; the name of the older was Leah, and the name of the younger

> *was Rachel. And Leah's eyes were weak, but Rachel was beautiful of form and face. Now Jacob loved Rachel, so he said, "I will serve you seven years for your younger daughter Rachel." Laban said, "It is better that I give her to you than to give her to another man; stay with me." So, Jacob served seven years for Rachel and they seemed to him but a few days because of his love for her. [Genesis 29:15-20 NASB]*

Laban insisted that Jacob work for him for seven years to earn Rachel's hand in marriage and Jacob agreed to do so. But Laban decided to pull fast one. Once the first seven years were complete, he would allow Jacob to marry the older sister, Leah, but he would have to work another seven years to get to marry Rachel, his chosen bride. So, let me put on my "prophecy interpretation glasses" for a moment and let me see if there might be something more significant that we can take from this.

The Bible, as we know it is two covenants, one was driven by the Law of Moses (the Old Testament), and the other was sealed by the grace we receive, by faith, through the death and resurrection of Jesus Christ two thousand years ago (the New Testament). I would equate the first seven years Jacob worked to the Mosaic Covenant, the Law. Not unlike Leah, it might not have been the desirable one or pleasing in the eyes of God, but it served a purpose. And it led to a second (and better) covenant, whereby Jesus became "the price paid" to become joined to the bride of His choice, the fair and lovely Rachel (or as we call it, His church). I would also equate it to our "awaiting the Bridegroom's return," that we may be forever joined to Him, so that where He is, we may also be for all of eternity. A bride must have patience and not lose hope, or she could give up on the promise. May it never be, Lord!

Therefore, I think it is reasonable to conclude that the Lord was willing to persist in pursuing us through two periods of "difficult days of preparation," to finally have the privilege of becoming one with His chosen bride, whom He proposed to at the Cross of Calvary. And there, He paid the full dowry with His blood, and promised to return at the appropriate time (of which we do not know the day or the hour) to take us to our "forever home.".

Isn't that so like our God? He was able to use the trickery of Laban (and we know Jacob was a bit of a conniver, himself) to bring about His ultimate will in that situation. While at the same time, He was painting a beautiful prophetic picture for us to better understand how and why He seems to be taking the long way around the block in coming back for us, while we lovingly long for His return.

Oh, one more point of interest from the story of Rachel and Leah. If we look at the twelve sons of Jacob, which became known as the twelve tribes of Israel, it should be evident that the first four sons of Jacob came through Leah, the older and less desirable of the two sisters. And the fourth son's name was Judah, the son through whom the bloodline of Jesus proceeded. So, I would conclude that the birth of Christ came under the old covenant, from the first wife, just as Judah did. The new covenant had not been sealed and ratified, as of yet. That came at the Cross.

Imagine that, the Chosen One did not descend from Rachel, but through Leah, the bride Jacob was tricked into marrying. I see this as just another example of what Paul taught us in Romans that "all things work together for the good of those who love God." [Romans 8:28 NASB] The devil may think he is "throwing God a curveball" with his trickery and deceptions, but he must not realize that our Lord is a master of "taking lemons and making delicious lemonade."

On a side note, you may not be aware of this (it was new to me too), but there is a tradition that exists to this day for traditional Jewish weddings that relate to the story of Laban and Jacob. It is called, "The B'deken" (aka...the veiling ceremony). You know how with modern weddings (at least, here in the West), it is considered bad luck for the groom to see the bride on the wedding day? Well, believe it or not, it is customary in Jewish wedding traditions that on the day of the wedding...the groom, both fathers, and the groom's attendants intentionally go into the bride's chambers to verify that, in fact, the bride the groom expects to marry will be the one behind the veil during the ceremony. Once they are assured, then the groom lowers the veil to cover the bride's face. It is a symbolic "tip of the hat" to how Laban tricked Jacob into marrying Leah first. Try doing that for a non-Jewish wedding, nowadays. My guess is, it would not go over very well.

And lastly, there is the parable of the wedding banquet in Matthew 22. A king is giving a wedding for his son, and he sends out his servants to invite his preferred guests, but they refused to accept the invitation, saying they were too busy with "other things." The king then told his servants to go out into the streets and "invite everyone you find," in other words "those who are willing to come." The servants did as they were asked, and the banquet room was filled with guests who were thrilled to be invited by the king.

I see this parable as pointing to those of the first covenant, the Jews who rejected Christ the first time He came, being too busy with their own concerns to embrace the invitation. And those on the streets as being the Gentiles, who the Apostle Paul said were invited because the Jews rejected Him. They were overjoyed to be invited and have the chance to attend the wedding feast for the king's son.

Now, mind you, I am sure there are going to be plenty of people of Jewish descent who will be sitting at the banquet table for the Marriage Feast of the Lamb, as well. But it will only be those who recognize Christ as Messiah and Lord and put their trust and faith in Him for their salvation, not their Jewish laws and traditions. As Jesus said Himself at the end of this parable, "For many are invited, but few are chosen." [Matthew 22:14 NASB]

So now, if I were to hypothesize that the institution of marriage was the Lord setting forth a pattern, an example for us to not only enjoy during our days on Earth, but a picture of how the Father views our relationship with Christ will culminate and remain far beyond the limitations of this world, would you consider that to be a stretch?

Consider these points:

- Marriage is a covenant relationship (sealed by vows made by the participants)
- It is meant to endure, as long as the two shall live. (and with Christ that means "forever")
- What God has joined, let no man put asunder. (Satan tried to keep us from Christ...bad idea)

- It is to be based on unconditional love. (it is for life, for better or worse, for richer or poorer)
- The Bridegroom promised to return for His Bride. (you can count on it…the Lord keeps His promises)

"FOR MANY ARE INVITED, BUT FEW ARE CHOSEN."
[MATTHEW 22:14]

CHAPTER SEVEN

TRIED BUT NOT FORSAKEN

According to most scholars, right around the same time as Abraham walked the earth, another great man of faith, one with quite a different story, was making his mark on the scrolls of biblical history, a man named Job. He was also righteous, just as Noah and Abraham were. Yet for some reason, he was treated quite differently by God. But as always, there was a godly purpose behind the events that took place.

> *Now there was a day when the sons of God came to present themselves before the Lord, and Satan also came among them. The Lord said to Satan, "From where do you come?" Then Satan answered the Lord and said, "From roaming about on the earth and walking around on it." The Lord said to Satan, "Have you considered My servant, Job? For there is no one like him on the earth, a blameless and upright man, fearing God and turning away from evil." [Job 1:6-9 NASB*

So, the story starts out with God, speaking of a man He refers to as "blameless and upright," having a discussion with Satan and his fallen angels. "Have you considered My servant, Job? There is no one like him on the earth." Satan replies by suggesting that the only reason Job is so righteous and seemingly faithful, is that God had greatly blessed him and even put a hedge of protection around him (we will be talking more about this concept later. It is very important).

God, then, agrees to allow Satan to bring hardship upon Job's livestock, his servants and even his family. But, at first, he does not allow Satan to touch Job (again, this is important, because we see that Satan has boundaries set by God and that is still the case and will be in the times of the end, as well). To no surprise to God, Job remains faithful, in spite of the hardships that Satan brought upon him, so God reluctantly allows Satan to go a bit further, to afflict him physically, but not kill him. Again, Job remains faithful. But, his wife begins to waver. In fact, she tells Job to "Curse God and die" at one point. Job rebukes her by saying she is talking like the foolish women who have no faith. He, however, does not waver.

But the fact of the matter is, God did not bring hardship upon Job and his family because Job had done evil in his sight. God allowed hardship to come for quite the opposite reason. Job had been righteous and blameless in God's eyes, and He wanted Satan to see just how unwavering his faith would be, even in the face of great pain and turmoil. I believe the Lord knew that Job would stay the course and come through it all just fine (after some bouts of crying out to the Lord and complaining about his circumstances, of course). But oh…what a testimony that would be to the one standing there, right in front of God, who had not stayed the course God intended for him…Satan.

One of the theories regarding the end times that I know many Christians embrace, these days, is called the "pre-tribulation rapture" theory (or as I call it, "the early departure plan"). And, one of the things I often hear those who teach it say is, "Our God is a loving God, and He would never allow the righteous to be forsaken." They refer to this early departure plan as the "Blessed Hope." I get it. If God takes us out of here before the real trouble starts, I guess that would be considered a great blessing, and it wouldn't make me mad if it happened that way. But hear me out, while I agree that God will never forsake the righteous, I never understood how that could be used as justification for a pre-tribulation rapture. The concept they point to is found in one of David's Psalms. Have a look:

I have been young and now I am old, yet I have not seen the righteous forsaken…For the LORD loves justice does not forsake His godly ones; they are preserved forever, but

the descendants of the wicked will be cut off. [Psalm 38:25, 28 NASB]

Yes, the Lord loves justice and will not forsake His godly ones. And yes, they will be preserved forever. I agree. David also said that in all his years, he had never seen the righteous forsaken, and I cannot argue with that. I never have either. I mean, yes, Job suffered greatly, and the Lord allowed it. But He never forsook him, and He will never forsake those of us who call on the name of Christ, either.

Even David, who wrote the Psalm, suffered greatly and God did not abandon him. However, when we assume that the psalm is evidence of a "catching away" of believers before the Great Tribulation, it sounds to me like we may have wandered into "the land of presumption." That goes beyond my comfort level. I do not see a connection between the two.

For me, this idea of being "forsaken by God" deals with two possibilities. One would be for someone (or even a nation) who is so hardened against God that they will never repent. I could see Him forsaking them. In other words, removing His hand of blessing and protection from them. I think Judas Iscariot would be a good example of that. Once he betrayed Jesus, his goose was pretty much cooked.

The second scenario would be with dealing eternity, as in those who will experience Hell and eternal separation from God. If we trust in Christ and receive the redemption He provided, we will never be forsaken for all eternity, as will the wicked. I trust in that. But I do not understand it to mean that the righteous, His redeemed ones, will not suffer hardship in this life. If that is what David meant, look around, there is plenty of evidence we could point to that might suggest, "God does not keep His promises," and I certainly do not believe that.

I also want to touch on the last portion of that passage from David's Psalm, if I may. It brings me back around to a point I made earlier when we looked at Noah and the flood. When Noah entered the Ark and shut the door, who was taken away? The wicked ones, not the righteous ones. Here in Psalm 37, King David says, "the godly ones are preserved (remain), but the descendants of the wicked will be cut off (removed)." That certainly is not what I was taught when I first learned about the early departure plan. The ones who subscribe to that theory believe the righteous will be taken (caught away) and the wicked will be "left behind." I've seen the movie.

This entire scenario reminds me of the famous parable about the wheat and the tares. After the crop started to grow, the slaves noticed some tares (weeds) growing among the wheat. They went to the landowner and asked him how they should proceed:

> ***The slaves of the landowner came and said to him, 'Sir, did you not sow good seed in your field? How then does it have tares?' And he said to them, 'An enemy has done this!' The slaves said to him, 'Do you want us, then, to go and gather them up?' But he said, 'No; for while you are gathering up the tares, you may uproot the wheat with them. Allow both to grow together until the harvest; and in the time of the harvest I will say to the reapers, "First gather up the tares and bind them in bundles to burn them up; but gather the wheat into my barn."'" [Matthew 13:27-30 NASB]***

Isn't that interesting? An enemy (let's call him Satan), according to the landowner, had mingled bad seed with the good and now, tares (weeds) were cropping up along with the good wheat. The slaves were wondering if they should not go out and go through the tedious process of removing the weeds from the wheat (notice…it doesn't say "gather up the good wheat," they were asking if they should gather up the bad stuff). But the landowner said, "No, you might damage the good wheat in the process of removing the bad. Let them grow together (until when?) until harvest time, then you can gather them up together (the good and the bad). Then, you can bundle up the tares and throw them into the fire, while you gather the wheat (preserve it) into my barn."

Once again, we see the bad crop being bundled up, taken away and tossed into the fire. Meanwhile, the good crop is protected and preserved in the barn. So, as I see it, the good crop was not forsaken at all. Only the tares were removed and destroyed. And remember, this is Jesus talking here. No mention of any urgency to gather up the good wheat out of the midst of the tares. Rather the landowner said, "Let them both grow together until the harvest." And I believe that is a beautiful picture of the age in which we are living. We are being cultivated, here, in this life on Earth, hopefully as the "good wheat." Meanwhile, all kinds of wicked weeds are being allowed to grow right next to us, but they will get their just rewards. Don't you worry.

I know I have asked the question, "Why would God allow evil to not just continue, but even flourish among us?" I believe the answer is, God has His purposes. Just as we saw with Job, it all had to run its course. All the hardships and even the tongue-lashings from his friends caused "spiritual brokenness and growth" in Job's life. Job was being sanctified, maturing spiritually through the process, as painful as it was. And in the end, he was greatly rewarded for enduring to the end. Let's look at one more verse, this one featuring the words of Jesus, Himself:

> ***"I am the true vine, and My Father is the vinedresser. Every branch in Me that does not bear fruit, He takes away; and every branch that bears fruit, He prunes it so that it may bear more fruit. [John 15:1-2 NASB]***

Are we starting to see a pattern, here? Jesus is referring to Himself as the vine and His Father as the vinedresser. And He specifically says that the Father does one of two things, He prunes the ones who are bearing fruit (so they can produce more fruit)., and the ones who are not bearing fruit, He cuts off. There it is again, the righteous remain and the unrighteous are taken away or cut off. It all seems quite clear to me, just as we learned about the two women grinding at the mill, one was taken, and one remained. The question is…which is which? If I am looking at the whole Bible, it seems the nature of God has always been to remove the wicked ones and preserve the godly ones. That seems to be the more consistent pattern.

But I do not want to wander too far off the path, however, from talking about the Book of Job and what prophetic significance it might hold. So, I will talk more about this whole idea of who stays and who goes later. For now, let's go back and see how Job's story unfolded.

Over the next thirty or so chapters, in Job, three friends of Job (Eliphaz, Bildad, and Zophar) offer him three speeches each and to each one Job responds. Each of these men suggests that Job is not being honest with them and probably not being honest with God

Almighty regarding the sinful deeds that either he or his children may have committed. They all claim that until he realizes that God does not afflict the righteous and he admits his wrongs, God will not forgive him and, thusly, cannot restore him.

Then, when these three men were done, as if that was not enough, a younger man named Elihu, who had been standing back and just listening, took his turn at adding his two cents worth of "tough love," also implying that Job should finally repent and seek God. They all meant well, I am sure. I do have to say, however, it seems to me that they had a funny way of expressing it.

Through it all, Job never wavered from proclaiming his innocence. Yes, at times he cried out to God and even wished God would just take him and end his suffering. And sure, he questioned why God would do this to him. Hadn't he been kind and loving to others who were hurting? Had he given in to the enticement of a woman other than his wife? Had he been harsh to his servants and his slaves? Had he put his confidence in his wealth above God? Had he walked in falsehood, or celebrated the hardships his enemies encountered? And maybe most importantly, he asked, "Had he sought to cover his sins as Adam did?

To all these questions, I believe in Job's heart that he truly believed he had not done any of these things, and therefore he felt had a right to question why God would allow suffering of this magnitude to come upon him. But the true purposes as to why God allowed all of this to happen had not been revealed yet. Let's not forget, this story of Job was recorded and preserved as a great example for us to learn from, regarding how we as believers should respond to adversity in our lives. And all along, of course, God planned to restore him and bless him with even far more than He had at first. Job had not been permitted to understand that all, just yet. It would have defeated the purpose of what God was trying to display to Satan. Let's move ahead, then, and look at how this story ended.

> **"Hear, now, and I will speak; I will ask You, and You instruct me. I have heard of You by the hearing of the ear; But now my eye sees You; Therefore, I retract, and I repent in dust and ashes." [Job 42:4-6 NASB]**

So, it only took forty-two chapters and a handful of speeches from four "well-wishing friends" (who lacked the compassion needed to become good grief counselors, I'd say), to finally bring Job to the point of being beyond self-pity, touting his own righteousness and questioning God's love and mercy towards him. And that brought him to a place where he was willing to finally surrender and say, "I have heard of you before, my God, but now my eyes can see You… therefore, I retract, and I repent…forgive me, Lord." And how did the Lord respond to this new-found repentance and brokenness in Job? He had a little talk with Job's so-called friends:

"My wrath is kindled against you and against your two friends because you have not spoken of Me what is right as My servant, Job, has. Now, therefore, take for yourselves seven bulls and seven rams, and go to My servant, Job, and offer up a burnt offering for yourselves, and My servant, Job, will pray for you. [Job 42:7-8 NASB]

God told Eliphaz that His wrath had been kindled against him and his friends for not telling Job what is right (meaning their presumptions were wrong as to why God allowed him to suffer). In addition, He commanded them to take seven bulls and seven rams to offer as sacrifices for themselves, as a way of showing Job they were sorry. And then, just to show them what kind of guy Job is, that he would not only forgive them, but he would graciously pray for them, as well (ah…the old "pray for your enemies" bit…I like it). I love the fact that God said that Job would pray for them, but He never instructed Job to do it (at least as far as we know). He just knew that he would. Amazing!!!

The Lord restored the fortunes of Job when he prayed for his friends, and the Lord increased all that Job had twofold. Then all his brothers and all his sisters and all who had known him before came to him, and they ate bread with him in his house, and they consoled him and comforted him for all the adversities that the Lord had brought on him. And each one gave him one piece of money, and each a ring of gold. The Lord blessed the latter days of Job more than his beginning; [Job 42:10-12 NASB]

And there it is...restoration cometh from above!! By the way, what happened when Job forgave them and even prayed for them? It says, "The Lord restored the fortunes of Job (wait for it) when he prayed." You see, God rewarded Job for responding the way he did, even though that is how He expected Job to respond eventually. No, restoration did not come right away. God is not a spiritual vending machine, where you insert a prayer and an ice cream sandwich pops out (ooh, that sounds good right now...I'll be right back!!).

Job had to be brought to a place of utter brokenness, even though he was considered a righteous man who loved God and worshipped Him in his heart. And I believe those of us who are alive when the final seven years are upon us will endure (and be preserved) through much hardship, as an example to Satan and his minions that God's chosen people are willing to fight the good fight and remain faithful unto the very end, no matter what.

What is the point of going through six thousand years of human pain and suffering, if in the end, you plan to take your team off the field before the ultimate test takes place? It does not line up, for me, with all the other examples we see in Scripture such as Noah, Moses, Abraham, David, Daniel, and so many others. They went through the hard times, and God brought them out victorious, not because of what they were able to do, but what He was able to do through them.

So, why did I share all of this? Yes, I probably dug deeper into Job's story than I needed to, but I felt there were some very important aspects of God's divine nature hidden in the details of this story:

1) Job was a man God called "blameless and upright," but that did not stop Him from allowing the rain of hardship to come in buckets.

2) Every step of the way, Satan was restrained in what he was permitted to do to Job, by God. And that hasn't changed.

3) God will never allow the righteous to be forsaken, in the end, but that does not mean we will be spared of life's pain and suffering as God sees fit. Paul said, "As Christ suffered, so shall we suffer for His namesake."

4) I believe in the days before Christ returns, the saints of God will again be tried, but God intends for them to be victorious (just as He did with Job) that they might display to Satan what true love and devotion to God looks like. I see no benefit in God removing His key players from the field at the beginning of the fourth quarter, with the outcome of the game still clearly in question. No, I fully expect Him to let it all play out, with His chosen ones standing their ground by faith and God granting them the power to do the impossible through the Holy Spirit because He told us He would never leave us or forsake us. And I believe that to mean, in this life and beyond.

Although it may be extremely difficult at times, God will be with us, He will not forsake us, and the reward for remaining faithful (for those who truly do) will be great. We, like the good wheat, will be gently gathered into His barn, His safekeeping…forevermore.

THOUGH HE SLAY ME, I WILL HOPE IN HIM
[Job 13:15]

CHAPTER EIGHT

I'LL TELL YOU WHAT I'LL DO

Up next, I would like to continue our journey through the days of Genesis (or 1st Revelation, as I sometimes call it), by taking a good look at the story of Joseph, the eleventh son of Jacob. I believe there are a couple of valuable principles of God's nature that will loom large in our later discussions of what is to come, which come to light in this interesting, yet revealing story.

1) I want to examine the concept of descendants and the importance of birth order, things that the writers of the Bible talked a lot about in Scripture, to see if they have any value as we consider the end of this world and the coming kingdom. I believe it does.

2) Since it is what we will be digging into next, I want to introduce the concept of prophecy, with an emphasis here on dreams and visions. As we move forward, I will be focusing more on the ways in which God has chosen to reveal Himself and communicate with those He created for His glory. So, this should serve as a good springboard, as we head into those topics.

Most of us are familiar with the story of Joseph because of the wonderful musical interpretation called, "Joseph and the Amazing Technicolor Dreamcoat," or maybe through the equally wonderful song by Dolly Parton called, "Coat of Many Colors," which was based on her childhood and a coat her Momma made for her. But, the idea of the multi-colored coat was inspired by the story of Joseph, of course.

First, let's see if we can discover why Joseph is so important, especially as we keep one eye looking towards the end times. Joseph is the eleventh son of Jacob, the grandson of Isaac, and the great-grandson of Abraham (the father of nations). For those of you who may not remember, Jacob fell in love with the beautiful Rachel. But her father, Laban, pulled a "switcheroo" and insisted he marry his older daughter, Leah, first. Then, Jacob had to work another seven years to earn Rachel's hand in marriage. But, once Jacob finally got to marry Rachel, the plot thickened. Although Rachel was beautiful and "the apple of Jacob's eye," she was unable to conceive. But God had another plan in mind:

> *"Now the Lord saw that Leah was unloved, and He opened her womb, but Rachel was barren, Leah conceived and bore a son and named him Reuben, for she said, "Because the Lord has seen my affliction; surely now my husband will love me." [Genesis 29:31-32 NASB]*

Well, isn't that interesting? Leah, the older and less desirable of the two, became the one that God chose through whom to bring about Jacob's firstborn son, Reuben. In fact, Leah bore Jacob's first four sons as Simeon, Levi and Judah came along shortly after. Then she stopped bearing children, and Rachel was jealous, so she gave Jacob her maid, Bilhah and she bore him two more sons, Dan and Naphtali. Not to be outdone, Leah gave Jacob her maid, Zilpah, and she bore Jacob two more sons, Gad and Asher. The Lord, then, allowed Leah to bear two more sons, Issachar and Zebulun. After that, Leah gave birth to Jacob's first daughter, Dinah. It was only after the first ten sons and one daughter were born to Jacob, that God opened Rachel's womb and allowed her to give birth to the eleventh and twelfth sons, Joseph and Benjamin. And that is how the "twelve tribes of Israel" came to be. Not exactly "The Waltons" or "Little House on the Prairie," was it?

Now, you may be wondering why I felt the need to share all of that. To me, it is truly amazing how far God will go to bring about His good and perfect will. There are no shortcuts with God. He certainly could have spared Jacob from doing two seven-year stints of serving Laban to earn his chosen bride, Rachel. God did not. It causes me to reflect on why the Lord chose to redeem His own chosen bride following two distinct periods of time, the Old and New Testament. They each revealed a bride of their own, an older and less attractive covenant (let's call her, Leah) and the younger and more beautiful covenant (Rachel-like), which brought forth the grace and mercy of God through His Son, our blessed Lord Jesus.

And it took ten sons and one daughter from Leah and the two maids before God allowed the first fruit of a union between Jacob and Rachel to be born. His name was Joseph (the name means "may He add," with the word "He" meaning Yahweh). It also can mean "increaser" or "doubler." And of course, Rachel was ultimately able to give birth to another son (increase or double her fruitfulness), Benjamin, to complete the twelve tribes. I would also suggest that it should be quite easy to envision God as "one who adds or doubles." Did he not tell Adam and Eve to "be fruitful and multiply?" Did we not see Him restore Job "twofold" in the last chapter?

Why is this important? I believe it is helpful in allowing us to see that God is not interested in quick, or easy fixes. But there is always a good reason for seemingly "taking the long way around the block." As we will see, God was writing a greater story that had many pieces and moving parts that all had to properly align for His ultimate will to be revealed. Joseph's is a story of how the Lord aligned some very key moving parts to do something miraculous.

Now Israel loved Joseph more than all his sons, because he was the son of his old age; and he made him a varicolored tunic. His brothers saw that their father loved him more than all his brothers; and so they hated him and could not speak to him on friendly terms. [Genesis 37:3-4 NASB]

It seems that, clearly, Jacob (Israel) loved Joseph more than the others and because of that, he gave him this special "many-colored tunic" we've heard so much about. But, although Scripture says his love for Joseph was because he was a son of his old age, I cannot help but think he was also special to Jacob because he was the first fruit of his beloved Rachel's womb. Needless to say, the cool jacket did not endear Joseph to his stepbrothers. Seeds of jealousy were beginning to sprout, but this was only the beginning.

So, what should we take away from all that, or maybe a better question is what did the Jews miss?

It seems to me that maybe the Jews missed the whole prophetic significance of there being two daughters of Laban, not one. Jacob had two serve to terms of seven years, not one, to finally be given the hand of his "desired bride." The Law of Moses was never intended to redeem anyone. It was only intended to show us that none are righteous, no, not one, and a newer and more beautiful covenant was needed to erase the stain of the sin that the first covenant identified. God always knew there would be a Rachel, a second more desirable covenant that would produce the apple of His eye, the one the Lamb would rejoice at the thought of being joined to for all eternity.

And speaking of that, the story of Joseph did not take any shortcuts, either. First, there was the long process of bringing him into the world, number 11 of 12 sons. Then, there was this fancy coat that might as well have had "Dad loves me more than you guys" printed across the chest. Another time, Joseph had brought his father, Jacob, a bad report on his stepbrothers, which certainly did not help things, but rather, they became the events that would cause Joseph to become someone they felt the need to deal with, once and for all. And eventually, they did just that.

When they saw him from a distance and before he came close to them, they plotted against him to put him to death. They said to one another, "Here comes this dreamer! Now then, come and let us kill him and throw him into one of the pits; and we will say, 'A wild beast devoured him.' Then let us see what will become of his dreams!" [Genesis 37:18-20 NASB]

God had given Joseph two dreams that implied that there would come a day when his stepbrothers would bow down to him. The first one dealt with sheaves in a field being bundled. Joseph said his sheaf stood up erect and the others bowed down before him. The second had the sun, the moon, and eleven stars...all bowing down to him. He told them they were his father and eleven brothers (pretty specific dream). His mistake was telling them what he saw. They were obviously quite angry with him to the point that they plotted to kill him. Only Reuben came to his defense and talked them out of killing him. So, they sold him to some slave-traders who were passing by. Then they dipped his fancy jacket in goat's blood and told their father, Jacob, that a wild animal had eaten him alive.

And lo and behold, many years later, Joseph had become the chief assistant of the Pharoah, in Egypt. When a great famine hit his homeland, his brothers came before him seeking help, not knowing it was Joseph who they were standing before. Sure enough, his father and stepbrothers did bow down before him, thus fulfilling the visions saw many years earlier. And that leads me to the second reason why the story of Joseph is so important to our study of eschatology. It introduces in vivid fashion one of the most important ways in which the Lord chooses to speak to His people, not only back then, but today as well. Prophecy. The prophet Amos spoke clearly about the Lord's fondness for advance notification:

"Surely the Lord GOD DOES NOTHING unless He reveals His secret counsel, to His servants the prophets. A lion has roared! Who will not fear? The Lord GOD HAS SPOKEN! WHO CAN BUT PROPHESY?" [AMOS 3:7-8 NASB]

Indeed, the Lord does like to call His shots in advance. He said, "Let there be light, and there was light." He said, "Let us make man in our image," and what do you know, He did just that. The Bible is full of examples of God foretelling His servants what lied ahead. And it always came to pass, just as He said it would.

It turned out Joseph was not just being arrogant or promoting himself above his brothers. God was warning the brothers, and Joseph too, as to what was coming many years down the road. The brothers, of course, didn't want to hear it and I am not sure Joseph even knew fully what the vision meant. But they did not need to know at the time the visions were revealed. That is one of the great things about true prophecy, many times the fulfillment of a prophecy doesn't come for many years, sometimes even thousands of years. But if it is true prophecy, it will come to pass.

Back in the days of Abraham, Jacob and Joseph, they did not have the Bible, of course, or a sacred written account of the things of God. So, God had to communicate by speaking, either through an angel, or a prophet or sometimes through signs and wonders like a flood or a burning bush that talks. He has His ways. I have always said, "I believe God has never created anything or anyone He is unable to communicate with directly, whenever He chooses."

So, here we are, thousands of years later, still looking back at the prophecies included in our Old Testament and, in many cases, still waiting for them to be fulfilled. We have records of the prophecies of Isaiah, Jeremiah, Ezekiel, Daniel, Joel and Zechariah, and many others, all painting this amazing picture of things yet to come. But even Daniel, himself, was told by an angel that some of the things he was being asked to record would be "sealed up until the times of the end."

Here is what Michael the Archangel told Daniel:

But as for you, Daniel, conceal these words and seal up the book until the end of time; many will go back and forth, and knowledge will increase." [Daniel 12:4 NASB]

There you have it. Some prophecies were given with no intention of them being fulfilled any time soon. In fact, some were meant, specifically, to remain hidden for hundreds or thousands of years. And Michael seemed to imply that people would go back and forth over what the words might mean for years until a day comes when knowledge greatly increased, and only then, would the true meaning become more evident.

Many Bible and prophecy experts point to the fact that we are living in times where knowledge has increased exponentially over the last one hundred years or so. They believe there has never been a time that seemed to be a more likely fit for the fulfillment of the things which Daniel wrote about. I happen to agree with them.

GOD IS NOT A MAN, THAT HE SHOULD LIE
[Numbers 23:19]

PARENTHETICAL PAUSE #1

A Gathering of the Summoned

For those who have spent any amount of time studying the Book of Revelation, it is common knowledge that these writings by the Apostle John, received in numerous visions from the Lord Jesus, Himself, were not recorded chronologically. There are what the scholars refer to as "parenthetical chapters" or "parenthetical pauses," such as Chapter 12 and Chapter 17 and 18, which do not fit, sequentially, into the timeline of end-time events. They are there to give us a "bigger picture" perspective on what is happening on Earth and in Heaven. As we know, God is not constrained by time, at least in an earthly sense. There may be some other manifestation of time in the supernatural realm, but we have no knowledge of it. God has us on a "need to know basis," and I am just fine with that.

As we move forward, from the historical chapters to the more prophetic chapters, I felt the need to put a few things into perspective, first. I thought I would add a short "parenthetical pause" here, to sort of "set the stage" for what we will be talking about next. And, I will add one more of these "pauses" in between Part Two and Part Three, to set the stage there as well.

For the next eight chapters, we are going to be talking about things that happened after the birth of Christ, and to a large degree, after His death and resurrection. Some would refer to this as "Church History," but as I will explain in this chapter, I am not all that comfortable with that term.

As I explained at the beginning of the book, I will be talking about "historical facts" that will help us to understand why we, as Christians, believe some of the things that we do, today, even if they are not biblical. And to do that, I need to talk about how the Catholic Church, and later the Protestant churches came to be. I will also point out why, in my opinion, some of these things, which are not based on sound biblical doctrine, are still practiced in Catholic, Protestant, and even many Evangelical churches, two thousand years later.

But, I do want to re-emphasize, I am not intent on attacking anyone's faith or where they gather to worship. As the Apostle Paul said, "The faith that you have is your own with God." It is purely a matter of choice between the believer and God Almighty, and it is up to the individual to "work out your salvation with fear and trembling," it says in Philippians 2:12. In other words, if we are to "be ready" for what is coming down the road, it is important that we get our facts straight. If you are going on a camping trip, and you don't know whether it is to Florida or Alaska, I suggest you ask a few more questions. Some "minor details" mean more than others.

So, let me start with a simple question, what is a church? Or, maybe better yet, for our discussion, what is "the Church?" As Christians, our lingo is filled with references regarding the word "church". We want to find a good church, attend a Bible-believing church, and we believe that as "the redeemed of the Lord," we are "the church of Jesus Christ." And for many students of the Bible, they believe that we are living in what is widely known as "The Church Age." That would be referring to what many call the time period between Christ's death and resurrection...and His promised return.

For me, as a naturally inquisitive person, that raises a question because I do not see that term in the Bible anywhere, and I never once read or heard about Jesus preaching on "the church," except where He told Peter, 'and upon this rock I will build My church" (and I will dig into that a little more, later in this chapter). No, quite the contrary. He was always preaching about "the Kingdom of God."

So, I want to do a little word study, if I may, on the word "church," and look at the origin of this widely used concept. And to do so, I want to kick it off with an excerpt from an article written by Christian author and speaker, Lonnie Lane. I believe she explains this far better than I could have:

To begin with, the King James translation uses the word "church" 112 times, having translated the word ecclesia to mean "church." First, let's look at where they got the word church. The word comes from the Old English and German word pronounced "kirche." In Scotland and Northern England, it was "kirk" and meant what we think of as church. Funny to think of someone, like Kirk Douglas as being named Church Douglas, especially since he was actually Jewish, but that's where the name Kirk derives from.

In the earlier Greek it was pronounced "ku-ri-a-kos" or "ku-ri-a-kon," a word that doesn't remotely resemble the Greek word "ecclesia," which it somehow replaced. The meaning of "ku-ri-a-kos" is understood by its root, "ku-ri-os," which means "lord." Thus, "kuriakos" (i.e. "church") means "pertaining to the lord." It refers to something that pertains to, or belongs to, a lord, not necessarily 'the' Lord.

The Greek "kuriakos" eventually came to be used in an Old English form as "cirice" (pronounced kee-ree-ke), which evolved to "churche" (pronounced kerke), and eventually to "church" as we use it today. A church, then, is correctly something that "pertains to, or belongs to, a lord."

The word "church" would have been an acceptable translation for the Greek word "kuriakos." But the translators inserted the word "church" in the English versions, even though they were not translating the Greek word "kuriakos." The word they were supposed to be translating was "ecclesia." Even the most liberal translator today would never find "church" as the acceptable translation for the Greek word "ecclesia." "Ecclesia" is an entirely different word with an entirely different meaning than "kuriakos."

The Greek word "kuriakos" actually only appears in the New Testament two times. It is found once in I Corinthians 11:20 where it refers to "the Lord's supper," and once again in Revelation 1:10 where it speaks of "the Lord's day." In both of those cases, it is translated "the Lord's," not "church." Even though the word does not appear again in the New Testament the word "church," as it has come to be known in the English language, has replaced "ecclesia."

"Church Douglas." I loved that!! Okay, so I am sensing a major problem here. The word "kuriakos" (which could, in certain settings, be correctly translated as "church") only appears two times in the New Testament. Yet, the word "church' appears 112 times. All the other times it appears, according to most Greek and Hebrew scholars, it is wrongly translated into English from the word "ecclesia," which means, as we have seen, something completely different. Hmmm... you don't say!! Most scholars would say the correct translation for "ecclesia" is either "assembly" or "congregation." But, isn't that what a church is? Well, those who have studied this matter say that "assembly" or "congregation" speaks more of the people. The word "church" points more to the building or organization. And, this will become even clearer as we move forward.

Not too long ago, I heard a preacher sharing his view of why he believes in the early departure plan. He said, "Have you ever noticed that after Revelation 4, there are no more mentions of the church to be found anywhere? That's because, after the message to the seven churches, the church is no longer present on the earth. We are long gone!!" Well, now that we have looked at the translation problems regarding the word "church," maybe there shouldn't be any mention of it prior to Revelation 5, either.

I would like to look at a well-known passage from Revelation 2 in a couple of older translations if we can. You know, the part about the "letters to the seven ecclesia," to illustrate my point a little further:

> **"Unto the messenger of the congregacion of Ephesus wryte: These thynges sayth he that holdeth the vii. starres in his right honde and walketh in the myddes of the vii. goldencandlestyckes"** *[Revelation 2:1 Tyndale New Testament 1526]*

The Tyndale New Testament (by William Tyndale, who was martyred for his faith before he could complete a full Bible translation in English) is regarded as the first English translation of the New Testament. I think it is important to see this clearly, but I would like to veer off-subject, just for a moment if I could, and tell a personal story. I found this to be quite amazing!!

About two years before this writing, I did a search of my ancestry on a well-known website specializing in such things, and to my amazement on my mother's side of the family, I found out that there were a number of well-known "reformers" to whom I am distantly related. One of them was a man named Reverend Rowland Taylor, who was also martyred for his faith by those loyal to the Church of Rome, and he was married to a lady named Margaret Tyndale who, you got it, is the sister of William Tyndale. She was my 14th great-grandmother, and that makes her father (and William's) my 15th great-grandfather. So, I am sort of indirectly related (I am more directly related to his sister) to the man who completed the first English translation of the New Testament. How cool is that?

Sorry, I just thought it was really great that while I have been pondering this matter of the overuse of the word "church" for years, but without a full understanding the translation problems, that one of my distant relatives produced the first English translation of the New Testament, and he also had issue with the improper translation of the word "ecclesia." Amazing!! Ok, I am done patting myself on the back, here.

Now, where were we? Oh yes, I remember… it should be noted that Tyndale was firm in his conviction that the word "church" was an improper translation of the Greek word "ecclesia," and refused to use the word "church," as those loyal to the Pope insisted. And we should also note that with the appearance of the King James Version (1610), which had no lack of Catholic influences involved in producing it, the word "church" takes center stage. Are we seeing a pattern, here?

Maybe we should also look at how the Hebrew scholars of the day viewed this problem.

> ***"To the malach (angel) of the Kehillah (Congregation) in Ephesus, write: These things says the One holding shivathakokhavim (seven stars) in the yadyamin (right hand) of him, the One walking in the midst of the shevamenorothazahav (seven golden menorahs):" [Revelation 2:1 Orthodox Jewish Bible]***

Once again, we see the Hebrew scholars were hesitant to use the word "church" to translate the word "kehillah," which again means "congregation" or "assembly." So fine, I understand there may be some problems translating from the Hebrew or Greek languages into English (which many say is a very limited language, by comparison), but what does have to do with a study on the end times and the eventual return of our risen Lord Jesus? I would say, "Only everything."

The most precise detailed interpretation of the word "ecclesia" from Greek into English was the phrase "a gathering of the summoned." We can think of that as "the elected" (as with our Congress), or "the elect" (if we think in Christian terms). But most would translate it to mean "assembly" or "congregation." It really means those who have been "called out" or "set apart" for a specific purpose…in this case, to be wholly serving the Lord Jesus Christ, not an earthly emperor or king.

In doing my research, I found out that the apostles were not primarily martyred for preaching something contrary to what the Romans or Jews believed (in religious terms). No, they were put to death because they were calling on people to "serve a different king or emperor," one not named Caesar. They were encouraging people to come under the lordship of Christ and be loyal to Him, as opposed to the Roman government and their laws. It was just like when Daniel was put into the lion's den. He was not abiding by the "rule of law" in Babylon, under Nebuchadnezzar. And that usually did not end well for those who tried such things, in Babylon or Rome.

And not surprisingly, if I look at the Tyndale New Testament and the Orthodox Jewish Bible again to see how they translated the words of Jesus, "upon this rock I will build my church," they both say "I will build my congregation (the OBL says "kehillah" which means congregation). It seems obvious to me, that somewhere along the line, someone decided that they want to emphasize the word "church," as in buildings, hierarchy, and organization. Hmmm, I wonder who?

So, what happens a few hundred years later, after Christ was born, died and was resurrected? In the 4th century, a man named Constantine, whose mother was converted to Christianity, became the emperor of Rome. And at the time, the Romans were being very hard on these

Christian "troublemakers." Many were put to death for not being loyal to Rome. Eventually, Constantine, himself (with some help from his mother...I suspect), became a Christian and then decided to try to make Christianity the "state religion," which did not sit too well with the pagans of the day. What about all their traditions, practices and holidays? They were just as serious about those traditions as the things in which these Christians believed. So, over the next century or so, there was a gradual merging of Christian and pagan beliefs and practices...many of which we, even as Christians who do not belong to the Catholic Church, still practice today.

Of course, this includes things like Christmas, Easter, Halloween, and the practice of using Sunday as a "day of worship," as opposed to the Hebrew practice of the Sabbath (decreed by God as the "day of rest") from sunset on Friday night to sunset on Saturday. But over the years, the hierarchy of the Church of Rome felt, especially once they formally introduced the Pope as God's primary spokesman upon the earth, that they had the power to make these changes as they saw the need. And things got even more heavy-handed when, on Christmas Day (believe it or not) in the year 800 A.D, when Charlemagne was named the head of "the Holy Roman Empire," the more political wing of the Church of Rome.

Then, a little over a thousand years after Constantine's conversion, in the 16th century, Martin Luther stood up to the Church of Rome, on of all days...October 31st, 1517 (coincidence??...I think not) and nailed his "95 Theses" (complaints) to the door of a Catholic Church in Wittenberg, Germany. By the way, have you ever noticed that Halloween (which is said to have demonic origins) happens every year on the eve of the Catholic holiday, "All Saints Day?" Again, is that just a coincidence? Think about it, Halloween is often called "All Hallows Eve" or "All Saints Eve" and is a night that some believe the souls of the dead come home for one night and must be appeased. So, we have this holiday that we still practice today, even involving our children, which has origins as the devil's mockery of the Church's "All Saints Day," and very few people give it much of a thought. Imagine that.

So, what we have is this gradual merging, or blending, of traditional, biblical Christian theology with practices that were the result of compromises between Christians and pagans to keep the masses happy. But what has resulted is a diluting of the truth that the writers of Scripture, inspired by the Holy Spirit, were led to pass on to us. It brings to mind what the Apostle Paul wrote:

"You were running well; who hindered you from obeying the truth? This persuasion did not come from Him who calls you. A little leaven leavens the whole lump of dough." [Galatians 5:7-9 NASB]

I have read that the Catholic Church, over time, began to think of itself as the one, true mediator between God and man. The Bible, however, presents quite a different view of this matter:

For there is one God, and one mediator also between God and men, the man Christ Jesus, who gave Himself as a ransom for all, the testimony given at the proper time. [1 Timothy 2:5-6 NASB]

It seems churches nowadays, even non-Catholic ones, have positioned themselves in a difficult spot. Do they adhere strictly to the Bible (which, admittedly, is hard because of the overt influence of the Church of Rome on our English versions of the Scriptures) as it was originally intended? Or, do we make room for tolerance of the compromises made along the way?

Listen, I am not trying to be "a Scrooge" here, or cry "Bah Humbug." My only intentions, in bringing up these things in this conversation is that they have had, I believe, very damaging effects on how we perceive the end times…as we will see shortly, here.

And Christ, Himself, insisted that we **"Seek, first, the Kingdom of God and His righteousness."**

Our Lord was all about establishing "His Kingdom," not empowering an earthly church that would serve as our only interpreter of the "things of God." May it never be. That role rightly belongs to the Helper, the Holy Spirit.

The Constantinian influence, and what followed, was all about building these huge and palatial buildings that they called "churches." They became "gathering places for believers to come and worship."

And that may be all fine and good, in and of itself. But it also gave them much power over the people and does to this very day. You didn't dare go against "the Church," an institution which had such influence and authority around the world, right?

The New Testament, however, teaches about the "ecclesia" as the gathering of the summoned, the ones who are "called out," "elected" to become separate from the world and its systems...even religious ones. You see, when I think of "ecclesia" or the Hebrew word, "kehillah," I tend to think of the people, the assembly, the congregation...a gathering of those "called to come out from the world systems and be separate."

When I think of the Catholic Church, the Lutheran Church, the Presbyterian Church, the Baptist Church, the Mormon Church (or fill in the blank with any religion or denomination), I think of an organization, a hierarchy...a religious system. And, as we know, Jesus was not fond of religious systems. The church (if we are going to use that word at all) is the people assembled or gathered in His name, not the building or organization.

So, as we go forward, I just wanted us to keep in mind that we need to be very careful about blending any "man-made beliefs" with the truth of God...and putting them on an equal footing. In the "end of days," we will be seeing another "worldwide church" (or one-world church) appear on the horizon preaching tolerance of all kinds of beliefs...whether they glorify God Almighty or not (usually not).

Am I suggesting that we should all leave our churches, choose not to be associated with any of them, because they may have allowed some of these practices with questionable origins to remain? I AM NOT. I want to make that very clear. My wife and I belong to a wonderful church, and we have no plans to stop attending or cease from being involved there. It's more about being aware and being diligent to protect the truth that God has presented us with, in the Scriptures. And, I believe as the days grow more wicked, that will become even harder. The devil is a master at "blurring the lines," so that the truth and the lies become very hard to distinguish from one another.

I will end this chapter with a word of encouragement from the writer of the Book of Hebrews:

> *"And since we have a great priest over the house of God (Christ), let us draw near with a sincere heart in full assurance of faith...not forsaking our own assembling together, as is the habit of some, but encouraging one another; and all the more as you see the day drawing near." [Hebrews 10:21,22,25 NASB]*

So, just as we believe it is God's intent for us to "be in the world, but not of the world," perhaps it should also be our goal to be a part of His "church" (a part of the "body of Christ" and an active part of the "gathering of the summoned"), but not of "The Church" (and by that I am pointing towards man-made religious organizations...not any one in particular.

JESUS SAID, "I AM THE WAY, THE TRUTH, AND THE LIFE."
[JOHN 14:6]

Part Two

GOD'S NATURE

IN
PROPHETIC PATTERNS

"The things which are..."

(Revelation 1:19)

CHAPTER NINE

"TEST THE SPIRITS..."

As we move into Part Two of this study, since the story Joseph pointed us to the subject of prophecy (dreams, visions, interpretations, and the like), I feel we need to look at the other side of this prophetic coin...prophecies and prophets not ordained by God to speak on His behalf. And I can think of no better teacher, for this subject, than the Lord Jesus Christ, Himself.

At the end of Chapter Seven, we talked about a passage from the Book of Amos that said, "God does nothing without first telling His prophets." We talked about how God prefers to "call His shots ahead of time," and this, we believe, is so that when these prophecies are fulfilled (and hundreds of them already have), it will build faith in those who seek to know God better.

But prophecy can also show us those who are working against God, the liars and deceivers among us. The Apostle John made it very clear that we should be very careful with messages said to be "from God," for not all so-called "words of prophecy" are divinely inspired.

> *Beloved, do not believe every spirit, but test the spirits to see whether they are from God because many false prophets have gone out into the world. [1 John 4:1 NASB]*

So, let's begin by going back to a well-known passage of Scripture from Matthew 24, a discussion between Jesus and His disciples. For many, this chapter represents the "high ground" of biblical prophecy because it is the Lord, Himself, revealing "the signs of His coming," or how His faithful ones will know when His return is drawing near. God does not want His children to be unaware. He wants them to be ready, waiting, and to be "about the Father's business."

> *Jesus came out from the temple and was going away when His disciples came up to point out the temple buildings to Him. And He said to them, "Do you not see all these things? Truly I say to you, not one stone here will be left upon another, which will not be torn down." As He was sitting on the Mount of Olives, the disciples came to Him privately, saying, "Tell us, when will these things happen, and what will be the sign of Your coming, and of the end of the age?" [Matthew 24:1-3 NASB]*

Jesus finished off Chapter 23 with what is referred to as the "Eight Woes," eight rebukes, pointing out the hypocrisies of mankind…and six of them started by saying, "Woe to you, scribes and Pharisees, hypocrites!" So, it was the religious leaders of those days that Jesus was most suspicious of. Surprise, surprise! You mean to tell me, Lord, that those who have the clout and authority of being deemed "men of God," might use that clout to spread false theology that benefits themselves? Who'd a thunk it?

Now, in Chapter 24, Jesus starts off by asking, "Do you not see all these things?" and He continues by telling His disciples that not one stone (of the Temple) would be left one upon another. And it was only a few short years later, of course, that Jerusalem was destroyed and the Temple was left in ruins, just as Jesus prophesied it would be. But, let me ask this, who was it that came and tore down the city, trashed the Temple, and caused the Jews to be scattered around the world, separated from their homeland for the next two thousand years?

Well, history tells us it was the Romans, of course. We should take note of that. I do not think it was purely coincidence, since the religious system that was founded and centered in Rome, in the years following Christ's first visit to this world, would become hugely influential in the centuries that followed, even in the days in which we now live and the days that lie ahead. But Jesus was not done. He had more to say about all of this.

> *And Jesus answered and said to them, "See to it that no one misleads you. For many will come in My name, saying, 'I am the Christ,' and will mislead many. [Matthew 24:4-5 NASB]*

Immediately after foretelling the destroying of the Temple, He is quick to point out that false prophets will arise among us…and will mislead many. And a little later in the chapter, He talks about this again:

> *For false Christs and false prophets will arise and will show great signs and wonders, so as to mislead, if possible, even the elect. Behold, I have told you in advance. [Matthew 24:24-25 NASB]*

If you ask someone an important question, as the disciples did of Jesus, and that person answers in such a way as to highlight one specific point three different times, I would say it's a big deal (at least to them). Therefore, as we wade into the waters of studying the prophecies, signs, and wonders that might help us to unravel the mysteries of the "end of days," let us not forget to "test the spirits," as John taught us, to make sure we are hearing from God, and not being deceived. Sometimes, it is really hard to tell the difference between the truth and lies, especially when they are coming from those considered to be religious or claiming to speak on God's behalf.

What I would like to do now, is take a "bird's eye view" of the most notable and influential false prophets in the Bible and throughout religious history, as we know it. I will skip over the first "false prophet," because we have already dedicated a chapter to his deceptions…the serpent who deceived Adam and Eve in the Garden of Eden. We will remember that he quickly tweaked God's words to lead them astray. He changed "if you eat of the forbidden fruit, you will die" to "Oh no… you will not die. You will be like Him…able to know good from evil." A very subtle change, you might say. But the ramifications changed the course of human history…and not for the better.

Let's take a look at a few more so that we can be aware of the strategies the enemy uses to lead us away from God. First, we should look at the "prophets of Baal," who were very prominent over the last one thousand years or so before Christ (and still are operating, today, around the world).

> *When Ahab saw Elijah, Ahab said to him, "Is this you, you troubler of Israel?" He said, "I have not troubled Israel, but you and your father's house have, because you have forsaken the commandments of the LORD and you have followed the Baals. Now then send and gather to me all Israel at Mount Carmel, together with 450 prophets of Baal and 400 prophets of the Asherah, who eat at Jezebel's table." So Ahab sent a message among all the sons of Israel and brought the prophets together at Mount Carmel. Elijah came near to all the people and said, "How long will you hesitate between two opinions? If the LORD is God, follow Him; but if Baal, follow him." But the people did not answer him a word. [1 Kings 18:17-21 NASB]*

King Ahab was one of the evil kings that ruled over the tribes of Israel, but his wife, Jezebel, was even more wicked. She is responsible for introducing and seducing the Israelites into worshipping Baal, which led to all forms of idolatry, sorcery and even the sacrificing of children to try and gain his favor.

Elijah, who was a true prophet of God finally called for a showdown where the prophets of Baal failed to invoke their false god to act. Elijah, then, called down the fire of God from heaven and it consumed the sacrifices. After that, Elijah called for the false prophets to be gathered up and put to death. But notice how when Elijah told the people to choose God or Baal, they did not answer. And Baal worship continued, not only through the rest of the Old Testament, but it remains even today, as many around the world still honor Baal. While it may be true that false gods are not alive, as is our God, they certainly seem to be hard to kill.

Next in line, strangely enough, would be the religious zealots within the Jewish religion. Remember, these are the ones Jesus was talking about at the end of Matthew 23…the hypocrites. But, another time, Jesus said something else about them that was quite telling, if you ask me:

> *"You search the Scriptures because you think that in them you have eternal life; it is these that testify about Me, and you are unwilling to come to Me so that you may have life." [John 5:39-40 NASB]*

What Jesus is pointing to here, is a classic example of "religion vs. relationship." The Jews trusted in the Law. So much so, that when the Messiah came (as they all believed He would someday), they failed to recognize Him. And so, even in modern times, there are religious debates and skirmishes over "legalism" (in other words…trying to earn salvation through good works or obedience), and those who believe in coming to God through faith in Jesus Christ, and knowing that He died for the sins of the world. It is believed that through His suffering, we are no longer held guilty under the Law. We are redeemed…now and forever. Thank you, Lord!!

Three-hundred years after Christ came to "set us free," there was a Roman emperor, named Constantine, who was persuaded to become a Christian. But it did not take long for things to veer off the path and into a religious ditch. The Pagans, who were prominent in the Greek and Roman cultures of those days, became quite upset because Constantine wanted to make Christianity the "state religion," which would have been a death knell to their feasts and religious traditions. Over the next few centuries, there was a gradual blending of the biblical truths of Christianity, taught by Jesus, and the false religious traditions and symbols of the Pagans (many of which were descendant from those who followed Baal, they just took on different names).

This process of blending eventually led to what we know today as the Roman Catholic Church, with its feasts (holidays), symbols, and practices which many deem unbiblical, by comparison. Then, about twelve-hundred years after Constantine's conversion, Martin Luther called out the Catholic Church, and the Pope, in what became known as his "95 Theses" (or complaints). This event, of course, was pivotal in bringing about the Protestant Movement, which I consider a "call to return to the Bible," as the only sound teachings upon which we should base our beliefs, and the only true gauge by which we can "test the spirits," and the truth against the lies.

This led to a heated debate, one which still rages on today in religious circles and one that we touched on with the Jews, as well. It is the struggle between "justification through works" and "justification by faith." The Apostle Paul was quite vocal about this, even two-hundred years before Constantine:

Where then is boasting? It is excluded. By what kind of law? Of works? No, but by a law of faith. For we maintain that a man is justified by faith apart from works of the Law. Or is God the God of Jews only? Is He not the God of Gentiles also? [Romans 3:27-29 NASB]

You see, the Law of Moses was given to the Jews. So, in a way, if salvation could only be obtained by obeying the written laws handed down through the generations, then only the Jews could be saved. Everyone else would be doomed. But God, of course, had a better idea. He intended to make redemption available to all mankind, all of His children…not just one nation or tongue. And that would be accomplished through the death and resurrection of His Son, Jesus Christ. For did not John write, "For God so loved the world…"? He did not say, "For God so loved the Jews" (which, of course, He does). But salvation is and will be available to all. And I believe that will continue to be true right up to the sounding of the final trumpet, when Christ returns, victoriously, to redeem us once and for all time. Praise be to God.

But there is one other prominent form of "false prophecy" at work in the world, even today. And that is, of course, those who still insist on denying the deity of the Lord Jesus Christ, meaning to refuse to believe that He was "God in the flesh." The Apostle Paul addressed it this way:

See to it that no one takes you captive through philosophy and empty deception, according to the tradition of men, according to the elementary principles of the world, rather than according to Christ. For in Him all the fullness of Deity dwells in bodily form. [Colossians 2:8-9 NASB]

I believe this makes it abundantly clear that Paul, who was a Jew, himself, had clearly come to know Christ as more than a prophet or a teacher. He considered Him to be God, "the fullness of Deity in bodily form." And it seems, in this passage, he is taking a page out of Elijah's book by saying, "See that no one takes you captive to philosophies and empty deceptions, according to the traditions of men." Different day, different times...same old lies. Then John, once again, adds in his thoughts on this problem of reducing Christ to merely a mortal, by denying He is God":

> ***I have not written to you because you do not know the truth, but because you do know it, and because no lie is of the truth. Who is the liar but the one who denies that Jesus is the Christ? This is the antichrist, the one who denies the Father and the Son. Whoever denies the Son does not have the Father; the one who confesses the Son has the Father also. [1 John 2:21-23 NASB]***

I can name numerous religions (but I won't), nowadays, who boldly say they do not believe Jesus is God. They may say they believe He is the son of God, a great prophet, or a profound teacher. But they stop short of giving Him the glory and distinction He deserves. John wrote that Jesus was the "Word of God that became flesh and dwelt among us." He even went one step farther by saying, "the Word was God." So, if you are looking out for modern day "false prophets," that is a great place to start. Do they acknowledge that Jesus Christ was, and is, God? That is extremely important, and another great "truth meter."

Matthew ends this pivotal chapter with the words of Jesus telling us, "Therefore, be on the alert." And he talks about a good and faithful slave who remains ready and is found doing as his master wishes when the master returns. But He also talks about an evil slave who does not. Let's look at what Jesus says will happen to that slave:

> ***"...the master of that slave will come on a day when he does not expect him and at an hour which he does not know and will cut him in pieces and assign him a place with the hypocrites; in that place, there will be weeping and gnashing of teeth." [Matthew 24:50-51 NASB]***

So, those who are not found doing what the master requires, when he returns, will be assigned where...and with whom? Jesus says they will be sent to a place where there will be weeping and gnashing of teeth (ooh, that does not sound good), to a place where the hypocrites will be also.

Wait, who did Jesus say, six out of eight times in Chapter 23, were the hypocrites? You got it...those deemed to be religious and speaking on behalf of God. Of course, I am not suggesting that all religious leaders or those who are presumed to be speaking on behalf of God are "false prophets." Not at all...but many, especially as we draw nearer to the time of Christ's return, will be trying to lead us astray through false words and deeds that they will claim are "ordained of God." So once again, as John suggested, we need to be very careful and "test the spirits." And the best way to do that, is by comparing the words they speak or write, against *"every word that proceeds from the mouth of God" [Matthew 4:4],* just as Jesus did Himself, when confronted by the devil.

Yes, it certainly seems that there was a pattern developing, over the centuries, regarding the lies coming from those who are not working for God but against Him. And that is why I also believe it is critically important to have a firm grip on solid biblical teaching and an awareness of church history if we desire to know how things will likely unfold in the future. Like I said in the earlier chapters, God is unchanging, and how He dealt with mankind in the past is how He will likely deal with us in the future.

Therefore, it should be quite apparent, now, why the Apostle John was so intent on warning us to "test the spirits." Deception can be very hard to spot, especially when it comes wrapped in religious dogma. That is why it is so important to hold the Scriptures, God's Word, in such high esteem. What is in black and white (and sometimes red), printed in our Bibles, not the opinions of any man or woman elaborating on them, is more than enough for us to come to an accurate and full appreciation of who God is and what He desires from us. Can I get an "Amen?"

"ALL SCRIPTURE IS GOD-BREATHED..."
[2 TIMOTHY 3:16]

CHAPTER TEN

GRECO-ROMAN WRESTLING

Once again, my "point of reference" for this study hangs on two principles. First, if we are to understand how the end times will unfold, we need to understand "who God is." We must learn of His nature, His character and how He dealt with mankind in the past, and in particular, how that might affect the ways in which He may deal with humanity in the future.

And secondly, for the sake of this study, I want to look at the Scriptures at face value, and not rely too much on the interpretations or teachings of any of those who preceded us. Although I do trust they "studied to show themselves approved" (as the Bible teaches) and had the best intentions of getting to the truth, just as I do, somehow over time, they drifted from it. But, as the Bible also says, "We know in part, and when the perfect comes, the partial will be done away with." So, none of us see the fullness of God and His glory with clarity and assurance to the point that we have it all figured. We are all, sort of, working on the same puzzle...and there are many pieces yet to be found...as God chooses to reveal them.

So yes, our opinions and conclusions are based on what we have seen and heard, and we all do the best we can to come to a full knowledge of the truth with the assistance of the Holy Spirit, the Helper, as Jesus called Him. And I put myself into that box, as well. I am sharing my opinions and conclusions, here, hopefully, to give you some "food for thought." But my views are just that, my views. What you do with this information, after you read this book, is between you and God. May He, who is "the light of the world" shine down upon us and help us to "separate the wheat from the chaff," the truth from the deceptions of the enemy. Sometimes they look a lot alike and only a trained eye can tell the difference. That is why we must be diligent to know our Bible…it is the only trustworthy measuring stick of divine truth.

Thank you, in advance, for your forbearance in these matters. I believe that when I present my conclusions later in this book, hopefully, they will all make sense. Or, at least, you will see how I came to my conclusions (whether you agree with them or not). Over the next few chapters, I am going to do a "deep dive" into what I have found, over the years, to be one of the most amazing chapters in the Bible (and one that holds a foundational place from my early years as a believer in my Christ)…Daniel Chapter Twelve.

But, before I do that, I need to address one very pivotal issue. An issue that, depending on where you stand on this one, will likely change everything else you believe regarding "the afterlife," the final chapters of man's earthly struggles, and the return of the Bridegroom to claim His eternal bride.

I have decided to call this chapter Greco-Roman Wrestling for a reason. To fully understand where I am coming from on these critical biblical issues, you need to have a solid grasp on where the originators of the philosophies that are so prevalent and widely believed, today, we're coming from…namely, ancient Greece and the early Church of Rome.

For the record, many things we believe as Christians today have derived from the deep thinkers of the Greek culture, like Plato and Socrates, and later found their way into the core beliefs of the Church of Rome. And, although there was a major effort to move away from some of these things, in the 16th and 17th centuries and beyond, there are a few deeply held beliefs that Christian churches, even Protestant ones, still held on to today. Two such issues are:

Is the human soul immortal (as that would apply to whether or not the soul leaves the body when we physically die, and whether or not our soul enters into God's presence immediately upon our death)?

Whether physical death is truly death (as God sees it) or is it a spiritual form of sleep, as Jesus, Himself, said in Matthew 9, "The girl is not dead, but asleep." The people laughed at Him, then, and some still laugh at the suggestion of it even now. But, the question remains. Is our understanding of physical death different from God's perception of it? I am inclined to answer, "Yes. I believe it is."

In this chapter, I want to look at the first question. I will address the second one a bit later. And once again, my reason for sharing these things is not to start some "strange new doctrines." Based on my studies, I believe that what many Christians believe nowadays, concerning these critical matters, are the "strange new doctrines." I do not believe that at the time the New Testament was written, that the Christians of the day believed that the soul goes immediately to Heaven when we die. But, don't take my word for it. Let's see what the Scriptures teach on the subject.

> ***Then the LORD God formed man of dust from the ground and breathed into his nostrils the breath of life; and man became a living being. [Genesis 2:7 NASB]***

By the way, I feel it is important to mention, the King James Version, the Wycliffe Bible, and the 1599 Geneva Bible all say, "living soul," (the Hebrew word "nephesh" is translated "soul" in some English translations, but others use "being" or "creature"...I believe because saying "soul" weakens the argument that the soul can be separated from the body and goes to Heaven immediately when we die). What we see in this passage is that a soul is what results when two other things are brought together (a body + the breath of life = a living soul). The Apostle Paul wrote this:

> ***Now may the God of peace Himself sanctify you entirely; and may your spirit and soul and body be preserved complete, without blame at the coming of our Lord Jesus Christ. [1 Thessalonians 5:23 NASB]***

So, if I understand this correctly, a body without breath is not a soul; and breath without a body is not a soul. And both body and breath must be present to form what is called in Genesis, "a living soul." I find it easier to think of the words "soul" and "being" as interchangeable, as the translators did. It is the whole of the parts, the body and spirit. It is what "has life." Ok, but when we die (physically), isn't there a third part (a soul) that immediately goes to be with the Lord?

Good question, I am glad you asked. I thought so, too, for many years. Looking at the above passage again, when does Paul say "your spirit, soul and body" will be preserved? He said, "at the coming of our Lord Jesus Christ," and I believe that happens when the last trumpet blast sounds. But wait, you might say, if the human soul is not immortal, then from where did we get this extremely popular philosophy?

Most accounts that I have read attribute it to Plato, a Greek philosopher, and his work, "Phaedo," which was depicting the death of his mentor, Socrates. It was written around 360 BCE and was widely embraced by many of the early church fathers. Here is what "The Catholic Encyclopedia" has to say about this:

"The great majority of the Christian philosophers down to St. Augustine were Platonists."

There was a problem, my friends. Greek philosophy largely considered this idea of an immortal soul to include the concept of reincarnation. That theory implies that the soul exists before we are born, enters our body at birth, and leaves our body at the time of our physical death to eventually inhabit another human body, and on and on it goes. The early church fathers, although onboard with the idea of a soul being immortal and going to be with the Lord at death, were not ready to fully embrace reincarnation as church doctrine.

So, over the course of many years, they finally decided to get behind the idea that the human soul originates with us, when we are born, and goes to be with God when we die. It was another compromise, one they believed the people would embrace. And that is what many Christians believe today. Let's face it; it is far more comforting to be able to think and say when a loved one passes away, "He (or she) is in a better place now," than "He (or she) is asleep in the grave awaiting the resurrection." Ooh, that does not sound pleasant. What if they are cold or feeling trapped? It is far better to believe they are in Heaven and in the arms of their glorious Maker, right? I agree. But is that biblical?

Let's examine a few of the key verses that are often used to support the idea of an immortal soul that returns to God, immediately, at the time of our physical death:

> ***Therefore, being always of good courage, and knowing that while we are at home in the body, we are absent from the Lord—for we walk by faith, not by sight—we are of good courage, I say, and prefer rather to be absent from the body and to be at home with the Lord. Therefore, we also have as our ambition, whether at home or absent, to be pleasing to Him. [2 Corinthians 5:6-9 NASB]***

When I hear people just focusing on one small part of this passage, it always sounds like they are quoting one of the Ten Commandments. "You know...to be absent from the body is to be present with the Lord." It sounds quite "matter of fact." But in reality, Paul is merely stating a preference. He said, "knowing that we are at home in the body (physically alive), we are absent from the Lord...we are of good courage, I say, and PREFER to be absent from the body and to be at home with the Lord." Amen, Paul, me too. Who wouldn't rather be at home with the Lord, as opposed to dragging around this body of death?

But, nowhere in this verse (or anywhere else in Scripture) does it say that the transformation, from this home to our heavenly home occurs at the moment of our physical death. That blank was filled in, years later, with the help of those who embraced the philosophies of the Greeks and the Romans, and very few have challenged it since. I am wondering if this, among other things, is this one of the matters that were to be "sealed up to the end," as Gabriel instructed Daniel in Chapter 12, part of what I call "The Daniel Twelve Factor?

Then, we have this popular verse where, again, only a small snippet of it is used to seemingly establish sound doctrine:

> ***One of the criminals who were hanged there was hurling abuse at Him, saying, "Are You not the Christ? Save Yourself and us!" But, the other answered, and rebuking him said, "Do you not even fear God since you are under the same sentence of condemnation? And we indeed we are***

suffering justly, for we are receiving what we deserve for our deeds; but this man has done nothing wrong." And he was saying, "Jesus, remember me when You come in Your kingdom!" And He said to him, "Truly I say to you, today you shall be with Me in Paradise." [Luke 23:39-43 NASB]

Once again, in my mind, there seems to be a question or three (lol). Most folks, nowadays, believe Jesus was telling the criminal that on this very day, that he would be with Jesus in Paradise. My first question is, "Was Jesus actually in Paradise on that day? Did He go to Heaven immediately upon His death, and did He take this criminal with Him?" Now, I understand that Jesus was forgiving his sins immediately and granting him redemption. I am just questioning the timing of this "trip to Paradise." Was Jesus saying it would happen that very same day (in earthly terms)?

In John 20, there is the story of Mary Magdalene encountering the risen Lord and He tells her to *"Stop clinging to me, for I have not yet ascended to the Father." [John 20:17 NASB]* That leads me to believe that Jesus did not go to Heaven between His death and resurrection. And we know it was a while before He did ascend into Heaven…forty days, to be exact (there is that number, again). That raises another question, what about those who were supposedly raised from the dead with Jesus, as we read about in Matthew 27?

The tombs were opened, and many bodies of the saints who had fallen asleep were raised; and coming out of the tombs after His resurrection they entered the holy city and appeared to many. [Matthew 27:52-53 NASB]

The Bible says that when Jesus died, there was an earthquake and even the graves were split open and "many bodies of the saints who had 'fallen asleep' were raised (from the dead)." Others say that they came back to life after Jesus was raised from the dead, three days later. Again., the timing is not entirely clear, but who were these people, and did they go to Heaven with Jesus when He ascended? Great question!!

Clearly, these people were among those "set apart for redemption" because they are called "saints." But it is not clear if they received glorified bodies, as Jesus did, or if they were just "restored to life" in the earthly sense…as with Lazarus (John 11), the daughter of Jairus (Luke 8), and the son of widow in the town of Nain (Luke 7). These are all examples of people "restored to physical life" after they had passed into death (or fallen asleep…as Jesus called it). As far as we know, they did not receive glorified bodies or go to Heaven with Jesus. We are led to believe that they resumed their normal lives, were seen and recognized by many, and eventually died again. So, I am inclined to believe that the ones who were raised with Jesus did not receive their glorified bodies at that time or ascend with Him forty days later. If we look at the account of His ascension (Acts 1), there is no mention of anyone ascending with Him.

This may be one of the most widely debated topics regarding the death and resurrection of Jesus Christ. And, I think, for a good reason. Scripture is not at all that clear on these things. Where did Jesus go between His death on the cross and His resurrection on the third day? Most say that He went down to Sheol (which some say is the name of the temporary holding place for condemned souls), but that raises a question, as well.

If I look up the meaning of the Hebrew word "Sheol," it is defined as "referring to the grave or the abode of the dead." But, which is it? There is quite a difference between being "in the grave" or being in "a temporary holding place of the departed souls," especially if there is a question about whether, or not, human souls are immortal and "live" beyond our physical death, right?

Remember when we talked about the sons of God, fallen angels, in Genesis 6 who took human women for wives and had children with them, which led to the "seed war" that was revealed when Adam and Eve fell, and God said there would be "enmity between the seed" of the serpent and the seed of God. Well, some say Jesus went to where those fallen angels (not humans) were being held "in prison" until the day of their destruction (1 Peter 3:19) to give them one more chance to repent. And that is why it says in Ephesians 4, "When He ascended on high, He led a host of captives…" It would seem, according to this passage that perhaps some of them did repent, renounce Satan and decided to follow Jesus, instead. Now, I cannot prove that, but the passage does seem to imply that someone who was "imprisoned" in some way, had now been set free. And I don't think it was the "saints" we talked about earlier. For we know that, *"if the Son sets you free, you will be free indeed." [John 8:36]*, not in some sort of prison (spiritual or physical) awaiting release.

And lastly, let us look at the most common objection to the idea that Jesus and the thief would be "in Paradise" on that very day. Before the original documents were compiled and translated into what we now call the Bible (which was originally done by whom…yes… largely by the Church of Rome…so take note), they did not contain punctuation, as we do today. The translators made decisions as to where punctuation should go, to try to best represent WHAT THEY THOUGHT was the true meaning of the writings. And if we keep that in mind, when reading this passage, it makes a huge difference. Let's read this verse using two possible applications of punctuation:

And He said to him, "Truly I say to you, today you shall be with Me in Paradise." [Luke 23:43]

This is the way almost all English translations applied it. It gives the impression that Jesus is saying that "today" (meaning that very same day), they would both be in Paradise…together. But, if we look at the common beliefs as to where Jesus was between the Cross and His resurrection, that should raise a giant "red flag," if you ask me. Let's look at another possible translation:

And He said to him, "Truly I say to you today, you shall be with Me in Paradise." [Luke 23:43]

Here, I have simply moved a comma (translator's discretion) to after the word "today," instead of before it. Now, it says something completely different. Jesus often started off His comments by saying, "Truly I say to you" or "I tell you the truth." So, this was not uncommon. But the thief is making a request, "Jesus, remember me when you come in Your kingdom." He was not asking Jesus to do something immediately, necessarily. He was asking Him to remember him WHEN He comes into His kingdom.

So, again, maybe just maybe, Jesus felt compelled to do Him one better (since as God in the flesh, He had the authority to do so, right then and there) and say, "Truly I say to you today, you shall be with me in Paradise." It is like He is saying, "Let me put your mind at rest right now, my good man. Fear not, I promise you, you will be with me in Paradise." Now that seems to make a lot more sense to me, especially if Jesus knew He was not going to be lounging around in Heaven for the next three days. Why would He promise something He knew could not be true? So, maybe He is saying to the thief, "When that last trumpet sounds and the dead in Christ are raised first, know this. You will be among them. You will join Me in My kingdom...you have My word.

Once again, I think as students of the Bible, we need to be very careful regarding how much weight we give to the commentaries, writings, and theories of men. I believe the Bible is certainly clear enough if we take it as a whole and properly "divide the Word of God," as we are instructed to do. We do not really need the opinions of other people (including yours truly), to help us understand the Scriptures or form our beliefs or doctrines. That is the job of the Holy Spirit, as John told us in John 14:

> **But the Helper, the Holy Spirit, whom the Father will send in My name, He will teach you all things, and bring to your remembrance all that I said to you. [John 14:26 NASB]**

"WHERE I AM GOING, YOU CANNOT FOLLOW"
[JOHN 13:36]

CHAPTER ELEVEN

"NOW I LAY ME DOWN TO SLEEP"

"Now at that time Michael, the great prince who stands guard over the sons of your people, will arise. And there will be a time of distress such as never occurred since there was a nation until that time; and at that time your people, everyone who is found written in the book, will be rescued." [Daniel 12:1NASB]

Now, that is an interesting place to start a chapter, "at that time… everyone who is found written in the book, will be rescued." Hang on to that thought, "at that time." It will be important as we progress, here, I promise. It makes you wonder what people the angel was referring to, right? Was it the Jews? Daniel was a Jew. But then it says, "everyone who is found written in the book." If he was speaking of the Book of Life (which I presume he was), I believe that would include many other people, namely all those who have trusted in the Lord Jesus Christ. Oh, this is going to get good (and we are only in verse one of "The Daniel Twelve Factor").

The Book of Daniel is one of the most amazing books of the Bible, especially with regards the prophecies that relate not only to the end of days, and how we understand them, but to the kings and kingdoms that would be on the world stage leading up to them, as well. But over the years, I have become quite intrigued by Chapter 12 for a number of reasons.

To set the tone for this chapter, I would like to tell a story of something that happened to me as a very young Christian. What I stumbled on, way back when, has loomed large in my view of future biblical events, ever since. If my memory serves me right, it had only been about two years since I had accepted Christ. And, although I had learned a lot about the Bible in my first couple of years of seeking God (I was like a kid with a new toy, I couldn't get enough), I had barely scratched the surface, especially regarding things like prophecy and the end times. Oh sure, I had heard and read about some of the basic beliefs regarding Christ's return and the events that would lead up to that blessed event, but I had not zeroed in on them all that much, at that point.

So, one night I was attending a men's discipleship group led by our pastor. Not sure how or why the subject came up, but the pastor brought up the subject of "the restrainer" that the Apostle Paul wrote about in 2 Thessalonians 2. The pastor asked, "You guys know who or what that is, right?" I said, without hesitation, "Sure, that is Michael the Archangel. It talks about him in Daniel 12." The pastor seemed a little shocked and turned to me and asked, "How did you come to that conclusion?" I responded, thinking I had screwed up, "Well, it just sort of makes sense. Michael was the one who helped Daniel's answer to prayer finally break through in Daniel 10, and we read about him again in Revelation 12, fighting with the dragon. So, he would most likely be the one Paul is referring to in his reference to a restrainer." He said, "I agree with you. I was just surprised to hear you say that." That is how I spell r-e-l-i-e-f…whew!!

From that point on, I guess you could say my hunger for learning more about prophecy and the End Times had officially begun to sprout, and it is still growing to this very day. The entire subject of prophecy and end-time studies began to intrigue me. And that certainly has deepened my faith in God and His redemptive nature towards all of mankind. For someone or something to be able to string together thousands of data points over thousands of years in such a way that, when connected and compared, they only seem to confirm one another...that is quite incredible. I can find no logical explanation other than there had to be a greater power at work to pull this off. No human or group of humans could have accomplished that. And I am certainly not alone in that conclusion.

But, getting back to the subject of Daniel 12, let's look a little more closely at verse 1 (above), it says, "Now at that time, Michael, the great prince who stands guard over your people will arise..." When I compared that to Paul's words, it seemed that "arise" could be another way of saying "taken out of the way." Let's take a look at the often-quoted verse from the Apostle Paul and let's take note of the fact that he writes "only HE who now restrains" and "until HE is taken out of the way."

> *For the mystery of lawlessness is already at work; only he who now restrains will do so until he is taken out of the way. [2 Thessalonians 2:7 NASB]*

Here, the Apostle Paul was saying that there is someone (not something, as in "the church"...the church would more likely be referred to as a "she") who seems to be restraining the evil one until the appropriate time set by God when he will be taken out of the way. Now some say, "The restrainer is the Holy Spirit. The Bible teaches that He is a person, so that fits." While I do agree with that, in part, He is a person. But, I do not agree that the Holy Spirit would be taken from the earth before the last trumpet sounds because there will still be people on the earth (Jews and Gentiles) who need to be saved.

Remember the words of Jesus, "those who endure to the end will be saved." One of the primary functions of the Holy Spirit is to convict us of our sin and show us our need for a savior. Plus, It sure sounds a lot like this warring angel, Michael, from Daniel 10 and Daniel 12, does it not? I mean, this restrainer is holding back the evil one from being released upon the earth. And when I read Revelation 12...there he is again:

> *And there was war in heaven, Michael and his angels waging war with the dragon. The dragon and his angels waged war, and they were not strong enough, and there was no longer a place found for them in heaven. And the*

great dragon was thrown down, the serpent of old who is called the devil and Satan, who deceives the whole world; he was thrown down to the earth, and his angels were thrown down with him. [Revelation 12:7-9 NASB]

It seems, in Scripture, whenever we read about demonic princes, angels or Satan himself, being confronted by God's angelic forces, it is primarily Michael the Archangel doing the contending or restraining. And as I look back on this story, in my heart, I have always considered this to be the first time in my life that I truly felt God had revealed something to me directly...not through a book or a sermon or another person. I just read about it in the Bible, and the Lord seemed to connect the dots. And it all seemed to make sense. And for that reason, Daniel 12 and references to Michael have always been special to me.

So why would the identity of this "restraining power" be important for us to be able to understand end-time events? Well, for one, those who believe in the early departure plan say that the one who keeps great tribulation from coming upon the earth is the Holy Spirit and the Holy Spirit dwells within those who believe in Jesus Christ, aka...the Church. They go on to say, that when the Church is "taken up" at the beginning of the seven-year tribulation period, the Holy Spirit will no longer be present on the earth and evil will be free to manifest itself fully in those days.

But, what about those who might not have come to Christ before this "catching away" happens? We know it will come like a thief, in the blink of an eye. There will not be time to repent, as when Noah closed the door to the Ark. Is all hope gone for them, at that point? I think not. For me, seeing Michael the Archangel as the restrainer solves that problem. The Holy Spirit will still be present during the tribulation, as will many be who still need redemption. Here is what it says, again in Revelation 12, about those believers who are to be redeemed out of the Great Tribulation.

Then I heard a loud voice in heaven, saying, "Now the salvation, and the power, and the kingdom of our God and the authority of His Christ have come, for the accuser of our brethren has been thrown down, he who accuses them before our God day and night. And they overcame

> *him because of the blood of the Lamb and because of the word of their testimony, and they did not love their life even when faced with death. [Revelation 12:10-11 NASB]*

The Gaither Vocal Band sings an amazing song called, "These Are They," which is taken from Revelation 7, where it says, "These are they who have come out of great tribulation, they have washed their robes in the blood of the Lamb." Powerful song, indeed (it is on YouTube, you should check it out…it's incredible!!) So yes, it is clear there will be some believers present during the seven years of tribulation. Now, if there is a rapture before the seven years start, since we know from Scripture that some will be born during those years, there should be opportunities for others to be saved after the rapture (as we saw in the movie, "Left Behind"), at least I would hope so.

My question is, if the Holy Spirit is no longer active upon the earth, how can anyone be saved? And that is, for me, where the entire theory falls apart. The Lord gave us the Holy Spirit that we would be "His witnesses" to a wicked and lost world. Why would He remove that from the equation for the final seven years? If the accuser, Satan, is thrown down and he brings great trouble upon the earth through his appointed one, the Antichrist, and we hear of these faithful ones who overcame him with their testimony and the blood of the Lamb, how does that happen if the church and the Holy Spirit are nowhere to be found (in this world, anyway). I cannot make sense of this, and believe me, I've tried. So, you can count me among those who are not convinced that "the restrainer" is the Holy Spirit or "the church." I believe it has always been Michael the Archangel who contends with Satan on God's behalf.

Now, as we move further into Daniel 12, I am going to hop back to something I talked about in the last chapter, the questions of the immortality of the soul and the question of what happens when we physically die. We covered the first one earlier. Now, here in Daniel 12, the second question begs to be addressed. For the record, this is the angel, Gabriel, speaking to Daniel:

> *"Many of those who sleep in the dust of the ground will awake, these to everlasting life, but the others to disgrace and everlasting contempt. Those who have insight*

will shine brightly like the brightness of the expanse of heaven, and those who lead the many to righteousness, like the stars forever and ever. But as for you, Daniel, conceal these words and seal up the book until the end of time; many will go back and forth, and knowledge will increase." [Daniel 12:2-4NASB]

In my first book, "Unlocking Creation," I made the case that God Almighty has woven into the wondrous things He created, aspects of His divine nature as a way of revealing Himself to us. So, when we look at things like "God created the universe and everything in it in six days, and then He rested on the seventh," did it truly take Him six days to create everything? I doubt it. I believe He could have done with a wave of His hand or one word from His mouth. Or...did He choose to allow it to take Him six days and then allow Himself to take a rest on the seventh, to reveal a pattern for us, one by which we were meant to live our lives? I vote for the latter. I believe He, quite often, was revealing patterns and mysteries that we could learn from, things that would help us to not only understand Him better, but ourselves as well.

So, may I suggest to you that when He designed us and made us in such a way that we need a good night's sleep, maybe He was leaving us a little hint as to how things would unfold at the end of our lives. I believe He did not have to make us this way. He could have designed us to function quite well without the need for rest or sleep, but He did not. He could have created the world in seven days and not taken a day of rest. He doesn't need a day off, we do. Same with eating, He designed us to desire food regularly, and water, or we die. Are there not also spiritual correlations there, too? We need to be fed spiritually and drink of the living water regularly, too, do we not?

And when we sleep, be it for twenty minutes or eight hours (should you be that fortunate), do we have a sense of time that has passed, or what is going on around us, while we sleep? Not if you are truly asleep, right? Could that be God's way of comforting us that when we die and are awaiting our resurrection, we will have no sense of time or surroundings then, either? We could be asleep in the grave for a thousand years, but when the last trumpet sounds and "the dead in Christ" are raised first, it will seem like a blink of an eye. I think King Solomon nailed it when he wrote these words:

> *"For the living know they will die; but the dead do not know anything." [Ecclesiates 9:5 NASB]*

In the same way, just as when we are sound asleep at night, I believe our physical time in the grave will seemingly pass in an instant, as well. To the one who has "entered their rest" (I do not think that it is a coincidence that those words were used, either), their body will be resting, awaiting the moment when they will all be changed "in the twinkling of an eye," made alive again and shall instantly be like Him." And those of us who are still alive at that time, we shall be changed in an instant, as well. Then, at that moment, we shall all come into the light of that glorious new day, and all will be well forever more. HALLELUJAH

In preparation for writing this chapter, I got out my Strong's Concordance and did a study on how many times the words "asleep," "sleep, "sleeps" and "slept" appeared in the Bible in correlation with death. I counted over fifty times. It is used all through the Old Testament when the patriarchs died, saying they "slept with their fathers." Then, in the New Testament, we find Jesus twice referring to people who had physically died as "only sleeping," once with the young girl whom He raised from the dead and once regarding Lazarus. Even Luke, when he wrote the account for the stoning of Stephen in Acts 7 referred to his death by saying "he fell asleep."

The common explanation for the use of the word sleep is that has long been used as a way to soften the concept of death by saying a person did not die, they merely fell asleep (implying that they will be alive again in the afterlife). But it seems to me that this was over thousands of years, with many different writers all choosing to use the same method of "softening" when they spoke of death. Isn't it more logical to think that death, as we see it vs. how God sees it, could be two very different things? I have to think that our time here on Earth, in the eyes of God, is merely a temporary assignment and that our earthly passing is not truly the end of anything. Rather, we live beyond the grave in one form or another, as it is mentioned here in Daniel 12…some to "everlasting life" and some to "disgrace and everlasting contempt." So, in God's eyes, the word "sleep" could be more appropriate. To Him, it may be simply a "time out," as we await the promised resurrection which, spiritually speaking, will be "our new day dawning."

I have often heard it said that the true biblical definition of the word "death" is "eternal separation from God." Our physical death, most certainly, is not that. I believe it is a time for all of us to wait for whatever eternity holds for us. As we have learned from as far back as Genesis, rest is something that was always part of God's plan for us. We have the Sabbath, the Sabbath week, the Jubilee year and, of course, the passing away of these temporal, corruptible bodies. I see it as the reason people have always said, "rest in peace." Is that not a fitting way to express your good wishes that the person who has died will one day be resurrected to eternal peace in Christ. I would say… absolutely.

I think that it is also very telling that the subject was raised again, a second time, by Gabriel at the end of Daniel 12 as we see in the verse below. It certainly does not sound like Gabriel thinks that Daniel will spend thousands of years in Heaven awaiting the second coming of Christ to Planet Earth.

"But as for you, go your way to the end; then you will enter into rest and rise again for your allotted portion at the end of the age." [Daniel 12:13 NASB]

So, Daniel will die, enter his rest, and then rise again at the end of the age. He is told he will receive his "allotted portion at the end of the age." Well, that seems quite clear, does it not?

I do want to share, if I may, one more passage of Scripture, before moving on, because I feel it goes a long way towards explaining why this idea of "resting in the grave, awaiting our resurrection" is so important in the big picture of things. This one is from the eleventh chapter of Hebrews, a chapter that pays tribute to so many of the "fathers of faith" who went before us. Have a look:

And all these, having gained approval through their faith, did not receive what was promised, because God had

provided something better for us, so that apart from us they would not be made perfect. [Hebrews 11:39-40 NASB]

All these amazing soldiers of faith, although they gained approval for their faith (God counted their faith as righteousness), they DID NOT receive what was promised, so that they would NOT be "made perfect" (receive their incorruptible bodies) apart from us. Let that one sink in a bit.

God, in His infinite wisdom and mercy, did not choose for them to "receive their promise"...before the rest of us. I believe that implies that at the time of the writing of Hebrews (which was after the death and resurrection of Christ), the Old Testament saints had not yet been raised from the dead and received the fulfillment of their promise of eternal life. Oh, they will, because they found God's approval, but not just yet. I believe at the sound of the last trump, all the dead in Christ will be raised together, from Adam to Billy Graham (and the rest of the dearly departed). And to them, it will seem like they had been asleep for only a matter of seconds and went home to be with the Lord immediately, anyway. It really is just a matter of perspective. In the big picture of things, it will matter not. We won't miss a thing.

You may be wondering why I believe these two subjects are so critical to our understanding of the end times? For me, that is an easy one to answer. If the soul is not "immortal," in other words, if our soul does not go immediately to be with the Lord upon our death, as so many believe, then there is no basis for believing in a pre-tribulation rapture. That would go against what the writer of Hebrews felt it was important to convey. God did not intend for some to be raised to everlasting life and receive their glorified bodies before anyone else who was yet to be redeemed. It is meant to be a "one-day event" that tops all other "one-day events" the world has ever known.

Yes, on that glorious day, the dead in Christ (the redeemed of all of human history) will be raised first, with those who are yet alive being "changed in the twinkling of an eye"...immediately after. It is all going to happen within a matter of seconds. I do not believe it will be like an "installment plan," where some are raised this month, some next month, and some the month after that...etc. No, I believe there will be one great big "Homecoming" at the sound of the last trumpet when Christ returns to vanquish His enemies and claim His eternal bride….His beloved. And as Phil Keaggy said in one of his classic songs many years ago…"What a day that will be." Amen to that.

"WE SHALL NOT ALL SLEEP…BUT ALL BE CHANGED"
[1 CORINTHIANS 15:51]

CHAPTER TWELVE

THINGS SEEN, YET UNSEEN

But wait, there is yet another astonishing thing revealed in the opening verses of Daniel 12. In verse 4, Gabriel tells Daniel to write all these amazing revelations down, apparently for future generations, and then he is told to seal up the book until the end of the age.

Imagine that, about twenty-five hundred years ago, during the Babylonian captivity of the Israelites, a man from among them named Daniel, found favor with God and was even contacted by a high-ranking angel named Gabriel, who revealed some amazing things that were to take place many years in the future. But then, Gabriel tells Daniel to "seal up the book," as these things were not to be revealed until "the time of the end." He is probably thinking, "Oh great, then I most likely will not get credit for it, either." I am kidding, of course. His heart belonged to God.

Then, Gabriel says, "many will go back and forth, and knowledge will increase." That seems peculiar. Why would the Lord do that? I mean, sure, many times prophecies are given that could have more than one fulfillment, a current one (for the present) and one that will come to light in the future. But, this situation does not seem to be one of those. These messages seem to be all about the future. Gabriel even says, "Now at that time…"

Aside from the reason stated in the text, that "knowledge will increase," the only other reason I can think of (since these prophecies were written down and are included in our Bible), is that it would cause those who came after, to keep their eyes and ears open. It is saying that there are more details yet to come, but they will not be revealed until the time is right. These things would, then, become yet another sign that the end times are drawing near.

Have you ever told someone, "Mark this down, I am just saying this now so when it happens, you will know I told you so." OK, I confess, I have. Maybe it's just me. But apparently, God also likes to tell us what will happen long before it does, too, so when it comes to fruition, we will know it is God's hand at work, helping us to "test the spirits." But, let's be honest, His motives are much purer than mine, no doubt. His ways are always pure and redemptive. Mine, well honestly, not so much.

In addition, I would say we are living in a day and age where human knowledge has increased exponentially, not just regarding biblical things, but in general. It has been said that knowledge has increased more in the last one-hundred years than the previous twenty centuries put together. It also appears the rate in which we are "increasing in knowledge" and making discoveries is only accelerating. Who knows what the world will be like in another hundred years, should the Lord tarry? It is a little scary, isn't it?

The Bible does say that if the time (the days of this world) were not shortened, all would perish. Could it be that the return of Christ may occur just before some catastrophic happening, some "extinction level event" like a nuclear war or a major meteor strike, one that could wipe us all out? It very well could be. But, even that would not surprise God. His plans are already in place, and as we have talked about repeatedly, He changes not…and He knows the beginning from the end, as we saw in Isaiah 46.

Let's face it, there are all kinds of things being considered and even developed nowadays that could be quite troubling. I am sure you have heard about some of them, like cloning and artificial intelligence, to name a few. I shudder when I think how these new technologies might be used in the days ahead. It reminds of the early days of Babylon when the people tried to build the Tower of Babel, so they could reach towards the heavens and communicate with their gods. How did that work out? Not so well, God intervened, and He will again, I have no doubt.

But, on the other side of the coin, if we look just at the studies of theology and Bible prophecy, the last century has revealed incredible amounts of new information. Just with the discovery of the Dead Sea Scrolls and all the other amazing archeological discoveries, we not only know a lot more about the Bible and the people chosen by God to be His messengers in Scripture, but we also have found plenty of confirmations about the things we believe, as well. And that is very comforting to know.

But is there more? What else does this chapter point to that we should take note of, as we continue in this discussion of the end times?" I am so glad you asked?

> ***Then I, Daniel, looked and behold, two others were standing, one on this bank of the river and the other on that bank of the river. And one said to the man dressed in linen, who was above the waters of the river, "How long will it be until the end of these wonders?" I heard the man dressed in linen, who was above the waters of the river, as he raised his right hand and his left toward heaven and swore by Him who lives forever that it would be for a time, times, and half a time; and as soon as they finish shattering the power of the holy people, all these will be completed. [Daniel 12:5-7 NASB]***

"How long will it be until the end of these wonders?" Isn't that the sixty-four-million-dollar question? Wouldn't we all like to know the answer to that one? I know I sure would.

The first thing I would be asking here is, "Who are these three figures that are talking?" Daniel says he sees "two men," which I assume are angelic beings, one standing on one bank of a river and the other standing on the other bank. And one is asking this question of a third figure, one who is positioned above the river, itself. My take on this is that there two angels standing on opposite sides of a river. And the third, I would presume, is a higher-ranking angel, possibly Michael again (because it says he "swore by Him who lives forever"...which is the Lord). And this higher-ranking angel replies, "a time, times and half a time and as soon as they finish shattering the power of the holy people, these events will be completed." This, of course, relates to periods of time, and as we have seen, this could be interpreted as days, years, or even thousands of years. But, more on that a little later.

And, as usual, one good question leads to another. Remember how Daniel 12 started off, saying "everyone in the book will be rescued?" Now, I need to ask, "Who are these holy people whose power will be shattered before these events are complete?" I want to be very careful here. It would be very easy to jump to conclusions, but as I said in my Introduction, I only want to take the Scriptures at face value, and not use "the interpretations of men" to color my conclusions.

So, this might be a good place to apply that prerequisite. Let me start by saying I looked at this verse in every Bible translation I could find and they all use the words "holy people." So, what does that mean? Some would say it speaks of the Jews, God's chosen people. Others would say, "Not so fast, it could also mean believers in Christ." For our purposes, here, I am not going to favor one or the other. Rather, I will stop and look at what the term "holy" means, in biblical terms. That might help, I think.

The Hebrew word for "holy" is "qodesh" which means "apartness, set-apartness or sacredness" or "things dedicated or consecrated to God or His purposes." So, for our discussion, let's say that the word "holy" means "set apart for God or His purposes."

Could this "set-apartness" apply to the nation of Israel...all the descendants of Abraham of which God spoke? I would say, "Yes, it certainly would seem to be a reasonable conclusion." Ok, then, how about those who have believed in Jesus Christ as their Savior and Lord? Have they not also been consecrated and set apart for God? I see that as being a reasonable conclusion, as well. After all, is it not the blood of Christ that sanctifies us, sets us apart for His purpose and makes us "holy?" I would think to assume anything less would be to minimize the work of Christ on the Cross.

So that presents a problem, does it not, as we look at the various end-time scenarios. Who are these holy people whose power will be completely shattered before the Lord returns at the sound of the last trumpet? Could he be referring to the Jews? Well yes, I believe the power of the Jewish people will be severely tested and even shattered in the final days before the Lord returns. During the last half of the seven years of tribulation, once the Antichrist assumes power, anyone who desires to seek and worship God will be rendered powerless (speaking in an earthly sense…God will still be mighty in their midst).

But I also believe those who have put their faith in Jesus Christ and are alive at that time, since they are "consecrated and set apart for God" through Christ, will be tested, as with fire, that they may be found to be sanctified and worthy, having persevered through a time of trial and tribulation, just as Job passed his test. Did not Peter tell us, in 1 Peter 4, to "be not surprised at the fiery ordeal among you?" That does not sound like we, as believers in Christ, will be immune to testing or trials. And again, did not Christ, Himself, say in Matthew Chapter 24 (a chapter that deals primarily with the end times), "But those who endure to the end will be saved." If we will not be tested, then what is there to endure?

I think we need to go back to the very first verse in this chapter, I believe, because Daniel makes it quite clear who these "holy people" are. They are "His people…everyone who are found to be written in the book." We are all sinners. But, we all can be "made holy" by the blood of Christ. Not unlike Paul, I see no distinction between Jew and Gentile. We all need to be redeemed by the blameless Lamb of God. I know of no one who is exempt from that.

Now, I know the idea of us, as believers in Christ, having to endure great tribulation before the Lord returns to claim His bride, is discomforting to many. But, as we look through the Bible, are there not many examples of people who God called to serve Him, yet had to endure great hardship, as well? Sure, there are. Why would we think that it would be any different with us?

What I find comforting is that the Lord promises to "never leave us or forsake us." And, just like the old saying teaches us, "If He has brought you to it…He will bring you through it!!" I think the saints of old like Noah, Abraham, Isaac, Jacob, Lot, Joseph, Job, Moses, Ruth, David and so many others would agree. Jesus said in Matthew 28, "Lo, I am with you always, even to the end of the age." I can only take that to mean that no matter what we are called to face in our lives, He is with us and we have nothing to fear.

So, I would say that we, as the ones set apart to be joined with Christ forever, may be rendered somewhat powerless (in the physical sense) during the reign of the Antichrist. But the power of life and death is in the hands of the Lord and He has promised to never abandon those that are His. Not now…not ever. That is good enough for me. That is a rock I can fix my feet on. But wait, there is more.

> *As for me, I heard but could not understand; so I said, "My lord, what will be the outcome of these events?" He said, "Go your way, Daniel, for these words are concealed and sealed up until the end time. Many will be purged, purified and refined, but the wicked will act wickedly; and none of the wicked will understand, but those who have insight will understand. [Daniel 12:8-10 NASB]*

I feel the need to point to something that leaped out at me as I dug deeper and deeper into Daniel 12. It is the following words, "Many will be purged, purified and refined, but the wicked will act wickedly, and none of the wicked will understand." It suggests that there will be two groups of people in those days, those who will be "purged, purified and refined," and "the wicked who will act wickedly." Once again, why are "the refined" not already out of the picture?

Those who believe in an early departure, before things get bad, might say, "We were purified by the blood of Christ, no need to do it again." OK, but just maybe God wants us to "show ourselves approved" to the enemies of God, in the face of great trials and struggles. I do not believe God forsook Job when he endured times of great hardship. And I do not believe He will abandon us, even if we go through the fire. May Your will be done, Lord, not mine. I place myself in Your hands. I trust you, no matter what.

Also, I cannot imagine the wicked being purged, purified and refined. For what purpose would they be refined. I would think only those whom God has deemed as "set apart for His purposes" would go through a purification and refining process that results in redemption and being fully ready to enter His eternal rest. The wicked are headed for destruction, no purification or refining is needed for that. So, in a sense, seven years of tribulation would be wasted on them. They are not going to repent, right? Why waste all that time on those who will never yield to the grace and mercy of God? Is it not times of great trial and suffering that lead many to turn to the Lord, and are there not many who remain alive during those seven years who need to be saved by His blood and the word of His testimony? Is that not how a great revival will likely come about? Have your way, Lord…both in us who have called on Your name…and those who are yet to believe!!

We do know, from Scripture, that some will come to know the Lord during these times of trial and tribulation. And even if it is one person who repents, I believe the Lord would say, "It is worth it?" So, I believe the Holy Spirit must be present on the earth, active and powerful, working inside of His people who remain to help bring about the redemption of those who are yet to come to Christ…even the Jews, of course.

"From the time that the regular sacrifice is abolished and the abomination of desolation is set up, there will be 1,290 days. How blessed is he who keeps waiting and attains to the 1,335 days." [Daniel 12:11-12 NASB]

At the end of this amazing chapter, Gabriel answers Daniel's question from verse 8, "What will be the outcome of these events?" And in doing so, it appears he is giving all those who suggest that "the Bible is full of contradictions" plenty of rocks to through in our path, to try and trip us up. What is up with all these different numbers we see in Scripture regarding these days. We see "time, times and half a time," 1260 days, 1290 days and now 1335 days. They cannot all be correct, right? Why all the confusion, Gabriel? Our God is not a God of confusion, so there must certainly be a good explanation, I'm sure.

Let me tell you, folks, in doing my research on all these different numbers, it seems there are more possible explanations than there are different ways of saying "three and a half years." I could not find one solid source for a definitive explanation on the subject. So, allow me to give you my take on all these different numbers as food for thought. I will try to simplify the confusion, just a little if I can:

1. First of all, since the writings of the Old Testament, there have been a number of different calendars used. The Hebrews went by the cycles of the moon, 12 months of 30 days each…360 days. And that meant they had to adjust every so often, by adding in a thirteenth month for certain years, to put the feasts connected to the harvest back where they should be. That meant you had some years with 360 days and occasionally, a "leap year" of sorts with 390 days. So, some have speculated that to measure the full seven years, it may or not be necessary to add in a "leap year", depending on when the seven years fall. So, it is likely that half of the seven years would be 1260 days (3 ½ x 360 = 1260), and the other half could add up to 1290 days, with that additional month added in, for adjustment sake. That would give us an entire seven-year period of 2550 days (counting one leap year). Fine, but this does not address the matter of 1335 days. And that leads me to the second possible explanation.

2. Some point to that fact that it is possible that, as Scripture teaches us, the second half of the tribulation period begins when the "abomination of desolation" is standing in the Temple, declaring himself to be God and he does away with the daily animal sacrifices. In this scenario, they suggest it is possible that the sacrifices had been restarted when the Temple was reopened and had been practiced for thirty days when the Antichrist shows up in the Temple. That would give us 1290 days, by adding in an extra thirty days before the sacrifices are stopped. This same theory, suggests that from the day Christ returns to vanquish His enemies, until Christ's millennial kingdom can be readied and established could take forty-five days (not sure where they get that

number from), giving us 1335 days from the time that the Temple sacrifices restarted until the time Christ kingdom officially begins on the earth.. Now, I do not, personally, put much significance on this theory. It seems to try too hard to make the numbers work out. But there is a third theory that does seem to make a lot of sense, if you ask me. And, since you are reading this book (thank you…btw), I assume you did ask me. I will do my best to answer, with God's gracious help.

3. We need to remember that Daniel was a Jew who was taken prisoner by the Babylonians and he lived the rest of his life in Babylon/Persia, history tells us. And it is known that Daniel was highly regarded as an astronomer. Not only was he gifted in interpreting dreams and visions, he also studied the sun and the moon and the stars, always looking for signs, since God instructed us in Genesis that the heavens were established as signs and ways of measuring the days, months and years. So, this theory points out that from the seven-year famine in Egypt (Joseph's time), there were 1150 years until the time that Israel fell to Assyria, 1260 years until God judged Assyria and they fell, 1290 years until Judah fell to Nebuchadnezzar, and 1335 years (539 BC) until God judged Babylon and they fell to Cyrus and the Persian empire took over. Knowing who Daniel was, his background and expertise, and the times that he lived in, it would make much more sense to me that these numbers would have a high-level of importance, not just to Daniel in his day, but also to how we might interpret what the angel Gabriel was telling him. Ah, another "double meaning." One that was relevant and made sense to Daniel at the time, and another that Daniel may not even have thought about, that had "end-time significance" and remains yet to be fulfilled.

So, I am going to go with "Door #3." Again, there are more theories on this than you can count. For the sake of our study, here, I believe that the timeline for Israel and Judah could very well have been ordained by God as a precursor to how things would unfold many centuries into the future. Plus, when the scholars of the final days (once knowledge has increased, as Gabriel said) are permitted to see these writings that were "shut up until the end," they might rejoice in having some tangible events in Israel's historical timeline, to help make sense of it all, looking forward.

Once again, we see that "the best predictor of future behavior is past behavior." If that applies to us, the ones He made in His image, why would it not apply to the Creator, as well? I believe it does. As we said before, "He changes not."

"TEACH US TO NUMBER OUR DAYS..."
[PSALM 90:12]

CHAPTER THIRTEEN

DO NUMBERS REALLY MATTER?

As I mentioned earlier, in my first book, "Unlocking Creation: God's True Nature Revealed," I looked closely at many well-known aspects of God's creation, to see if He had woven into them certain aspects of His divine nature that He desired us to both discover and learn from. I looked at things like light vs. darkness, hot vs. cold, consonant sounds vs, dissonant sounds...and even topics like male and female, and the miracle of human birth. And believe you me, I learned every bit as much as the reader did, as the Lord unmasked some amazing attributes of His divinity through my research.

Funny how these connections were there all the time, but it took a little curiosity and effort to bring them to light. Isn't that how God is? I believe it is part of His nature to desire to be sought, and to hunger to be discovered and understood, just as we do. After all, we are made in His image, are we not? So, I guess we should not be surprised. What I want to do now, is spend a little time unpacking this whole concept of "biblical numerology." Now, trust me, an entire book could be written on this subject alone (in fact many have), but I am only going to touch on a few of the key ones that relate to end times studies. And make no mistake about it, numbers play an important role.

Have you ever noticed that a handful of numbers show up in Scripture over and over again? We see, three and four used quite regularly, as is six, seven, eight, ten and twelve. And the number forty seems to pop up quite a bit, as well. So, let me give a quick overview of these numbers and highlight what significance they may hold:

One: This one should be fairly obvious. There is One true God, one maker of Heaven and Earth, and there is one name by which we are saved, Jesus Christ. So, the number one is generally attached to things connected to deity, to God Almighty, and implies that no one else or no other thing on Earth or in Heaven compares to Him.

Two: The number two usually is used in connection with things related to relationship. The most well-known of these is probably the one used to describe marriage, "And the two shall become one." Hold on to that thought, because as we dig deeper into Christ's return and what comes after, the importance of what I would like to call "two-ness" will loom large.

Three: Once again, we do not have to look very far to see an example of what role the number three plays. Think of the number three as number two on steroids, or let me say it this way, God "one-upping' us. If two is the number of "relationship," then three points to the ultimate relationship, the three-person Godhead or Triune God. In Ecclesiastes, Solomon wrote, "Two are better than one, they get a good return for their labor. But a three-strand cord is not easily broken." Just as the Godhead is more secure because of the three firm legs on which it stands, our duality (in our relationships) becomes much stronger when the third and strongest strand is added, through Christ, to be an intricate part of them.

Four: Here, we instantly think of things like four seasons, four corners of the earth, four winds, four horsemen, etc. So, I would suggest that the number four denotes "totality" in one form or another. When the Bible uses the number four, it generally is talking about things that are all-inclusive or complete. The whole enchilada, if you will.

Six: Most people point to the six days of creation, the six days of the week on which we are permitted to work, or the number 666, which is the number of the beast (the antichrist). But, it is also thought that the number six is "the number of man" and 666 would be the opposite of the Holy Trinity (the devil likes to imitate the things of God), a trinity of evil (Satan, the Antichrist, and the False Prophet) if you will. But, we will be talking about six, mainly as it applies to the days of creation and the days of the week since the end times seem to rely heavily on that theme.

I am going to skip over the number seven, for a moment, since that is what my main focus in this chapter will be.

Eight: This number seems, often, to be attached to thing denoting "new beginnings." There were eight people saved on the Ark, Noah and his seven family members. David was the eighth son of Jesse, Jesus was dedicated to the Lord on the eighth day, and of course, the Jews see the "eighth day" of certain feasts as implying a "fresh start."

Ten: This is an odd one, in that the number ten is often used regarding things that get broken down into two groups of five. Ten fingers, ten toes, ten commandments. ten virgins, etc...etc. We can think of it pointing to two groups that when added together, make one larger group. God loves to join pieces together to make something better!! Try swinging a golf club or tying your shoes with just one hand. A few years back, I had shoulder surgery. I found out very quickly that only having the use of one hand makes many simple things very difficult. God is quite smart in that way. He'll give you five things and then say, "But it works better if you have five others to help." I love it.

Twelve: This is a number that also implies completeness (after all it is three times four), especially relating to things that are of an eternal nature or things that will continue beyond this temporal world we live in. Israel was made up of twelve tribes, and thusly, we read of the woman who has twelve stars above her head. Jesus had twelve disciples, who became the twelve apostles. New Jerusalem will have twelve gates and, of course, the 144,000 is made up of 12,000 times twelve. Also, the twenty-elders who are seated around the throne of God are often thought to be situated with twelve to the right and twelve to the left of Him. Although the identities of the twenty-four elders are not revealed in Scripture, many have concluded that they may represent the twelve tribes of Israel (there were twelve precious stones that made up the breastplate for the high priest) and the twelve apostles (who were the foundation stones for the spreading of the Gospel of Jesus of

Christ). The important part for our discussion is that, again, we see the number twelve representing things that will remain long after this world has passed away.

Forty: Here we have a number that is most often associated with struggles, or difficult times. The flood rains during Noah's day continued for forty days. Moses hid from Pharoah for forty years and then led the Israelites to the Promised Land for another forty years. He died when he was 120 years old, so apparently, his first forty years were no picnic either (Isn't it interesting that the life of Moses unfolded in three forty-year periods?). Goliath taunted Saul's army for forty days before David showed up and ended his bullying. And, we also know that Jesus fasted for forty days and forty nights and was tempted by the devil during that time. So, when you see the number forty in Scripture, it is very likely that something bad, or at least trying, is happening.

But the number I want to take the closest look at, here, because it plays such an integral part in how things will unfold during the final days is, of course, the number seven.

Seven: This is a number, like twelve that is presumably pointing to completeness, but it is pertaining more to temporal things, or things of this world...not eternal ones. Think of some of the common things we know the number seven is attached to seven days in a week, seven colors in a rainbow, seven seas, seven continents, and you have probably heard of the seven deadly sins. If we think in biblical terms, the list is quite long, as well. There are the seven feasts, seven churches, seven lampstands, seven seals, seven trumpets, seven bowls (or vials), and of course, the seven years of tribulation, to name only a few.

Multiples of seven are also noteworthy, like the seventy years that Israel was held captive in Babylon, Daniel's seventy weeks, and the Romans destroying the Temple (as Jesus predicted) in 70 AD.

So what kinds of things should we be looking for, with regards to the end times, things that might help us see things a little more clearly? To answer that question, I would like to discuss a few key passages, if I may:

> *Thus, the heavens and the earth were completed, and all their hosts. By the seventh day, God completed His work which He had done, and He rested on the seventh day from all His work which He had done. Then God blessed the seventh day and sanctified it because in it He rested from all His work which God had created and made. [Genesis 2:1-3 NASB]*

As we jump back into Genesis, for a moment, we see it didn't take long for the Lord to set a precedent that the number seven may have significance. He created the universe and all that is in it in six days, and then He rested (that is key) on the seventh day. But here in Genesis 2, it goes a step further. It says, "Then God blessed the seventh day and sanctified it because, in it, He rested from all His work. Ok, so it seems He is putting a double emphasis on this seventh day. You might be guessing there is more than meets the eye, here, and you would be right.

The first way in which He chose to honor it, was by setting aside the seventh day and making it holy. This became what we now know as the Sabbath. I will talk more about that shortly, but for right now, I would like to look at the second way in which I believe this day of rest would become significant.

Then, the Apostle Peter talked about it in his second epistle, using a concept he gleaned from Moses's Psalm 90 (which also uses the number seventy (years) as the length of our days on Earth, or eighty if our strength does not fail us):

> *But do not let this one fact escape your notice, beloved, that with the Lord one day is like a thousand years, and a thousand years like one day. [2 Peter 3:8 NASB]*

So, we have here a principle that Moses wrote about in the Old Testament, and Peter wrote about in the New Testament. That always helps to strengthen the case for legitimacy and it also once again confirms…God changes not.

Now, let me see if I can draw a clear connection to how this principle may apply in the days yet ahead of us.

1) As we discussed earlier, there has roughly been six thousand years of biblical history from the time of creation until now. That would equate to six days if we applied Peter's measuring stick.

2) The Lord sanctified the seventh day as "a day of rest," and the Bible teaches us that when Christ returns, He will set up His Kingdom here on Earth and reign for one thousand years. And during those days, we know that Satan will be bound and unable to tempt or harm God's chosen ones. I would call that a day of rest, a truly amazing day of rest, to give it proper weighting.

3) When those one thousand years are over, or right at the end of them, we are taught that Satan will be released for a short while and then he and those who followed him will be cast into the lake of fire. That is when the New Heaven and New Earth will be unveiled, hence a new beginning and the ultimate "eighth day." One that lasts forever.

So, I guess you can see just how important numbers might be, especially the number seven, in making some sense of the symbolism and mysteries that have baffled students of the Bible for years.

Up next, I would like to stay in the same ballpark, here, by digging a little deeper into some of the traditional applications of the number seven to things of importance in Hebrew tradition, like the Sabbath, the Year of Jubilee and the Seven Feasts. I believe you find this very helpful when we get into the details of how things may unfold before and after the Second Coming of Christ.

"EVEN THE HAIRS OF YOUR HEAD ARE NUMBERED"
[Luke 12:7]

CHAPTER FOURTEEN

THE IMPORTANCE OF SEVENS

So, as we saw in the last chapter, the Lord was quite quick about establishing the number seven as "something special," and it was not very long before He began adding to that specialness to drive home the point of just how special it is. Let's examine the Jewish tradition of the Sabbath since the basis for so many of the other references to the number seven seems to be tied to these ideas of "rest" and "completeness." And what do you know? We need to look no further than the Ten Commandments:

> *"Remember the sabbath day, to keep it holy. Six days you shall labor and do all your work, but the seventh day is a sabbath of the LORD YOUR GOD; in it, you shall not do any work, you or your son or your daughter, your male or your female servant or your cattle or your sojourner who stays with you. For in six days the LORD MADE THE HEAVENS AND THE EARTH, THE SEA AND ALL THAT IS IN THEM, AND RESTED ON THE SEVENTH DAY; THEREFORE, THE LORD BLESSED THE SABBATH DAY AND MADE IT HOLY." [EXODUS 20:8-11 NASB]*

And to take it one step further:

> *"Every sabbath day he shall set it in order before the LORD continually; it is an everlasting covenant for the sons of Israel." [Leviticus 24:8 NASB]*

Make no mistake about it, the Sabbath rest is a big deal in the eyes of God. And I, for one, believe that in our modern society it has been ceremonially "kicked to the curb." When I was young, there were very few places of business that were open on Sundays. (I will abstain from wading into the whole Saturday vs. Sunday debate at this time as it has little bearing on our larger discussion of the end times).

While we are on the subject, I would like to "tip my hat" to Chick-fil-A, which has always remained faithful to this observance and kept their doors closed on the Lord's day, as many refer to it. Maybe it is no wonder, then, that they have endured so many attacks by the media and those who do not understand the significance of making God a priority. But I am sure the Truett family understand why it happens. Jesus said that just as they attacked Him, they will attack those who do His will, as well. However, He will never leave or forsake us, no matter what comes our way. And He will surely reward those who endure to the end.

But, there are two things I would like to chew on a little bit more, here. One is that the Sabbath is considered "holy" (which means "set apart" or "special"). In other words, it certainly was not a suggestion. And secondly, the verse from Leviticus bangs the drum a little harder by making it clear that the Sabbath was not a temporary or part-time thing. It was something to be observed by God's people in all generations. Truthfully, in my own heart and mind, I believe that over the years and centuries since God proclaimed the Sabbath as holy, the concept (and hence, it's the deeper meaning of "rest" and "completeness") of keeping the seventh day holy has been compromised greatly. But take note, there is yet another layer to this onion:

> ***The Lord then spoke to Moses at Mount Sinai, saying, "Speak to the sons of Israel and say to them, 'When you come into the land which I shall give you, then the land shall have a sabbath to the Lord. Six years you shall sow your field, and six years you shall prune your vineyard and gather in its crop, but during the seventh year the land shall have a sabbath rest, a sabbath to the Lord; you shall not sow your field nor prune your vineyard..." [Leviticus 25:1-4 NASB]***

So, not only does the sabbath rest apply to our weeks, but it also has an application to years. After six years of working in the fields, God instructed His people to let the land lay for a year, to let it "rest," if you will. One of my favorite authors, Rabbi Jonathan Cahn, wrote an entire book on the subject of the Sabbath year. It was called, "The Mystery of the Shemitah." The word "shemitah" (or "shmitah") is a Hebrew word that means "the year of release." And it applies to this Jewish tradition of a year of rest, of sorts, because along with allowing the land to rest from sowing for a year, the Shemitah year is also a year where the Jewish people were to release those who are captive and in debt (as the word "release" would seem to imply). In other words, the Sabbath year or Shemitah was looked at as a year of rest for the land and sowing and harvesting, for sure, but more symbolically it was about "setting the captives and those in debt free". It was looked at as a "year of forgiveness."

But, ah yes, there is yet another application of the number seven and its multiples, one that is all about forgiveness and rest, as well:

"You are also to count off seven sabbaths of years for yourself, seven times seven years, so that you have the time of the seven sabbaths of years, namely, forty-nine years... You shall thus consecrate the fiftieth year and proclaim a release through the land to all its inhabitants. It shall be a jubilee for you, and each of you shall return to his own property, and each of you shall return to his family. You shall have the fiftieth year as a jubilee; You shall not sow, nor reap its aftergrowth, nor gather in, from its untrimmed vines. For it is a jubilee; it shall be holy to you." [Leviticus 25:8-12 NASB]

Seven times seven, of course, equals forty-nine (I think there may be added significance that this is the square number of seven, as we often speak of foursquare with regards to churches and other things...and of course four means completeness or totality (like the four points of the Cross of Christ meaning "It is finished"). Even the New Jerusalem is in the shape of a square, twelve hundred by twelve hundred miles, and twelve hundred miles high, just to put an exclamation point on it all. So yeah, I take the significance of numbers in the Bible quite seriously, as we talked about earlier, "Nothin' is for nothin'."

Let's recap…a week is seven days with the seventh day being one of God-ordained rest. A shemitah is a period of seven years with the seventh year being a year of rest or release, also ordained of God. And now we come to a group of seven shemitahs that add up to a total forty-nine years, and that leads to the fiftieth year which is referred to in Scripture as the year of Jubilee. We should not be surprised. Sevens always carry a lot of weight, prophetically.

And the Jubilee year, of course, celebrates the beginning of another fifty-year cycle, another "fresh start." God is all about "fresh starts." He is redemptive to His core. Remember back when we talked about the different numbers and what they may mean, symbolically? The number eight was said to be the number of "new beginnings." Well, that is interesting, here, because the number fifty also often points to things that mark new beginnings. It marks the beginning of a new seven-year period (a week of years), and the start of another Jubilee cycle. We can also think of Pentecost; it was the fiftieth day after Jesus ascended into Heaven. It marked another "new beginning," as the Holy Spirit was poured out upon believers as a sign that His power would still be with us (as I believe it will, again, in the seven years of tribulation). And, wouldn't you know it, there is an Old Testament correlation to this, as well:

> ***You shall count fifty days to the day after the seventh sabbath; then you shall present a new grain offering to the Lord. You shall bring in from your dwelling places two loaves of bread for a wave offering [Leviticus 23:16-17 NASB]***

This feast, as I will talk more about a little later, is called the Feast of Shavu'ot (or Pentecost). And again, this passage highlights counting fifty days until what? The end of the seventh weekly Sabbath and a new harvest to be thankful for. Well, it certainly appears the Lord is diligent about nailing down a concept, especially when He deems it to be extremely important.

Since I sort of "stuck my toe in the water" slightly, regarding the Jewish feasts, let me close out this chapter with a birds-eye view of these special times on the Hebrew calendar, and briefly point to their prophetic significance in the bigger picture of the Lord's plan of redemption and restoration of His people and His Kingdom.

First, let's take a look at the four Spring feasts:

1) Passover (Pesach): This, of course, originated from the tenth plague when Moses was trying to acquire the release of the Jews from Pharoah, and the Lord decided to strike dead all of Egypt's first-born sons and allowed the angel of death to "Passover" the houses of the Jews who had applied the blood to the doorposts. The significance of this feast, prophetically, is always attached to the death of Jesus on the Cross, because we are released from the sentence of eternal death when we apply the blood of Christ to the doorposts of our heart.

2) Unleavened Bread (Chag Hamotzi…from which the word "matzah" is derived from): The making of bread without leaven (or yeast) signifies the absence of sin since in Scripture yeast is often correlated with sin or evil. So, the Feast of Unleavened Bread, prophetically, is attached to the fact the sacrifice of Jesus Christ at Calvary would mark the end of the stranglehold that sin and death would have on God's people. During this feast, the Jews were to remove anything from their homes that would be displeasing in the sight of God, who of course would later take care of that matter once and for all by offering His Son in exchange for the cancellation of the debt of sin.

3) First Fruits (Reishit Katzir): It says in Leviticus 23:11, that on the first day following the Sabbath of the Feast of Unleavened Bread (which would be the eighth day, not surprising), they were to bring the first of their harvest and wave them before the Lord as a way to give thanks Him for providing the harvest. This, prophetically, points to the resurrection of Christ, who was the "first fruits" of those to be raised from the dead and from whom a great harvest

is yet to follow. But have no fear, God always keeps His promises. Hallelujah!!

4) Pentecost (Shavu'ot): It says "On the day following the seventh Sabbath (which would be the fiftieth day from the beginning of Passover), Pentecost celebrates the summer harvest for the Jews. In the New Testament, we know that Pentecost is when the Holy Spirit fell upon the believers gathered in that upper room. Talk about new beginnings. And just as in the Old Testament, both Pentecosts marked the beginning of an eighth week, for the Jews it was since the beginning of Passover and for Christians, it marks the beginning of the eighth week, at which time Christ rose from the dead (Easter Sunday). Oh, and one other quick point, the two loaves are said to symbolize the Jews and Gentiles becoming one in the eyes of the Lord, which certainly can be said of the underlying impact of the giving of the Holy Spirit to believers in Christ (whether of Jewish descent or Gentile).

This marks the end of the Spring feasts, which was followed by a considerable length of time (one hundred and forty-six days or one day short of the completion of twenty-one Sabbath cycles) until the beginning of the Fall Feasts (or the actual Sabbath of the twenty-first cycle). And the first fall feast is the Feast of Trumpets. Many believe, including yours truly, it is on the Feast of Trumpets, that the seventh and last trumpet will sound to announce the Second Coming of Christ and all that comes afterwards. Needless to say, this will mark, prophetically, the beginning of the seventh day, followed by the ushering in of His Millennial Kingdom, which is most certainly a time of great rest and restoration:

5) Trumpets (Teruah): This is where it gets really exciting for those who are interested in prophecy. The seventh trumpet, no matter which end-time philosophy you ascribe to, is a big deal. It marks the end of the seventh year of the Great Tribulation, and everyone agrees that is when Christ will come again in victory as He destroys all who oppose God and sets up His Kingdom here on Earth for one thousand

years, while Satan is bound and no sin, evil or death will be present. Now, that is what I call a Sabbath rest!!

6) Atonement (Yom Kippur): This one should be fairly obvious to all. On the tenth day (think Ten Commandments) of the seventh month, they were called to have a day of confession and an offering made by fire to the Lord (a sin offering, if you will). It says in Leviticus; it was a day to "afflict your souls," which I would suggest means repentance. Of course, for Christians, our repentance occurs when we give our hearts to Christ and turn from our sinful ways. But the "transfer of title," you could say, officially takes place when Jesus returns and claims His bride at the sound of the last trumpet. As with marriage, getting engaged is only the promise of a new life. The blessed day that the loving couple is "joined as one" is the fulfillment. The past is gone, the new life has come and "the two have begun one," permanently. When we are raised to be with Him, and the goats and the sheep are separated once and for all, we will finally be adorned with a white robe, no more stains or no more holes or frayed edges. We will be clothed in His righteousness.

7) Tabernacles (Sukkot): This may be my favorite feast to talk about, because of the symbolism. This was a beautiful feast, and it is still observed in Israel to this day, where tents are set up, just as the Jews set up a tent of meeting when they were in the wilderness. But the feast also looks forward, just as the Israelites did back then, to a permanent dwelling place for the Lord God to reign and dwell among His people. And that, indeed, will happen first, when Christ sets up His Kingdom in Jerusalem for those one thousand years. And then, ultimately, when the New Heaven and New Earth is unveiled, where we will be with Him forever more. Can you say "Maranatha" (which means, "The Lord is coming" or "Come, Lord Jesus")? I sure can. That will be beyond what we can even think or imagine, for sure.

There you have it, a parade of special sevens, culminating with a look at the seven feasts of Israel. But, as with all of the sevens we looked at, there always seem to be an eighth day attached, a new beginning. And, I believe there will be at "the end of days," as well.

I did not want to leave out Chanukah, which celebrated the rededication of the Temple in 165 BC. Although it is not officially counted among the seven feasts, it has a noteworthy prophetic implication, as well. As we know, the Temple has been built twice. Once by Solomon, who built it for his father David, who was denied the privilege of seeing that come to fruition because of his sin. The second time, it was rebuilt following the decree of King Cyrus of Persia, who helped the Jews gain freedom from Nebuchadnezzar and not only decreed that they rebuild the Temple, he helped to fund it. That Temple was, then, completed under King Darius around 515 BC. This Temple was later refurbished by Simon the Just around 200 BC and was, then, rededicated around 165 BC, which is now celebrated by the feast of Chanukah. And to this day, the Jews celebrate Chanukah (Hannukah) looking back to the rededication of the second Temple, but also looking forward to the dedication of the Third Temple.

The Third Temple, of course, will be rebuilt in Jerusalem, following the peace agreement that begins the seven-year period of great tribulation. This Temple, however, will not be able to function for very long as the Antichrist interrupts things about three and a half years after the peace agreement bringing about the dreaded Abomination of Desolation. And that kicks off the second half of the tribulation period when things get really bad for the next three and a half years until the seventh trumpet blows and Christ return.

But once He sets up His Kingdom, it says there will no need of a Temple, as He will be our fourth (completeness) and final Temple. And that is what I believe Chanukah points to, prophetically, the arrival of our eternal Temple where we will dwell with Him (the eighth day...a day of new beginnings).

"I DID NOT SEE A TEMPLE IN IT..."
[REVELATION 21:22]

CHAPTER FIFTEEN

"RAPTURO" IS A LATIN WORD

Let me make one thing crystal clear, if I may before we move into this very important chapter. I have heard many who are convinced that there will be a "catching away," or a "rapture" prior to the seven years of great tribulation say, "Those who say they do not believe in a pre-tribulation rapture are generally inclined to not believe in a physical rapture or catching away at all." While there may be some who think that way, I am not one of them.

I firmly believe there will be a distinct moment in time when, in the blink of an eye, the dead in Christ will be raised first and those who yet are alive will instantly be changed from corruptible to incorruptible, as well. I have no doubt that we will "meet in Him in the air," and I have no problem calling that glorious occurrence "the blessed hope." It will be a blessed day and a glorious transformation that is for sure!!! I do, however, have a few bones of contention" with the concept, as some portray it:

1. I disagree with the timing of this blessed event, as others see it. I do not believe it will happen at the beginning of the seven years of trouble, but rather at the end, when the last trumpet sounds.

2. I do not think that just because the saints are not gathered to Him before those terrible days, that it means God has forsaken the righteous. I believe quite the opposite. I believe the Lord will do miraculous things through His people, in the midst of all the pain and suffering. And through it all,

many will be saved in numbers too great to count. Hardships have a way of getting people's attention. Many of us came to know Christ during the darkest days of our lives. When things go beyond what we can handle, that is when we look to Heaven for help. I do not see that changing, going forward.

3. The only way the Lord can raise the flag of victory over His enemies, once and for all, is by having those who chose to follow Christ no matter what, endure to the end...prevail by the power of His blood and the word of His testimony. I do not think that disappearing into thin air right before things get tough would accomplish that goal.

4. And, last but not least, I do not believe Christ is going to return to the earth two more times. So, I do not think it is biblical for Him to return to "meet us in the air" at the beginning of the seven years...and then to return a third time at the end of those seven years when the last trumpet sounds and He appears on that majestic white horse... coming and conquering. Correct me if I am wrong, but if the Lord doesn't return before the final seven years, we cannot "meet Him in the air" before the final seven years. So, this presents a problem. Either He comes at the beginning of the seven years or the end. It cannot be both, in my humble opinion.

And, let me also say, I do not get hung up (as so many do) that the word "rapture" does not appear in the Bible. The word "trinity" does not appear in the Bible, and for that matter, neither does the word "Bible." Even the word "church" did not come into use until the Reformation, in the late 1500s, as we talked about earlier. We always need to keep in mind that so many of the things we currently hang our Christian hats on, these days, were tweaked by the Catholic Church, and the Bible translators who gave us the English versions we have today. That has had a huge "domino effect" on the perceptions that many people have regarding the Second Coming, especially the when and the how of it all. I, for one, want to believe as Christ and His closest followers believed. Don't you? But I agree that it is very hard to do, at times. It can be difficult to cut through the "smoke and mirrors" of man-made religion...and arrive at the truth of God. Rest assured, I firmly believe the concept of a day when the saints of God will be gathered unto Him in the twinkling of an eye and be with Him forever more is entirely biblical. And it is not just talked about in the New Testament, either.

For starters, we just talked at length about Daniel Chapter 12, and we know that at the beginning of that chapter, Gabriel tells Daniel of a day when "those who sleep in the ground will awake...some to everlasting life...some to everlasting contempt. Then we have this passage from Isaiah that many suggest is evidence of a pre-tribulation rapture. It is a little long, but we need to read it in context, to get the full picture, I believe:

> *Your dead will live; their corpses will rise. You who lie in the dust, awake and shout for joy, for your dew is as the dew of the dawn, and the earth will give birth to the departed spirits. Come, my people, enter into your rooms and close your doors behind you; hide for a little while until indignation runs its course. For behold, the LORD IS ABOUT TO COME OUT FROM HIS PLACE to punish the inhabitants of the earth for their iniquity; and the earth will reveal her bloodshed and will no longer cover her slain. [Isaiah 26:19-21 NASB]*

Some point to the part that says, "Come, my people, enter into your rooms and close the doors behind you; hide for a little while indignation runs its course," as justification for God's people to believe we will be hidden away for a short time until the storm clouds pass. And yes, I can see how that might be the case. Yet, I would point to a few key phrases that raise doubt, when taken in context. First, this chapter is a song that Isaiah says will be sung in Judah one day. He is saying that the dead will come to life again, and those who sleep in the dust will awake again (just as Gabriel revealed to Daniel), and shout for joy. Also, if we look at the woman in Revelation 12 (who most believe is symbolic of Israel), we see her being taken "out of the way' and protected from the evil one, too. So, this could be alluding to that, as well.

Then, at the end of this passage, he is saying, "The Lord is about to come out from His place (Heaven) and punish the inhabitants of the earth for their iniquity..." But we know from other Scriptures that there will be godly people yet alive on the earth during these dark days. So, saying "to punish the inhabitants of the earth for their iniquity" is problematic, if there are believers still on the earth in the midst of them. So, when does "the Lord come out of His place to punish the iniquity of those on the earth?" As far as I can tell, that happens at the end of the tribulation period, while at the same time, those that are His are being protected, just as Noah and his family were during the flood.

Let us also not forget that following those seven years of great trouble, when Christ sets up His Millennial Kingdom on the earth, death will not have ended because we know there will be many who will be born and die during His reign on Earth. How do we know that? Well, we know that Satan will be loosed one more time at the end of those thousand years, and those born during that time, who were not tested as we have will be tested, just as we were. It is talked about in Revelation 20:

> *When the thousand years are completed, Satan will be released from his prison, and will come out to deceive the nations which are in the four corners of the earth, Gog and Magog, to gather them together for the war; the number of them is like the sand of the seashore. And they came up on the broad plain of the earth and surrounded the camp of the saints and the beloved city, and fire came down from heaven and devoured them. And the devil who deceived them was thrown into the lake of fire and brimstone, where the beast and the false prophet are also; and they will be tormented day and night forever and ever. [Revelation 20:7-10 NASB]*

So, I cannot help but conclude that, if Satan is going to be released one more time, those new souls (beings) who are on the earth will have a choice, just as we did in our time. And, therefore, before they can enter God's eternal kingdom, they need to be tested. Since Satan was bound for most of the thousand years, temptation was not present on the earth, so sin was rendered powerless. But, once he is set free again, temptation will again come. I do not believe that means those of us who were already tested will be tested a second time. God help us!! No, I am speaking primarily of those born during those years. You can all exhale now. I did not mean to startle anyone.

So where did this idea of a pre-tribulation rapture come from? What is the biblical basis for it? Although the idea was first advanced by the Catholic Church, who were looking to distance themselves from the views of the Reformers (which predominantly aligned with the post-tribulation view), it later surfaced in the Scofield Reference Bible and by others like John Darby, who were also advancing the dispensationalist point of view. More recently, the idea became much more popular following the release of books like "Late, Great Planet Earth," by Hal Lindsey and the "Left Behind" series by Tim LaHaye and Jerry Jenkins.

Yes, however, I do believe that are many passages and biblical stories that could lead one to believe that God would possibly take His faithful ones out of the "line of fire" before things get bad (and I do not know any Christians who doubt that they will get extremely bad). Even Jesus said, *"there will be a great tribulation, such as has not occurred since the beginning of the world until now, nor ever will."*

This is the reason I felt so strongly that this book needs to be written. We all know that it is quite easy to find a handful of Scriptures that make a convincing case for just about any theory one would choose to believe. That is why I insisted that we take the time to look at the whole Bible and take the Scriptures at face value...not allowing the interpretations and opinions of other godly men to influence our thinking. So, here are a few of the stories and verses from the Bible that many believe support a pre-tribulation rapture, and why I believe there might be some reason for concern.

Noah and the Ark: Many believe that this is evidence of God saving Noah and his family out of a wicked and perverse generation. Some even call it "the first rapture." My reason for not seeing Noah's story as evidence of a pre-tribulation rapture is the fact that, as we discussed at length earlier, Noah and his family remained on the earth...it was the wicked who were "snatched away."

The two men in the field and the two women at the grinding mill (Matt. 24): It does say, in both cases, one will be left, and one will be taken. However, right before that is the verse where Jesus says that in the end times, "it will be as in the days of Noah." So, why would the Lord use a story where the evil ones are taken away, and the righteous remain on the earth...then turn around only a few verses later, and tell two stories about the exact opposite? That does not make sense to me. I believe Jesus was either teaching about the evil ones being taken away, or He was talking about how the righteous will be removed, and evil ones being "left behind." It cannot be both, again, if you ask me. And since he tied these two examples to the story of Noah, I believe the wicked will be removed, not the righteous. Then, we get to hang around in the restored Garden of Eden for a thousand years or so. Works for me!!

David said, in Psalm 37, "I have never seen the righteous forsaken." That sounds like a great point, I have never seen the righteous forsaken either. But, would the possibility that believers in Christ may not be raptured before the tribulation period starts (including the "dead in Christ"), mean that God has forsaken us? Absolutely not, may it never be. God did not forsake Noah to the Flood, did He? God did not forsake Shadrach, Meshach, and Abednego in the fiery furnace or forsake Daniel in the lion's den, right? Those were times of great trial, I would say. And most importantly, God did not spare His own Son from suffering and dying on the Cross. All of these were used mightily to display God's power, and grace in the face of great troubles, not one of them was forsaken by God. And I do not believe, if God chooses for us to go through the tribulation of those final days that He will be forsaking us, either. That is never gonna happen...no not ever. Just sayin'.

At this point, I would like to share one passage of Scripture from John 17, which many call "the greatest prayer ever prayed" (and I agree). In this chapter, Jesus is praying directly to His Heavenly Father, just prior to His arrest and crucifixion. During this prayer, He focuses a lot on praying for His disciples, not only those who were with Him in those days, but also *"those also who believe in Me through their word."* That would be you and me, and all the saints who surrendered to Christ since His death and resurrection. And in this beautiful prayer to His Father, He makes a very telling request, if you ask me:

> ***"I do not ask You to take them out of the world, but to keep them from the evil one. They are not of the world, even as I am not of the world." [John 17:15-16 NASB]***

Let's let that one stew for a moment. Jesus is asking His Father to NOT take "those that He has given Him" (that is us) out of the world, but rather, keep them from the evil one. Let's see, did God take Noah out of the world? How about Daniel and his three companions? And I guess we could toss David in there, too. Did God pluck him from the earth when Saul was chasing him with the distinct purpose of killing him? The answer to all those questions is, of course, "No." But, we are supposed to believe that God is going to treat us differently in our day of trouble than He treated those great men of God? I am sorry, I do not see it. No, Jesus promised us that there would be trouble for those that follow Him…and I have certainly found that to be true in my life. Can I get an "Amen?"

And who is this "evil one" of whom Jesus was speaking? Ok, it could be Satan in general, I guess. But, in the end times, I am led to believe that Satan will empower a man who we have come to understand to be the Antichrist, who will unleash a great evil upon the earth…and make war with the saints of God, according to Revelation 13 (wait…I thought the saints are supposed to be long gone already). So, could it be that Jesus was praying that His beloved, the ones who the Father has given Him, would not be taken out of the world when great evil comes upon it, but rather, kept safe from the evil one during this time of great tribulation? That, my friends, is what bears witness to my heart.

Like I have so often said, "My flesh is hoping for an early departure…but my spirit is being readied to endure to the end, no matter what." It breaks my heart to think how many Christians might be crushed to wake up one day and see that the tribulation period has already started, and their Redeemer has not yet come for them. It says in the Bible that in those days "men's hearts will fail them." I am inclined to believe that some of those folks will be people who have trusted Christ but are deeply saddened to the point of death when the rapture fails to come and save them from what is about to come upon the earth.

So, to close out this chapter, I would like to look at the words that are commonly used in connection with a rapture, or a "catching away." To help us do this, we should look at the passage that most strongly points to a "catching away" of believers in Christ:

> **For the Lord Himself will descend from heaven with a shout, with the voice of the archangel and with the trumpet of God, and the dead in Christ will rise first. Then we who are alive and remain will be caught up together with them in the clouds to meet the Lord in the air, and so we shall always be with the Lord. [1 Thessalonians 4:16-17 NASB]**

It is the second half of this passage, verse 17, that gets quoted the most, and the part we will talk about first. The words "caught up" point to a gathering together (a rapture, if you prefer) of those who have trusted in Christ as Lord and Savior. I have no doubt about that. As I said earlier, I believe and look forward to being raptured, either from the grave, as one of the "dead in Christ," or if I am still alive, to be changed in the twinkling of an eye. Yes, I anxiously await that day. Don't get me wrong, I love my life, my family and friends and all that God has blessed me with. But I also know that what comes after this life and after our resurrection, is beyond imagination. So, when He is ready for Me…I'm ready to go!! There is a good friend of mine who was sick for a long time before he passed away. We would sometimes talk about why the Lord would not take him sooner, and why he allowed him to suffer so long. I would joke, "The Lord is obviously not quite ready for you yet, Guy…just sayin'."

Now, the Greek word translated into "caught up" in English is "harpazo." It means to be seized by force, taken, or snatched away. But most translators use the words "caught up," and I am fine with that, but I would not describe being "caught up to meet the Lord" as being "taken by force." Would you?

However, in Latin, the word would be "rapturo," which is where we get our word "rapture." Why is that important? Which religion predominantly used Latin until just recently? You got it, the Catholic

Church. And which religion first used the idea of an "immortal soul" to make a case that we go immediately to be with the Lord, when we die? The Church of Rome. Are you starting to see a pattern, here?

So, that leads me to ask a very important question. If the soul is not immortal, as the Catholics believe, and even many Protestants now believe that. And, we do not go to be with the Lord when our last earthly breath is breathed, does that negate any possibility of a pre-tribulation rapture? I would say, "Absolutely." That theory is totally dependent on the soul being immortal and going to be with the Lord, immediately, when we die.

Let's think this through, for a minute. Our fleshly bodies are certainly not going to Heaven. So, if there is not an "immortal soul" that is separate from the body and spirit (as many believe), what, if anything, goes to Heaven when we die? I think King Solomon answered this quite nicely in the Book of Ecclesiastes:

> **Remember also your Creator in the days of your youth, before the evil days come and the years draw near when you will say, "I have no delight in them"...For man goes to his eternal home while mourners go about in the street... then the dust will return to the earth as it was, and the spirit (breath of life) will return to God who gave it. [Ecclesiastes 12:1, 5b-7 NASB]**

Well, what do you know, we have come full circle. Here, Solomon is commenting on the aging process and, I believe, poking a little fun at himself by saying, "while the mourners go about in the street" (anticipating his death, I presume). But, remember when we talked about how in Genesis 2:7, and I suggested a simple mathematic equation (body + spirit = a living soul) to help us grasp what the Bible was saying on the subject? The son of David seems to be reflecting on it all the same way...the body returns to dust, the spirit (breath) returns to God who gave it, and he makes no mention of the soul, which apparently does not exist when the body and spirit are separated. At that point, we are no longer a "living being" or "living soul." We are awaiting our resurrection...waiting to be made "alive" again!!

It all seems so simple and makes perfect sense when we look at the beginning, as well as the end. When God created man, He breathed the "breath of life" into his nostrils, and he became alive. And we learned that the Greek word for breath and spirit is the same word, "pneuma."

So yes, God breathed life (spirit) into Adam, and he became a living soul (being). And when we die, the spirit (breath of life) returns to God who gave it in the first place, and we are no longer physically alive. We are no longer a living soul either, because a body cannot live without breath and we need both to become a living soul. We are from dust, and to dust we shall return, awaiting that new and improved body, which will surely come in what will seem like "the blink of an eye" to the one who has passed away. It will be like being on a long, tedious flight, while you were asleep the whole time. You wake up, and you have reached your destination. Praise be to God.

"YOU ARE THE GIVER OF LIFE"
[PSALM 36:9]

CHAPTER SIXTEEN

"AN ENEMY HAS DONE THIS..."

As we close out Part Two, there is one more critical piece of the puzzle I want to elaborate on. Back in Chapter Four, "Catching Away," where we talked about Noah, and who was snatched away and who was left behind, I briefly mentioned my favorite parable of Jesus, one that I think is paramount in showing God's nature regarding the end times and how things will unfold, the parable of the wheat and the tares.

Just in case you don't know, tares are weeds. So, in this story, Jesus tells us of a landowner whose slaves come to him and report that weeds are growing up alongside of his wheat crop. In my second book, "The Red Letter Parables," I talked about how these weeds looked very similar to the good wheat plants, and could only be properly separated at harvest time. And that, my friends, is where the plot thickens.

Since this parable is one of the longer ones in the Bible, I would like to look at it piece by piece because there are so many key points made in this story that are extremely important to consider, when we are forming our end-time viewpoints. Let us have a listen to the Master Storyteller, Jesus Christ:

> *Jesus presented another parable to them, saying, "The kingdom of heaven may be compared to a man who sowed good seed in his field. But while his men were sleeping, his enemy came and sowed tares among the wheat, and went away. But when the wheat sprouted and bore grain, then the tares became evident also". [Matthew 13:24-26 NASB]*

As a basis for this explanation, I want to first, state the obvious. Jesus is telling a story, a parable, about a landowner who I feel comfortable viewing as God the Father because Jesus said we can equate this story to the kingdom of heaven. He is painting a prophetic picture, I believe, to help us better understand what God's perspective on all of this might be.

So, we have a man who owns much land, enough to justify having workers who plant and maintain his fields. Notice that Jesus said the man sowed "good seed" in his field. Let's, then, assume when God created the earth, He was sowing goodness, not evil. Sometimes we hear people say that all the problems in the world, these days, point to a failure by God. That is why I wanted to highlight this point, Jesus is very clear in saying what His Father was sowing was good, and I believe that with every fiber of my being.

Secondly, take notice of the fact that his workers were sleeping (not dead, actually sleeping on the job), as in "not keeping a watchful eye on the fields." They certainly could have taken turns napping, with one of them watching the fields, at all times. But, apparently, from what we see in Scripture, they did not. And I would suggest, just as in this parable, our slackness or laziness regarding the things of God gives an open door to the enemy, who is not lazy or passive about his mission. The Apostle Peter warned us about the tirelessness of our enemy, the devil when he wrote the following words:

Be of sober spirit, be on the alert. Your adversary, the devil, prowls around like a roaring lion, seeking someone to devour. [1 Peter 5:9 NASB]

One of the most common knocks against the modern churches of the western world is that they have been lulled into letting down their guard by allowing the enemy to switch the focus of their faith away from being all about putting the Lord first. We have veered away from serving Him with our whole hearts, and being very aware that there is a deadly enemy constantly on the prowl, looking for ways to deceive us into disobeying God (as he did with Adam and Eve).

We have been coaxed into seeing our faith as something that is primarily designed by God to makes us happy, prosperous and safe in this life, and not as a spiritual battle that has been going on since the beginning of time. This war, by the way, is one that we are involved with whether we know it or not. Even unbelievers have been drafted into this fight, unknowingly of course. But they are not fighting on behalf of God, unfortunately, which means what, then? Jesus said, **"He who is not with Me is against Me." [Matt. 12:30]**

It's been said that whoever is not spreading the seeds of belief in God, they are spreading seeds of unbelief. Look around, the world has no shortage of "evangelists of unbelief" working hard at it 24/7 in the media, TV, movies, music and yes, even in the name of religion. The enemy is extremely clever and very subtle, like the Bible says, "Satan disguises himself as an angel of light." There should be no doubt then, since Jesus warned us of false prophets, and John told us to "test the spirits", that the devil has managed to mingle a message of unbelief into the words and teachings of many how claim to be ambassadors for Christ. Think about the popular phrase, "God helps those who help themselves." There are many who might say the quote is from the Bible, or maybe that they heard it in church. But, is it a biblical statement…does it portray an accurate picture of who God is? I would say, "Absolutely not." But the enemy has succeeded in spreading a message of deception, regarding God, and passing it off as truth when it is not. That is what the enemy specializes in…slight deviations that sound right, but are not only wrong, but very dangerous.

So, whatever we do as followers of Jesus Christ, let us not get caught "catnapping" while the enemy is on the prowl, amen? The enemy doesn't take any time off, my brothers and sisters. Peter was right, we need to sober (some translations say awake) and alert, spiritually, every minute of every day. Or you could become the roaring lion's next victim.

> *"The slaves of the landowner came and said to him, 'Sir, did you not sow good seed in your field? How then does it have tares?' And he said to them, 'An enemy has done this!'" [Matthew 13:27-28a NASB]*

So then, if God only sows goodness, yet evil (or in this case… weeds) pops up among the good stuff, where did it come from? According to the words of the landowner in the passage above, and I would assume we could apply the same response to the evil in this world that us "growing up among the good wheat." An enemy has done this. I can almost hear Flip Wilson and his famous retort, "The devil made me do it." But he was right on the money, if you ask me. Satan, Lucifer (or whatever name or title you want to attach to him) is the source and originator of sin, rebellion and all forms of disobedience towards God. The Lord, I believe, has only delayed Satan's destruction for a season, to allow him to be a sower of temptation and wickedness. Those things cannot come from a righteous God, so there had to be a willing adversary. Let's look at what James, the half-brother of Jesus, had to say on this subject:

> **My brethren, these things ought not to be this way. Does a fountain send out from the same opening fresh and bitter water? Can a fig tree, my brethren, produce olives, or a vine produce figs? Nor can salt water produce fresh. [James 3:10b-12 NASB]**

When I read this verse, it occurs to me that James is making sure we understand that one stream or fountain does not produce sweet and bitter water. It is either one or the other. And since we know that God only sows goodness…sweet not bitter…then the bad stuff has to come from another source. And that is key…Jesus said, "an enemy has come and mixed in his bad seed with the good." The landowner did not sow both. It all has to do with the source. It is either good or bad. It either truth or lies. Hence, a good source and good seed will only bring forth good fruit…not rotten and useless crops. It was the enemy who mingled the bad seed among the good, and he still does that today.

This memorable parable causes me to reflect on the ongoing "seed war" and how it started. The first two humans, formed by God's own hands, were "good seed." The enemy lied to them about what God meant, and they believed the lie. Then, in Genesis 6, we saw that fallen angels had intermingled with the daughters of men, creating hybrid offspring known as the Nephilim. Hence, the good seed became tainted, sort of like mixing a little poison in with your iced tea. The whole batch becomes deadly, none of it is good to drink any longer. But, in the case of this parable, the bad seed was only sowed into the ground alongside the good seed. The good wheat did not become tainted, but there were weeds mixed in that looked very much like the good wheat. It was hard to tell them apart.

And the reason this is so important, when we think of future biblical events, is that it should be crystal clear that two things have to happen before we can enter our eternal rest:

1. At some point, the crops need to be harvested.
2. And at some point, the wheat needs to separate from the chaff...the weeds.

So then, a very important question comes to the forefront. Should the good and the bad yield be harvested together, or at two different times? I am so glad you asked.

"The slaves said to him, 'Do you want us, then, to go and gather them up?' But he *said, 'No; for while you are gathering up the tares, you may uproot the wheat with them.'" [Matthew 13:28b-29 NASB]

It seems the workers were asking the same question. "Master, should we go now and gather up the weeds and dispose of them, so that they do not choke out the good wheat?" Now, the decision falls to the landowner, who understands that there could be some danger in leaving the weeds there to continue growing alongside the wheat. Some of the good wheat could indeed be choked out. But it is also true that some of the good wheat could be damaged if the workers try to harvest the weeds from among the wheat.

I believe that is precisely the decision our precious Lord will be facing when the day arrives that a great darkness is going to fall upon the earth, right before He breaks through the sky on His white horse with salvation in His hands. But He also knows that the greatest tests, for His chosen ones, still lies ahead...and that is where the greatest victory is won. This might be the single most important reason I cannot put my hope in a "catching away" that happens prior to the final seven years. The game is not over. The battle has not been won just yet. God's ultimate prevailing over evil has not yet been achieved. And I believe He desires for us to not only be present...but overcomers.

Again, Jesus said. *"Those that endure to the end will be saved."* But...the end has not come yet.

What do you call it when one team cannot, or chooses not to finish a game? A forfeit.

There is no way, in my mind or in my heart, I can come to grips with God Almighty, who "causes all things to work together for the good of those who love God," bringing this world to a close by forfeiting and allowing His enemies to go unopposed for the final days leading up to His return. For you see if, as many believe, that all the believers in Christ will be raptured before the tribulation and the Holy Spirit (who lives inside us, as believers), is no longer present on the earth, from where can any further salvation come? How can anyone, be they Jew or Greek, be saved? I believe many will believe in Christ after the tribulation period starts. But for that to happen, I believe the Helper, the Holy Spirit must be present and active. So, what did the landowner decide to do? It obviously was not an easy decision, with plenty of reason for concern, no matter which option he chooses.

> ***"Allow both to grow together until the harvest; and in the time of the harvest I will say to the reapers, "First gather up the tares and bind them in bundles to burn them up; but gather the wheat into my barn.""*** *[Matthew 13:30 NASB]*

He chose to allow both, the good seed and the bad seed, to remain until harvest time. He did not opt to harvest twice, gathering up the good and bad crop separately. That would require two separate harvest times, not one. But, let me point out one other thing that I find revealing in this parable. Jesus told of two options. One, the workers offered to gather up the weeds first so that the good wheat would not be choked out. And secondly, the landowner decided to leave both until harvest time. Then separate them, after it all was gathered up.

Did Jesus suggest a third option, one where the workers gathered up the good wheat first, and allow the weeds to continue to grow until harvest time? Of course, He did not. Why would He suggest that the wheat be harvested before it reached full maturity? I don't believe He would ever do that. The goal is to yield a mature, ripe, ready-to-be-harvested wheat crop. Gathering it before the appropriate time defeats the entire purpose of planting it in the first place. Neither Jesus nor the landowner saw any benefit in taking the wheat before it came to fruition. That option was not even suggested.

To close out this chapter then, I want to point out the similarities in what Jesus is saying, here, in this well-known parable, and what the angel, Gabriel, told Daniel back in Daniel Chapter 12. Here, the landowner decides to let the good seed and bad seed grow together until the appropriate harvest time, so as not to damage the good crop by trying to gather the weeds.

In Daniel 12, we see Gabriel telling Daniel that "those who sleep in the dust of the ground will awake (the good seed and bad seed), some to everlasting life, but others to disgrace and everlasting contempt." So, neither was harvested (for eternity) before the other. Both remained until the fullness of time had passed. This gives us an Old Testament example and a New Testament example of the exact same scenario...one harvest time...for both the good and the bad. Then they will be separated where some will find the warmth of the master's barn...and the others will find a blazing fire.

And why does this happen? Why are there weeds sprinkled in among the good what? The Lord told us quite plainly, "An enemy has done this." And, for that reason, both will be judged when the Lord returns to sit on His throne, and the sheep are separated from the goats as we read about in Matthew 25.

"THERE IS ONE FATE FOR THE RIGHTEOUS AND FOR THE WICKED"
[ECCLESIASTES 9:2]

PARENTHETICAL PAUSE #2

LOST IN TRANSLATION

Among the folks who know me best, it is no surprise that I rarely miss an opportunity to give my opinion, especially if it is something I feel strongly about. What might be a surprise to some, is that I do not have to believe my view is absolutely right and true, beyond a shadow of doubt, before I decide to share it. I know…I know…that sounds a little crazy. Now, I would never share something untrue intentionally, of course, but unknowingly? Guilty as charged. However, are you aware that what I just said is based on a biblical principle? I'm guessing not. Sure is. It comes from the Apostle Paul:

> *For we know in part and we prophesy in part; but when the perfect comes, the partial will be done away…For now, we see in a mirror dimly, but then face to face; now I know in part, but then I will know fully just as I also have been fully known. [1 Corinthians 13:9-10, 12 NASB]*

Wait a second, is that the Apostle Paul, a devout student of the Law, suggesting that someone may "prophesy in part? Is that not a sin worthy of death? It is indeed. Certainly, he is not suggesting that it is acceptable to be "willy-nilly" about speaking on behalf of God, right? What gives here? Well, as I see it, he is talking about the fact that none of us can fully know the mind of God. In our current human state, it is just not possible for us to perceive the deep things of God. Some things have been left, intentionally by God, to be revealed later. It is up to each of us to diligently seek the truth, to do our best to "rightly divide the Word of God." After all, the Bible says in Hebrews 11, *"He is a rewarder of those who diligently seek Him."*

But Paul wraps it up nicely by saying, "Thank God, when the perfect comes (I take that to mean when Christ returns and establishes His Kingdom), we will be free from these mortal bodies and our limited human minds. We will finally see Him as He truly is, in all the fullness of His divine and eternal glory. No guesswork will be needed. How amazing will that be? I, for one, can't wait. As I said before, I love my life, my wife, my kids, my grandchildren, my church, my friends, my hobbies and projects. But, it all pales in comparison to being able to see Jesus face-to-face. Maranatha!! That is my story… and I am sticking to it!!

So, before we move into the "nuts and bolts" of my view of the end times, I want to take a look at a bucketful of passages from Scripture that many people have used for centuries to frame their expectations of what the final chapters of the story of Planet Earth might look like. In particular, I am referring to the matters of life, and death, and the eventual return our true Blessed Hope, Jesus Christ.

NOTE TO THE READER: This chapter, as you may have noticed, is quite long, but I think it serves a purpose, at this point. The compilation of passages that I have included, here (and have made brief comments on), provide a basis for much of what we are going to be talking about in the upcoming chapters. So, I felt that taking the extra time to lay the groundwork, here, would prove worthwhile as we continue forward. Think of it as "reference chapter" or an "addendum." You can skip over it for now, if you like, but I believe this will serve as great clarification, now or even in the future, as to how I have reached my conclusions regarding both God's nature and the end of the age (hence the title of the book). So, bear with me, if you will, as I share my thoughts ahead of time, rather than stopping at numerous points along the way to explain how I came to my personal views on these matters.

Now, for the record, I do not see these as "pre-trib verses," "mid-trib verses," or "post-trib verses." I see them as the Word of God. As I have said a number of times here, already, I want to look at the Scriptures at "face value," without using the interpretations of godly men and women to "fill in the gaps." And that includes my opinions, here, as well. I am certainly not one to say, "I am right, and everybody else is wrong," or claim that God has chosen to reveal to "little ol' me" things that He has not chosen to reveal to anyone else, over the centuries. But, with His help, I am going to try to not "color these verses" one way or the other. I want to simply read the passages, themselves, and then talk about what they reveal to us...plus or minus nothing. That's the goal in this experiment...to let the Scriptures speak for themselves. Oh, and by the way, I intentionally arranged these passages sequentially, in the order in which they appear in the Bible as not to show any partially or try to manipulate a certain outcome. So, with no further ado...off we go:

The LORD SAYS TO MY LORD: "Sit at My right hand until I make Your enemies a footstool." [Psalm 110:1-3 NASB]

This one has caused many debates over the years. What does that mean, "The Lord says to my Lord?" Most scholars agree, it is King David writing about God the Father saying to the One he will send as Messiah and Redeemer (David uses "my Lord" to show that the Messiah will be worthy of the word "Lord," as well), "Sit at my right hand until I make Your enemies footstool." As I understand it, the Lord returns to destroy His enemies at the end of the seven years of "great tribulation," not before. So, we see here that God is saying that our precious Lord Jesus will remain with Him, in Heaven, until the day comes that God, the Father, makes the enemies of His Son a footstool." It does not suggest He will come back to Earth before God's enemies are defeated. In fact, I believe it suggests quite the contrary.

It will come about also in that day that a great trumpet will be blown, and those who were perishing in the land of Assyria and who were scattered in the land of Egypt will come and worship the LORD in the holy mountain at Jerusalem. [Isaiah 27:13 NASB]

Here, in Isaiah (somewhere around 2700 years ago), the prophet writes of a day when a great trumpet will sound, and those who had been "far off" will return home and "worship in the holy mountain at

Jerusalem." Of course, the Jews came home from around the world, beginning in 1948 when Israel was declared a nation again. But, they are still not free to fully worship as they see fit on the Temple Mount. Plus, another Temple must be built there, which most agree will happen once "the covenant with the many" (from Daniel 9) is signed, and there is peace in Israel. But, more importantly, I believe this speaks of Christ's Kingdom here on Earth, where He will reign for a thousand years (the "day of rest") once His enemies are defeated. That is why it says, "...in the holy mountain at Jerusalem"...and not "on the holy mountain." Remember, back in Part One, I said that the name "Jerusalem" could be translated as "God will see His peace?" One day, in the not too distant future, He will surely see His peace "in that holy mountain"...the New Jerusalem. But keep in mind, Isaiah said this will be kicked off by the sounding of a "great trumpet." That's important.

> *Then the Lord said to me, "The prophets are prophesying falsehood in My name. I have neither sent them nor commanded them nor spoken to them; they are prophesying to you a false vision, divination, futility and the deception of their own minds. [Jeremiah 14:14 NASB]*

This one does not require much explanation. The end will come at a time when false prophets are speaking "the deceptions of their own minds," not the word of the Lord. And just based on that, as we have already said, it appears that time may be very near if it has not started already (I believe the "false prophet" part clearly has).

> *Again, He said to me, "Prophesy over these bones and say to them, 'O dry bones, hear the word of the Lord.' Thus says the Lord God to these bones, 'Behold, I will cause breath to enter you that you may come to life. I will put sinews on you, make flesh grow back on you, cover you with skin and put breath in you that you may come alive; and you will know that I am the Lord.'" [Ezekiel 37:4-7 NASB]*

One of the things about prophecy is that it is not "time specific." And sometimes, a word of prophecy could be fulfilled more than once.

But for this passage from Ezekiel, many scholars agree (and I do too) that this most likely refers to the rebirth of Israel, for sure. But, many also believe that the specific reference to the "dry bones" and the need for them to be made alive again also refers to the Holocaust, and the killing of six million Jews by the Nazis. And that, many believe, led to the world finally agreeing that it was time for Israel to become a homeland for the Jews, just as the Lord decreed many, many years ago. Many say, as well, that the rebirth was the single-most most important fulfillment of prophecy since the birth, death, and resurrection of Jesus Christ. And I wholeheartedly agree with that.

> *Then He said to me, "Son of man, these bones are the whole house of Israel; behold, they say, 'Our bones are dried up, and our hope has perished. We are completely cut off.'* [12] *Therefore prophesy and say to them, 'Thus says the Lord God, "Behold, I will open your graves and cause you to come up out of your graves, My people; and I will bring you into the land of Israel." [Ezekiel 37:11-12 NASB]*

This, of course, is the Lord explaining the prophecy to Ezekiel. But not to be redundant, I shared this portion to point to the fact that the ones being brought back to life would come from where, their graves…not from Heaven, where they might be patiently waiting with the Lord to bring them back down to Earth (what a "let down," huh?). But yes, this passage paints a picture of "a people being reborn, a nation brought back from the dead." It is not saying that the Jews who were so ruthlessly killed will miraculously come back to life. I believe it is talking about the rebirth of Israel. I wanted to make that clear.

> *"Seventy weeks have been decreed for your people and your holy city, to finish the transgression, to make an end of sin…Then after the sixty-two weeks the Messiah will be cut off and have nothing, and the people of the prince who is to come will destroy the city and the sanctuary. And its end will come with a flood; even to the end there will be war; desolations are determined. And he will make a firm covenant with the many for one week, but in the middle of the week he will put a stop to sacrifice and grain offering;*

and on the wing of abominations will come one who makes desolate..." [Daniel 9:24,26-27 NASB]

Here we learn of the infamous "Seventy Weeks of Daniel." It has been understood by most scholars that the seventy weeks equals four hundred and ninety days....and those days will prophetically point to four hundred and ninety years, which began (according to many scholars) with the proclamation by King Artaxerxes to Jerusalem in 457 BC. Hence, the first week of years, (49 years) ended when the rebuilding of Jerusalem was finished in 408 BC, and the first sixty-nine weeks ended in 27AD (with the death and resurrection of Christ), leaving only a final seven years (one week) yet to be fulfilled in the final days of the world (as we know it). And the final seven years are broken into two 3 ½ year periods, with a breakpoint that Daniel called "the middle of the week." So, naturally most of our attention, now, is laser-focused on those seven years. When will they arrive? What will happen right before them? What happens during the first half, and the second half? And to be sure, what happens after those seven years are completed?

"And there will be a time of distress such as never occurred since there was a nation until that time; and at that time your people, everyone who is found written in the book, will be rescued. Many of those who sleep in the dust of the ground will awake, these to everlasting life, but the others disgrace and everlasting contempt." [Daniel 12:1-2 NASB]

As we discussed at length earlier, Daniel ended his writings with the angel Gabriel talking about this time of great distress. I also would suggest we take notice that, not unlike the parable of the wheat and the tares, Gabriel is saying both the wheat (the good seed) and the tares (the bad seed) will awake and be judged at the same time. That begs the question, are the redeemed of God and those who refused God's grace and mercy both going to be resurrected before the time of great distress? I have never heard anyone suggest that. So, in my mind, Gabriel can only be suggesting that this will happen at some point following the "time of distress." I believe this speaks of the second resurrection and the judgement that follows, because the "bad seed" are not harvested at the first resurrection. But, again, at the first resurrection, when Jesus returns, no one is going directly to Heaven. He is coming to set up His earthly Kingdom. It is following the second resurrection and the thousand-year reign of Christ on Earth that the judgement comes, and the New Heaven and New Earth are revealed... and we finally enter into eternity.

> *"But as for you, go your way to the end; then you will enter into rest and rise again for your allotted portion at the end of the age." [Daniel 12:13 NASB]*

Then, for a little "icing on the cake," Gabriel tells Daniel to go his way, and the appropriate time he will "enter his rest" (I believe that to mean to sleep in the grave) until he is resurrected to receive his "allotted portion" at the end of the age...not before. I believe that will apply to all of us. We live on this planet, until the time for us to "enter our rest" and to await resurrection at the end of the age, at which time we will receive our just rewards (both the good and the bad).

> *Then the Lord will appear over them, and His arrow will go forth like lightning; and the Lord God will blow the trumpet, and will march in the storm winds of the south...The Lord of hosts will defend them...And the Lord their God will save them in that day as the flock of His people; for they are as the stones of a crown..." [Zechariah 9:14-16 NASB]*

Once again, we now see the prophet Zechariah pointing to a time when the trumpet will blow and "the Lord will appear over them (us)." And, the Lord their God will save them (us) when? In that day, when the trumpet has sounded, and the Lord appears, "coming in the clouds."

> *"Behold, I send you out as sheep in the midst of wolves; so be shrewd as serpents and innocent as doves...You will be hated by all because of My name, but it is the one who has endured to the end who will be saved." [Matthew 10:16, 22 NASB]*

Here, Jesus is saying that He knowingly is sending out his faithful ones as "sheep among wolves," That does not sound as if He believes they will not see trials and tribulations, quite the opposite, I would say. And then the Lord adds, knowing the trials they will face, "the one who endures to the end will be saved." Knowing the truth, we should all feel sorry for the wolves. They have no hope of victory!!

> *"Then they will deliver you to tribulation, and will kill you, and you will be hated by all nations because of My name."* [Matthew 24:9 NASB]

Here in Matthew 24, the epicenter of end-time prophecies for many who study such things, the Lord specifically tells His disciples, "they will deliver you to tribulation." Is He seemingly disagreeing with other Scriptures that say "I have never seen the righteous forsaken," or that those who are to trust in Christ will never be subjected to the wrath of God? Or is He? I would say no, He is not at odds with Scripture with these ideas, because I do not believe those seven years are God's wrath. That comes at the end of the seven years when Christ returns to vanquish His enemies and establish His Kingdom on Earth.

We know that Michael the archangel, according to Revelation 12, is taken out of the way so that the serpent could be cast down to the earth. Yes, those seven years are the unleashing of great evil upon the earth and the people who live in it. I would call that Satan's wrath, not God's wrath. Michael is standing aside and releasing the "evil one" to come down to earth to cause much trouble. God's wrath will indeed come, but later, at the end of the seven years. And yes, at that time, the redeemed of the Lord will be protected from His wrath. I believe we have His promise on that.

> *"Many false prophets will arise and will mislead many... But the one who endures to the end, he will be saved. This gospel of the kingdom shall be preached in the whole world as a testimony to all the nations, and then the end will come."* [Matthew 24:11, 13-14 NASB]

Once again, we see our Lord pointing to the rise of false prophets, misleading messages that do not line up with the word of God. But, He reminds us again, to stay the course, remain faithful and endure to the end. And to do that, we need to be diligent about knowing the truth, so we can tell the difference when the lying voices come, and they will.

> *"But immediately after the tribulation of those days the sun will be darkened, and the moon will not give its light, and the stars will fall from the sky, and the powers of[the heavens will be shaken, and then the sign of the Son of Man will appear in the sky, and then all the tribes of the earth will mourn, and they will see the Son of Man coming on the clouds of the sky with power and great glory." [Matthew 24:29-30 NASB]*

Let me zoom in on the Lord Jesus Christ specifically commenting on His own glorious return to Earth, *"But immediately after the tribulation of those days...then the sign of the Son of Man will appear in the sky..."* I honestly doubt that I could find a clearer answer than the one the Lord gave regarding Himself, "I will return to Earth after the tribulation of those days." Pretty convincing, if you ask me.

> *"Truly I say to you, this generation will not pass away until all these things take place...But of that day and hour no one knows, not even the angels of heaven, nor the Son, but the Father alone. For the coming of the Son of Man will be just like the days of Noah." [Matthew 24:34, 36-37 NASB]*

Since we will be talking more about this later, let me quickly point out that when Jesus said "this generation," I believe He was talking about the generation that would be alive when the fig tree (Israel) would bloom again (or...become a nation again). That, my friends, has already happened. That prophecy has been fulfilled as of 1948. So, we are seventy years (as of 2018) into the what the Lord would call "the last generation." That is why so many people who were not interested in such things before are trying to learn all they can about what the Bible says about these events. Our eternal future (as individuals...and as a world) depends on it. And what other sign does He point to in this same passage? "For the coming of the Son of Man will be just like the days of Noah." So, He was suggesting that if you want to know how things will unfold in the last days, look to the beginning. Just as God interacted with us back then, that is how He will interact with us in the future. God changes not. Hey, that sounds familiar. Where have I heard that before?

> *And He said to them, "Rightly did Isaiah prophesy of you hypocrites, as it is written: 'This people honors Me with their lips, But their heart is far away from Me...But in vain do they worship Me...Teaching as doctrines the precepts of men...Neglecting the commandment of God, you hold to the tradition of men. [Mark 7:6-8, 13 NASB]*

Here we have Jesus, as recorded by Mark, once again quoting the prophet Isaiah, talking about lying lips and hearts that are far from God, trying to teach others based on the traditions of men and not on the truth of God. This was obviously a high priority subject for our Lord. He warned us many times about false prophets and false teachings. And yes, they are coming, and many are already here.

> *You will be hated by all because of My name, but the one who endures to the end, he will be saved. [Mark 13:13 NASB]*

And yet again, this time recorded by Mark, we hear "the one who endures to the end, he will be saved." If the Lord is going to make sure that the same statement gets into the Gospels, three or four times, I believe we should take note. It's important.

> *"Truly, truly, I say to you, an hour is coming and now is, when the dead will hear the voice of the Son of God, and those who hear will live...Do not marvel at this; for an hour is coming, in which all who are in the tombs will hear His voice, and will come forth; those who did the good deeds to a resurrection of life, those who committed the evil deeds to a resurrection of judgment." [John 5:25, 28-28 NASB] (Jesus confirms Daniel 12)*

The dead will hear the voice of the Son of God, and those who hear will live, and all who are in the tombs (and He is not just talking about the saved...He said ALL), just as Daniel heard from Gabriel... some to a resurrection of life (eternal) and others to a resurrection of eternal judgment. It seems these same themes are getting confirmed over and over again, does it not? But wait, how did the Lord start off this statement, "Truly, truly, I say to you..." It is just like what He said to the criminal on the cross. Don't take my word for it, folks. Do the "2 Ps"....pray and ponder. Ask the Lord to make it clear for you, one way or the other. I believe He will.

> *"In My Father's house are many dwelling places; if it were not so, I would have told you; for I go to prepare a place for you. If I go and prepare a place for you, I will come again and receive you to Myself, that where I am, there you may be also." [John 14:2-3 NASB]*

And here, He is talking about "going away to prepare a place for us." He even says, "if it were not so, I would have told you," I believe He was going to prepare a place, just as He said. And that place very well may be what He referred to as Paradise. But, the time for that place to be revealed has not come because the Bridegroom has not returned for His Bride. The new dwelling place is not revealed before that. See how the pieces all seem to fit?

> *"I have given them Your word; and the world has hated them, because they are not of the world, even as I am not of the world. I do not ask You to take them out of the world, but to keep them from the evil one." [John 17:14-15 NASB]*

I have already talked about this one. Jesus is telling the Father, regarding the ones He has been given, "I do not ask you to take them out of the world, but to keep them (protect them) from the evil one." What are we to make of this rarely quoted passage (I wonder why)? Two things, Jesus is saying there is an "evil one." It is not a fairy tale. And we, as believers in Him will need to be protected from it...in the midst of the hard times (obviously), not taken out of the world so we would not be available for duty, having been "taken off the field when the game is truly on the line."

I'm guessing that if we could ask Noah, Joseph, Job, Moses, David, Daniel, and Shadrach, Meshach and Abednego, they would say, "What? You think God will pop you off the face of the earth before the bad stuff starts happening around you? Whatever gave you that idea?

That is not how things went down with us. We went through the trials and tribulations. Yes, the Lord was with us and protected us. But no, we were not removed from the earth to spare us the pain. And now, if He does that for you folks, we might have reason to be a little miffed, wouldn't you say?"

> *"Therefore repent and return, so that your sins may be wiped away, in order that times of refreshing may come from the presence of the Lord; and that He may send Jesus, the Christ appointed for you, whom heaven must receive until the period of restoration of all things about which God spoke by the mouth of His holy prophets from ancient time." [Acts 3:19-21 NASB] (confirming Ps 110:1)*

Here Peter says, referring to Jesus, the One who sits at the right hand of the Father, "whom heaven must receive until the period of restoration of all things (including the Garden of Eden, I believe), pretty much confirming the words of King David in Psalm 110. I do not believe the Scriptures teach that the Father will send His Chosen One back before the restoration of all things (or as David said, "until I make Your enemies Your footstool"). And that, almost everyone agrees, will happen at the end of the tribulation.

> *After they had preached the gospel to that city and had made many disciples, they returned to Lystra and to Iconium and to Antioch, strengthening the souls of the disciples, encouraging them to continue in the faith, and saying, "Through many tribulations, we must enter the kingdom of God." [Acts 14:21-22 NASB]*

This passage appears in Acts when Paul and Barnabas were going from town to town preaching the Gospel and doing acts of wonder through the power of the Holy Spirit. And the people reacted with "mixed reviews." Some said of them, "the gods have come down to us in human form," to which they responded by saying, "No, we are men just like you," But others stoned Paul and dragged him out of the city, thinking he was dead. So, this was either Paul or Barnabas encouraging the disciples by saying, "Through many tribulations, we must enter the kingdom of God."

And if we think about it, 11 of the 12 disciples were put to death for their faith. Only John was not, but he was taken captive and banished to the Isle of Patmos, where Jesus revealed to him the visions we know of, today, as the Book of Revelation. So, it is hard for me to imagine that these godly men would embrace any idea of "believers being whisked away to spare them of hardships." It just does not bear witness with me. These men persevered through the trials and tribulations until their last breath. And the fruit of their faithfulness was many souls being won to Christ. Now that does bear witness with my soul, because I believe God, in His heart, is redemptive.

> *He who did not spare His own Son, but delivered Him over for us all...Who will separate us from the love of Christ? Will tribulation, or distress, or persecution, or famine... just as it is written, "For Your sake we are being put to death all day long; We were considered as sheep to be slaughtered." [Romans 8 32:35, 36 NASB]*

"He did not spare His own Son but delivered Him over for all of us..." 'Nuff said...there.

> *But now Christ has been raised from the dead, the first fruits of those who are asleep...Christ the first fruits, after that those who are Christ's at His coming, then comes the end, when He hands over the kingdom to the God and Father..." [1 Corinthians 15:20, 23-24 NASB]*

And pertaining to the resurrection, what does Paul say He is? The first fruits. Ok, but the first fruits of what? He says Jesus, when resurrected, became "the first fruits of those who are asleep." Now, I have heard many folks say, "Oh sure, many times in the Old Testament, we see people equating death with sleep...that is how they spoke of it back then. When someone would die, they would say they "slept with their fathers." It seemed to be a softer, easier way of talking about death. Well, here is Paul in the New Testament, not only talking about those who are dead as being "asleep." He is suggesting that Jesus was one of them, in fact, the first one (of many to follow) to be resurrected to life again. I did try, but I was unable to find a single verse that stated Jesus was waiting in Heaven, with the Father, until the time of the resurrection. In John 20:17, Jesus told Mary Magdalene not to cling to Him, why? Because He had "not yet ascended to the Father." Think about that, Jesus...after being raised tells Mary Magdalene, "I have not yet ascended to My Father..." So, since Christ was our example, does it make sense that He was not carried away to Heaven to await His resurrection, but we will be? Not to me, it doesn't.

> *Behold, I tell you a mystery; we will not all sleep, but we will all be changed, in a moment, in the twinkling of an eye, at the last trumpet; for the trumpet will sound, and the dead will be raised imperishable, and we will be changed.*
> *[1 Corinthians 15:51-52 NASB]*

So then, IF...we are asleep and awaiting our resurrection, THEN... when should we expect the trumpet to blow (just as when we sleep at night, we perceive no passing of time or anything happening around us while we sleep. Solomon wrote, "the dead know nothing."). Paul makes it very clear by confirming what the prophets like Isaiah and Zechariah said many years earlier, and what I believe Jesus revealed to John on the Isle of Patmos, years later. The dead will be raised at "the sound of the seventh and last trumpet." No sooner and no later. And no man knows the day or the hour...remain watchful...and be ready.

> *Therefore, being always of good courage, and knowing that while we are at home in the body we are absent from the Lord...we are of good courage, I say, and prefer rather to be absent from the body and to be at home with the Lord.*
> *[2 Corinthians 5:6, 8 NASB]*

This may be another one that led me to call this chapter, "Lost in Translation." There is maybe no other passage that has been quoted more often, to suggest that we have an "immortal soul" (as the Greeks and Romans believed) and that when we die, we are immediately in the presence of our Blessed Savior, Jesus Christ. And like I have said before, if what I believe is wrong and after I take my last breath, in the blink of an eye, I will be in His glorious presence...that works for me!! I, however, do not see that in the Scriptures.

How often have you heard the phrase, "The Bible says, "to be absent from the body is to be present with the Lord?" Countless times, right? Let's go back and read this passage again. Does it say that? No, it does not, and not in any other translation, either. Paul is saying, "Sure…we are of good courage, I say, and prefer to be absent from the body and at home with the Lord." I agree with Paul. I would prefer to be at home with the Lord, too, and one day we will be. But this does not say that is what happens, immediately, when we die. That is an interpretation that some people have attached to this passage… an assumption. I am not willing to base my faith or my theology on assumptions. I am quite comfortable with what the Bible teaches, plus or minus nothing. If something is God's will, it is good enough for me!!

> ***But we do not want you to be uninformed, brethren, about those who are asleep, so that you will not grieve as do the rest who have no hope. For if we believe that Jesus died and rose again, even so, God will bring with Him those who have fallen asleep in Jesus. [1 Thessalonians 4:13-14 NASB]***

Ah, 1 and 2 Thessalonians!! Ground zero for many of the passages that help form this idea that we will be whisked away before the great tribulation period begins. As we look at these verses, please keep in mind that these were all penned by the Apostle Paul under the influence of the Holy Spirit. These passages were not written down by different people. It was all Paul, here. And here he says, "We do not want you to be uninformed about those who are asleep…for if we believe that Jesus (the first fruit) died and rose again (physically rose from the dead)…even so, God will bring with Him those who have fallen asleep in Jesus." Ok, fine, so God will raise us…just as He raised His own Son from the dead when the time was right.

> ***For the Lord Himself will descend from heaven with a shout, with the voice of archangel and with the trumpet of God, and the dead in Christ will rise first. Then we who are alive and remain will be caught up together with them in the clouds to meet the Lord in the air. [1 Thessalonians 4:16-17 NASB]***

Now, Paul is saying that the resurrection of those who are asleep will happen when? With a shout, with the voice of the archangel, and yes...the sound of the trumpet of God. That is when "the dead in Christ" will be raised, and those who are yet alive will be instantly changed immediately thereafter. I do not remember reading or hearing that there will be a shout, the voice of the archangel and the sound of the trumpet of God being attached to a rapture that might occur just before the final seven years. In fact, many who are looking forward to that call it "the Secret Rapture." I do not believe there will be anything "secret" about the second coming of Christ. The Bible says, "Every eye will see Him" and "every knee will bow." That does not sound very "secret" to me.

But since we are of the day, let us be sober...For God has not destined us for wrath, but for obtaining salvation through our Lord Jesus Christ...so that whether we are awake or asleep, we will live together with Him. [1 Thessalonians 5:8-10 NASB]

Here, Paul is pointing out that "God has not destined us for wrath," and I agree. God's wrath is what comes, again, at the end of the seven years. It is where the enemies of God get what's been promised to them. It is Satan's wrath that is let loose on the earth during those troublesome years. In Revelation 12, it says he has come down to earth "to make war with the saints." If you believe that only the Jews remain, do you think the Lord would refer to the Jews as "the saints?" I do not. Yes, there are Messianic Jews who have put their faith in Christ as Messiah. But, if there is a pre-tribulation "a catching away of the saints of Christ," they would be among them. Those are not the Jews who would remain during the final seven years.

Now we request you, brethren, with regard to the coming of our Lord Jesus Christ and our gathering together to Him...it will not come unless the apostasy comes first, and the man of lawlessness is revealed. [2 Thessalonians 2:1, 3 NASB]

Paul, again here, speaks of "the coming of our Lord Jesus Christ" and "our gathering together to Him." I fully believe in both of those things. Yes, as I said earlier, I believe there will be a rapture, a "catching away" of those faithful to the Lord. I simply disagree with the timing of the "catching away," as others see it.

But Paul, however, does give the Thessalonians a few hints:

1) Apostasy must come first (some say that happened when the Constantinian believers began making many theological compromises with the pagans of the day…I do not go quite that far. I think there is yet another great apostasy to come and we may already be seeing the signs of it happening all around the world, especially here in America).

2) The man of lawlessness (the Antichrist) must be revealed. That, obviously, has not happened yet, although many believe that he is alive, somewhere on the earth today. And that has some credibility, especially if you believe (as I do) that the rebirth of Israel marked the beginning of the final generation before Christ's return. So, we can conclude here, that according to Paul, until the Antichrist is revealed, Christ cannot come back. And most believe his revealing happens at the middle of the seven years with the appearance of "the abomination of desolation" standing in the rebuilt Temple (hasn't happened yet) and claiming to be "equal with God." And again, almost everyone agrees that does not happen prior to the final three and a half years.

And you know what restrains him now, so that in his time he will be revealed. For the mystery of lawlessness is already at work; only he who now restrains will do so until he is taken out of the way [2 Thessalonians 2: 6-7 NASB]

We talked about this when we talked about Daniel Chapter 12. I am thoroughly convinced that "the restrainer" is Michael the Archangel…not "the church" or the Holy Spirit. If we look at Paul's writings to the Thessalonians as a whole, I believe the picture is quite clear. He is not teaching them of a "catching away" that will happen before the final seven years of tribulation. Many things must happen first. And boy, have they ever!!

> *And all these, having gained approval through their faith, did not receive what was promised, because God had provided something better for us, so that apart from us they would not be made perfect. [Hebrews 11:39-40 NASB]*

This one is also "a biggie" in my mind. Hebrews 11, of course, is the "Faith Chapter." It talks about all the old-time saints who displayed great "acts of faith" before Christ came to save us. So, imagine if you can, we have the writer of Hebrew (who I tend to believe was Luke) saying that these blessed Old Testament saints "gained approval for the faith...but DID NOT receive what was promised (which I believe is their resurrection and their glorified bodies). And he goes on to write that God did it this way, "so that apart from us, they would not be made perfect (immortal)." Let that sink in. God is looking forward to one glorious day, where all the saints of God who have ever lived will pass from "that which was corruptible...to that which is incorruptible." It makes sense to me because the Bible also teaches that "God is not a respecter of persons." I believe that means to favor one above another for any reason than a person is either "in Christ" or not "in Christ." So, why would He allow some to proceed into His glorious presence before others? No, I tend to believe He would prefer His children come to Him all at once. One big "resurrection party" (or maybe a great wedding feast!!). At least, that is how I see it.

> *For Christ also died for sins once for all, the just for the unjust, so that He might bring us to God, having been put to death in the flesh, but made alive in the spirit; in which also He went and made proclamation to the spirits now in prison, who once were disobedient, when the patience of God kept waiting in the days of Noah, during the construction of the ark, in which a few, that is, eight persons, were brought safely through the water. [1 Peter 3:18-20 NASB]*

Ooh, this is a juicy one. I have plenty to say about this important passage, but I will try to keep it brief. We already talked about the fact that between the crucifixion and the resurrection of Christ, our blessed Lord did not go to Heaven to be with the Father, per His own words recorded John Chapter 20. So where, if anywhere, did He go during those days? Did He just quietly lie in the tomb, awaiting His resurrection? This passage seems to point to something else that we don't often talk about.

Remember the "seed war" that I mentioned a few times. It sprang from God's judgment towards Eve that there would be "enmity" (opposition, anger, hostility) between her seed and the seed of the serpent (Satan). Well, it appears here that Peter believed that some of Satan's followers, the angels who rebelled with him (we can call them the "bad seed"...I am comfortable with that) were in some sort of prison and that Christ went and made a proclamation to them there, sometime between the crucifixion and resurrection. Many believe He was giving the fallen angels one more chance to repent and once again become loyal to God Almighty.

Whether some of them took Him up on the offer, we do not know. There is that verse says "He brought captives with Him," so maybe some did repent. Again, this would be more evidence that Christ did not go immediately to Heaven when He physically died, but also it would imply that He had not yet prepared that place He promised He would prepare for us. I am inclined to think that will be Paradise, or we could call it the restored Garden of Eden. And that makes it more likely that Jesus was not telling the criminal they both would be in Paradise that very same literal day. But again, one day, we shall see.

So again, I have questions about this idea that Jesus or anybody else might instantly pass from Earth to God's presence at the moment that we cease to "physically live" here. And based on all the Scriptural support, I tend to think I am not alone (although I believe I would be in the minority of Christians, today, who think that way). But what I am searching for is the truth. I am not interested in being aligned with the popular side of a debate. That has no eternal value. Being aligned with the truth of God, on the other hand, has great eternal value. May His will be done...that is my only priority in these matters.

For if God did not spare angels when they sinned, but cast them into hell and committed them to pits of darkness, reserved for judgment; and did not spare the ancient world, but preserved Noah, a preacher of righteousness, with

> *seven others, when He brought a flood upon the world of the ungodly; [2 Peter 2:4-5 NASB]*

Two things worth elaborating on here: 1) God did not spare the angels (the bad seed) when they sinned and put them in some form of holding a place, reserved for those headed for judgment. But he brought Noah and seven members safely through the flood. He did not have to remove them from the earth to protect them, while He punished those who were rebellious and disobedient prior to the Great Flood.

> *The Lord knows how to rescue the godly from temptation, and to keep the unrighteous under punishment for the day of judgment, [2 Peter 2:9 NASB]*

And lastly, this passage is a very important one, when thinking of God's divine nature regarding the end times. He, I believe, is more than able to judge many upon the face of the earth, while at the same time protecting many others in the midst of it all. He is able to rain on some and not others at the same time. He can cause the wind to rip one house apart and leave the house next door relatively untouched. One passenger in a car wreck can be killed instantly, while the other passengers only suffered minor injuries or maybe even none at all. God can do that. The military likes to use the word "surgical strikes." I think God invented the idea. His movements are very swift and precise, with no accidental or "unintended consequences" left in the wake of His actions. No collateral damage, if you will.

Now, I know that was a long list of passages and explanations and thank you so much for putting up with all of that. I believe it will be very helpful as next, we go into Part Three of this book, where I will finally reveal my views and my timeline regarding the end times. I will reveal where I think we are now on that timeline and what I believe happens next...and then beyond, up until and including the return of Christ and the revealing of our eternal home, once the one-thousand-year reign of Christ on the earth has been completed.

All the passages in this chapter provide the basis for everything we are going to talk about from here on out. So, I thought it best to compile them neatly in one place. This will provide the foundation upon which I hope to build, sort of like a reference chapter or addendum that you, the reader, could come back to at any time, now or in the future, to refresh yourself as to my reasoning for some of the conclusions I have reached. And some of them, of course, I realize are not in line with the majority of Christians today. But, that is why I felt so strongly that I needed to write this book may be, just maybe, I have touched on a few things that you have not considered before. And it is possible that it could either change how you see these things or, at least, cause you to dig deeper into them for yourself.

The bottom line, at least in mind, is that we should as the Bible teaches, "Be diligent to present yourselves approved to God... accurately handling the word of truth." I believe God wants us to keep digging and to learn all we can while we are able to do so. That is why He made the mysteries of God to be such that no one, in human form, will ever completely understand or comprehend. He wants us to stay hungry and keep digging. No one ever regretted, at least to my knowledge, getting to know God better.

And I, for one, have no desire to stop trying.

"SEEK THE LORD WHILE HE MAY BE FOUND"
[ISAIAH 55:6]

Part Three

GOD'S NATURE

IN FUTURE EVENTS

"The things which will take place..."

(Revelation 1:19)

CHAPTER SEVENTEEN

THE WEEK IN REVIEW

Well, we have finally arrived (at long last) at the crux of the matter. It's time to talk about how I believe the final chapters of "life on Earth as we know it" will unfold, and how the principles of God's nature will play into it all. And from the bottom of my heart, thank you for bearing with me as I laid the groundwork for my explanations of "what I believe will happen," "when I believe they will happen," and maybe most importantly, "why I believe these things." I believe understanding the past, as they apply to "end-time matters," is crucial to understanding future events

These conclusions have taken me forty years to solidify (and there is still much to learn, I'm sure). And now, I feel it is time to put my findings out there. God has laid these things heavily upon my heart because I truly believe the day of our Lord's return is quickly drawing near, and I do not want to be "uninformed," as the Apostle Paul said, regarding these things.

But, before we look ahead at what will be coming in the days, weeks, months and years that lay before us, I feel we need to take a quick look at how we got here and establish exactly where I believe we are, right now, regarding the timing of "the last days."

Remember back in Chapter One, when we talked about creation and how the Lord created all things in six days and rested on the seventh? I wrote about the "high priority" I felt God was putting on this "day of rest" by establishing it as a pattern for us to follow all the days of our lives, and through all generations? We are about to see why I believe that is so important to Him. The entire span of human history and our interactions with the Lord were based on this "seven-day plan." As we have seen, there was the Sabbath Day, the Sabbath Year and the Year of Jubilee, all based on this "six-plus-one" concept. Six days of work…one day of rest. For there to be so many different applications in Scripture and biblical prophecy, surely there must be something of great importance to which all these things are pointing. This idea that all of one's labors are to be followed by a period of rest and ceasing from striving, well, it must be quite precious in the eyes of the Lord.

We talked about how twice in the Bible, once in the Old Testament (Psalm 90:4) and once in the New Testament (2 Peter 3:8), we have been taught this biblical "rule of thumb" that states that in the eyes of the Lord, "one day is as a thousand years and a thousand years is as a day". And wouldn't you know it, if we look at the genealogies of the Bible, or a timeline of human history (as we know it), it reveals that we have tarried here on Earth for roughly six thousand years (4000 before Christ and 2000 after Christ).

Have you ever wondered why our calendar switched gears from BC to AD (or from BCE to CE, as some prefer) two thousand years ago? The Jews, who did not recognize Jesus as the Messiah, did not change their calendar. They still count forward from the day of creation. For them, 2018 is 5778. So, is it just a coincidence that "the powers that be" decided the birth of Jesus Christ was the suitable time for that dividing line to be drawn? I do not think so. I think it was "divine providence." The birth of Christ changed everything, why not our calendar?

So, what I would like to do right now, is take a brief, birds-eye view of the six days (6000 years) we humans have endured while highlighting some of the pivotal events that happened on each day. I am guessing you have never seen it done this way before. I know I have not. But this will be fun, and I promise to be brief, so we can finally look forward!!

Oh, by the way, the numbers will be representing the years counting forward from Adam and Eve until Christ (as the Hebrews do), and then from Christ forward, I will use both the Hebrew year and the Gregorian calendar we use today, introduced by (you guessed it), Pope Gregory XIII. Rome strikes again!!

DAY ONE

Adam and Eve (0): Day One begins with God creating order out of chaos, and before you know it, His masterpieces (humans) have given the power back to chaos through their sin and disobedience.

Seth (Adam's son) (130): Following Abel's murder by Cain, if the bloodline of the Messiah was to be protected, God had to provide a replacement. A third son had to be given to Adam. Seth was that divine replacement through whom the Savior of the world was to come.

Enoch (622-987): He was not only the first person to be taken to Heaven without tasting death, He was also one who was quite prolific in writing about the Watchers (the fallen angels who intermingled with the daughters of men) and, of course, the "seed war" we have talked about quite frequently, here. And that "seed war," I believe, will play a major role in the final days of Earth, before Christ returns.

Conclusion: Day One started with some glorious events, God creating the Universe and making mankind "in His image." But it was not long before sin entered the picture and the "seed war" was on!! Hence, the rest of Day One reveals a gradual, yet steady decline into wickedness, with mankind becoming more and more evil as the days and the years passed. Something had to be done.

DAY TWO

Noah (1056): As the world became exceedingly evil, the Lord decided to hit the "reset button" on humanity. He chose eight highly-favored ones to be "left behind" (that's interesting) and repopulate the earth. The wicked ones were removed from this world. Keep that in mind, going forward.

Nimrod (1800): He was the great-grandson of Noah, the grandson of Noah's son, Ham, who did not follow in the ways of God or his own earthly father. Nimrod became the first "Antichrist" type of world leader. He became the father of Babylon and the builder of the Tower of Babylon. Oh yes, we will be talking about Babylon again later, for sure. It is important enough to take up two parenthetical chapters in the Book of Revelation, so you can count on it.

Abraham (1948): He was the one God chose to be the father of a great nation. Through Abraham's seed came God's people, and his own grandson, Jacob (who God would later rename Israel). When Abraham was in the womb, his father (Terah) chose to hide Sarah and the baby from Nimrod, who would have killed him. He believed a male child was about to be born who would one day take his throne.

Conclusion: Day Two got off to a positive start, once again, with the birth of Noah, the one God would use to preserve the seed of His great nation, while He eliminated the evil ones among them. Remember, God can do both at the same time…preserve His righteous ones in the midst of great trouble, while holding His enemies under judgment. And, of course, there were challenges to God's plan on Day Two. But God, as always, was in control.

DAY THREE

Isaac (2048): The promised son of Abraham and Sarah became the one God told Abraham to sacrifice. And had not God provided a suitable replacement, he would have obeyed God and willingly sacrificed his son…just as God Himself would do years later.

Jacob (2008): He was said to be the one who "wrestled with God and prevailed," and therefore, it was then that God changed his name to Israel.

Joseph (2100): A favored son of Jacob, a multicolor coat, and a bunch of jealous brothers provide us with a miraculous story that teaches us that what God says will happen, will indeed happen (whether others believe it or not).

Moses (2478): Saved from death as a baby (as Abraham was) and chosen by God to lead His people out of Egypt and to the Promised Land, Moses was not permitted to enter the land because of his own sin. Sin has consequences.

Conclusion: Day Three began with the birth and possible sacrifice of Isaac. And it ended, with God supernaturally saving and raising up a deliverer of His people through Moses. And through him, the Law was given to the people of Israel as a way for them to measure themselves against the righteousness of God. Not surprisingly, they (as we all do) fell miserably short of being righteous, and therefore, we are all in need of a Savior, a deliverer, and we know that the Lord provides. And I believe He will provide again, and again, until the final day when He appears to deliver us once and for all, just as He promised He would do two-thousand years ago.

DAY FOUR

David (2990): At the beginning of the fourth day, prophetically speaking, God raised up a king from Bethlehem, named David, who would face giants and fight valiantly on behalf of His people, not unlike our King Jesus, who was yet to come…and will come yet again.

The Prophets: The fourth day was full of attacks against Israel and Judah. But they brought them upon themselves by disobeying God's commandments, seeking false gods, and ignoring the likes of Isaiah, Jeremiah, Ezekiel, Daniel, and many others who God sent to warn His people before judgment eventually came. And God still does that today. Amos 3:7 says, **"Indeed, God does nothing without revealing His counsel to His servants, the prophets."**

Conclusion: As we have seen in each of the previous days, God provided mankind with a "promising start," first Adam, then Noah, then Isaac, and of course, David. But, each time, it was not long until the enemy appeared on the scene to try to squash the hopes of God's ultimate promise, Jesus Christ, from coming to fruition and ending Satan's reign over the earth, once and for all time. But each time, although it may have looked like he had won a battle or two, he was forever doomed to ultimately lose the war.

DAY FIVE

Jesus Christ (4000/4 BC): A descendant of David, also born in Bethlehem, but also a Nazarene (as prophesied), born of a virgin who God said, **"This is my beloved Son, in whom I am well-pleased."** Not a bad way to start Day Five.

The Fall of Jerusalem to Rome (4074/70 AD): Just as the Lord Himself prophesied, the Temple was destroyed with **"not one stone**

left upon another" and the Jews were scattered, not to return home for 2000 years.

Constantine (4300/300 AD): This emperor was converted to Christianity and decided to make it the "state religion" for the entire Roman Empire. That did not go over well with the pagans. And that led to many compromises over the next hundred years or so. Those compromises eventually led to what we know today as the Catholic Church. BTW: the word "catholic" means "worldwide." That will be important later, as well, when we talk about the appearing of another "one-world religion."

The Holy Roman Empire (4800/800 AD): A man named Charlemagne was crowned emperor of the Holy Roman Empire, which was the more "political wing" of the Catholic Church and became, like the European Union today, a governing authority over much of Europe. We will something very similar in the days yet to come.

Conclusion: Well, I would say Day Five got off to the best start ever (although Day Seven sounds pretty darn good, too) with the birth of Jesus Christ, whose name actually means "Yahweh is salvation." Imagine that, the Savior is given a name which means, "I am your salvation," and the people still missed it. Maybe they should have put it on a t-shirt that Jesus could have worn or made a hashtag out of it. But back then, they did not even dare spell out the name God. They would write G-d, or YHWH, to avoid being blasphemous. And Day Five, of course, ends with another enemy uprising in the form of the Holy Roman Empire and its stranglehold on the nations of the world. It was the second "one-world government" we have seen, so far (The first one was Babylon). And one more is coming, for sure. In fact, if we read Revelation Seventeen, we see the name Babylon surfaces again. Coincidence? I think not.

DAY SIX

The Gutenberg Bible (1455): The invention of the Gutenberg Press was said to be the most impactful developments for helping to spread the Gospel of Jesus Christ around the world. One of the first things that this new printing press was used for was to print the first Bible, in Latin (of course). The Holy Roman Empire was still in charge.

Martin Luther's Ninety-Five Theses (1517): These ninety-five complaints, by Luther, became the beginnings of the Reformation and led to a very long and bitter battle between Protestants and Catholics, the effects of which are still being felt around the world today.

The Tyndale New Testament (1526): William Tyndale produced the first English version of the New Testament but was put to death before he could finish the Old Testament. And as I mentioned earlier, he was the brother of my 14th great grandmother on my mother's side, Margaret Tyndale...so yes, his work is special to me. You knew I just had to fit him in here somewhere, right?

America is Born (1776): I would not underestimate the birth of the United States when looking at impactful events regarding the things of God during the sixth day. America has become the biggest exporter of the Gospel to the world at large through missions, TV and radio ministries and, of course distributing Bibles in many languages. And, we are also Israel's greatest friend in the modern world. And I believe that will be huge as the day of the Lord's return approaches, as well.

Communist Manifesto (1848): God's enemy, Satan, is always quick and active in counteracting anything good that God brings upon the earth. America brings "freedom and liberty" and a limited federal government. Communism offered the exact opposite.

Israel is Reborn (1948): This is probably the most impactful prophetic fulfillment since the resurrection of Jesus Christ. Most scholars agree that this marks the beginning of the final generation before Christ returns. And, so far, we are about seventy years into it. So how much longer can it be? Only God knows for sure.

Jerusalem Reunited (1967): The Six-Day War brought the enemies of Israel against them, but Israel quickly prevailed and recaptured all of Jerusalem and the Temple Mount.

The Rise of Radical Islam (1948-present): Probably the most recent prophetic development is the rise of radical Islam and their desire to re-establish the caliphate (which would be, should that happen, the third one-world government after Babylon and Rome). And, we certainly saw the teeth of this uprising on September 11th, 2001. But, many say their battles with Israel and America (their best friend) on one hand, and other Muslim groups and nations, on the other hand, are far from over and will only escalate.

Conclusion: Ok, so maybe the sixth day did not start off so well, with the Crusades and the like. Religion was not just something you could be shunned for, back then. Powerful people were more than willing to kill others in the name of religion. But unfortunately, it was not God's Word, or will, that was guiding their decisions. Remember the "eight woes" from Matthew 23? Who was Jesus pointing to as the hypocrites? Once again, it was man-made religion and watered-down versions of the truth. Over the last 2000 years, false prophets and tainted truth have been on the rise. But, have no fear, my friends, the sixth day is going to have the best ending of all. MARANATHA... Come, Lord Jesus, come!!

DAY SEVEN

Some say that the tribulation period has already begun. Some say, it could come at any moment, because as the Lord said Himself, "No man knows the day or the hour of His coming." Others suggest that there are some key events that must happen first. Almost all Christians believe, however, that we are very close to seeing those prophecies fulfilled. So, praise God, it will not be terribly long before that final trumpet sounds.

All we can do at this point is pray, share the Good News with as many as will listen, seek the Lord with all our hearts, and do the very best we can to be ready when the Bridegroom comes for us. BTW, did you ever take notice of the fact that the Lord's Prayer includes, "Thy kingdom come, Thy will be done on Earth as it is in Heaven?" Some people think it is selfish for Christians to pray for Christ to return and for the end of this world as we know it. But Jesus taught His disciples to pray for Him to come back and establish His Kingdom. He wanted His redeemed ones to constantly be looking forward to His return, and to live accordingly. Are we doing that?

But, in closing out this chapter, there is one more view of when the "last days" will begin out there. And while it is not my personal view, it is one that in a way, has some merit. The theory suggests, as we talked about, that the Lord implied that our "earthly mission" would last seven days (seven thousand years). Six days of labor followed by a glorious "day of rest." And, if we follow the logic of this theory, we are at or nearing the end of the sixth day.

Now, those who give credence to this theory, then, are quick to point out that Christ's return will mark the end of our human struggles (or time of testing) and the beginning of a glorious "day of rest" at the beginning of Day Seven. And, since "the last days" cannot mean one day, it would be reasonable to think of the fifth and sixth days as "the last days." So, they would conclude that we have been in them, now, for roughly two thousand years. They believe the arrival of the Messiah began what they point to as the "last days." And, to some degree, I can understand that logic.

These same folks would point to Constantine and the emergence of the Catholic Church as "the great apostasy" (or "falling away") that the Lord warned us about. Many of the Reformers believed that. And many folks think that someday, probably sooner rather than later, a Pope who is in power when the Holy Roman Empire is revived will become the Antichrist. As for me, I do not see things unfolding quite that way. I do not believe a Pope will become the Antichrist. But, more on that a bit later.

So, as we begin to move into a more specific look at the end times and how things may unfold, where would I say we are, right now, on the timeline of end-time events?

Jesus taught, when "the fig tree blooms again" (the rebirth of the nation of Israel), that would start the clock ticking on the final generation before the Lord comes back to Earth to defeat His enemies and gather His elect. We are now seventy years beyond the rebirth of Israel, so it raises the question, "How long is a generation, biblically speaking?" I have heard forty years, seventy years, and one hundred and twenty years. No one knows for sure. Let's just say the end of the last generation is quickly drawing near (for the sake of our discussion) and leave it at that.

So, I believe we are seventy years into what I would call "the last days." I believe they started on May 14th, 1948, when Israel once again became a nation. And, as it says in Amos 9, ***"I will also plant them on their land, and they will not again be rooted out from their land which I have given them," says the LORD YOUR GOD...*** this time they are home for good. And, I believe things are gradually inching towards the final mysteries…hundreds of end-time prophecies finally being revealed.

Jesus said, "My sheep know My voice," and when He returns and calls us to Himself, we will hear that call (whether we are asleep or yet alive). And then, and only then, will we joyfully "meet Him in the air" and forever be with Him. For me, "when" is not that important.

Ultimately, I am quite comfortable letting Him work out the timing of all these things. I just need to be ready!!!

I can almost hear Peter, Paul and Mary (not the biblical ones) singing in the background, "All my bags are packed…I'm ready to go…I'm leaving on a jet plane…Don't know when I'll be back again."

Ok, not exactly that…but you get my point.

"I TELL YOU…NOW IS THE DAY OF SALVATION"
[2 CORINTHIANS 6:2]

CHAPTER EIGHTEEN

"SUMMER IS NEAR..."

We are now going to launch head-long into my explanations for these things we call, "the End Times." Many people have given millions of sermons and written countless books about these days that are promised, in the Bible, and said to be coming upon the earth at some point. Some say sooner rather than later. As the Lord told us, no one knows when, of course. But that does not stop us from speculating, strategizing and doing our best to connect the dots and untangle "the mysteries of the ages," and I am no different. I have been itching to put "my two cents worth" into this debate for years. So, love it or hate it, here we go!!

The way I would like to do this is a little different (otherwise, why would I have chosen to write this book, right?). Over the next few chapters, I am going to use the "Ground Zero" of end-time prophecy, Matthew 24, as our roadmap. I think the Lord did a masterful job (why not, He is the Master) of laying things out in a somewhat sequential order of events that will help us identify the stepping stones on the path to His ultimate return.

Then, in each of these chapters, I will reference the different prophecies in the Book of Revelation and from the other prophets, that I believe tie into each stepping stone. Hopefully, that will give us a clear and simple "chain of events" that we can be on the outlook for, as these things begin to appear on our spiritual and physical horizons. Are you ready? I hope so. I know I am!!

So, as Matthew 24 gets started, the disciples ask Jesus the "sixty-four-million-dollar question." "When will these things happen?" As I see it, the question was broken into two parts. So, I want to take the first part here, in this chapter. Then we will address the second one in the next chapter. Here's the first part, as recorded by Matthew:

> **As He was sitting on the Mount of Olives, the disciples came to Him privately, saying, "Tell us, when will these things happen?" [Matthew 24:3 NASB]**

What is interesting to me, in this chapter, is that the Lord Jesus does not give any specific times or dates. Rather, He points to "stepping stones" or indicators that can be seen with our eyes and discerned with our hearts, that will tell us where on the path we are, timewise.

For starters, there is one stepping stone that the Lord pointed to which I believe serves as a great starting point. It is like those maps we see in the mall that say, "You are here." It is hard to tell where you want to go next if you do not know where you are at the time. So, let's start there:

> **"Now learn the parable from the fig tree: when its branch has already become tender and puts forth its leaves, you know that summer is near; so, you too, when you see all these things, recognize that He is near, right at the door. Truly I say to you, this generation will not pass away until all these things take place. Heaven and earth will pass away, but My words will not pass away. But of that day and hour no one knows, not even the angels of heaven, nor the Son, but the Father alone.' [Matthew 24:32-36 NASB]**

As I said in the previous chapter, knowing where we are right now is best understood by looking at the rebirth of the "fig tree," Israel. We are seventy years (as of this writing) beyond the day Israel was once again declared a sovereign and independent nation on May 14th, 1948. Jesus, then, referred to the fact that this event would mark the beginning of the last generation by saying, "this generation will not pass away until all these things take place."

Some would say, "Well, if this generation is seventy years old right now, how much longer can it be before He returns?" I would say, "Great question!!" And, don't we all wish we knew the answer. Apparently, the disciples were thinking the same thing when they said, "Tell us when…"

But, at least for me, one more question remains. How can we be sure that when Jesus referred to the fig tree, He was referring to Israel? Well, there are a few hints. He had just recently cursed a fig tree that would not bear fruit. Israel certainly was that, before they were scattered around the world. But we also have this passage from Jeremiah that seems to confirm our assumption:

> *"Thus says the Lord God of Israel, 'Like these good figs, so I will regard as good the captives of Judah, whom I have sent out of this place…For I will set My eyes on them for good, and I will bring them again to this land; and I will build them up and not overthrow them, and I will plant them and not pluck them up." [Jeremiah 24:5-7 NASB]*

Well, that seems to firm things up a bit. The Lord prophesied through Jeremiah, that the captives from Judah would be thought of as "good figs" (even though they were not always obedient, hence their exile into Babylon) and He promises to bring them back to their homeland when their seventy years of captivity were finished (seventy years…that is interesting). By the way, shout out to my brothers, George L. and Terry W. I always thought "The Good Figs" would be a great name for a Christian band. What do you think?

Now, these verses also say that they will build again, and not be overthrown; He will plant them in the land and will not pluck them out again. And, I believe, that applies to another return to the homeland, not their return from Babylon. And this second fulfillment came to fruition in 1948. So, I am comfortable in referring to the fig tree as Israel, for the sake of your discussions here.

> *"So it shall be when all of these things have come upon you, the blessing and the curse which I have set before you, and you call them to mind in all nations where the Lord your God has banished you… then the Lord your God will restore you from captivity, and have compassion on you, and will gather you again from all the peoples*

where the Lord your God has scattered you. [Deuteronomy 30:1,3 NASB]

Even in Deuteronomy, many years before their troubles with Assyria and Babylon, the Lord was telling them that they would endure both blessing and curse (which they surely did) and that they would reflect on all that God had done for them, even while they were yet in captivity. And then, He would restore them to the land He promised them, have compassion on them, and regather them from where they were scattered. In 1948, it happened, just as it said in Deuteronomy.

"Also, I will restore the captivity of My people Israel, And they will rebuild the ruined cities and live in them; they will also plant vineyards and drink their wine and make gardens and eat their fruit. I will also plant them on their land, and they will not again be rooted out from their land which I have given them," says the LORD YOUR GOD. [AMOS 9:14 NASB]

THOSE WHO HAVE HAD THE CHANCE TO VISIT ISRAEL SINCE THEIR RETURN, ESPECIALLY IN RECENT YEARS, SEEM TO ALL SAY WHAT AN INCREDIBLE NATION IT HAS BECOME. THEY ARE WORLD LEADERS IN MANY CATEGORIES OF AGRICULTURE, MEDICINE, AND TECHNOLOGY. AND YES, SOME GREAT WINES NOW COME FROM THEIR FERTILE FIELDS, FIELDS THAT WERE, NOT THAT LONG AGO, DESOLATE AND BARREN.

"Who has heard such a thing? Who has seen such things? Can a land be born in one day? Can a nation be brought forth all at once? [Isaiah 66:8 NASB]

Yes, modern Israel came to be a nation in one day, thanks to a vote at the United Nations which was strongly advocated by the United States under President Harry Truman. But, in reality, this did not come about overnight. There were Zionists who had been campaigning for the return of the Jews for more than a century, and in 1917, a man named Arthur Balfour (the United Kingdom's Foreign Secretary) sent a letter extending what he said was a show of "sympathy with Jewish Zionist aspirations" that they should once again have a homeland. By the way, it is interesting to note that 1917 was as Year of Jubilee, according to the Hebrew calendar, and Jubilee years are said to be about "returning the land to its rightful owner." I should also mention that the 1967 War, which brought about the reunification of Jerusalem also occurred during a Year of Jubilee, as did the U.S. decision to recognize Jerusalem as Israel's capital in December of 2017. How is that for "putting a little frosting on the cake?"

Then, of course, there was the rise of Adolph Hitler and Nazi Germany, which led to one of the most horrific tragedies the world has ever known. It was an event we have come to know as the Holocaust, where two-thirds (six million people) of all the Jews who were scattered throughout Europe were put to death…men, women, and children… simply because they were Jews.

And I would say that the fact that Hitler was defeated and killed at the end of World War II was, to some degree, God's retribution on Hitler and the Nazis for the senseless slaughter of His people. We have talked many times, throughout this book, about the "seed war" that began in the Garden of Eden. The goal of the seed of the serpent has always been twofold:

1) To corrupt the bloodline of the Messiah and prevent Him from being able to become the "blameless Lamb" that would redeem those that are His.

2) To keep the promises of God from being fulfilled and one of the biggest promises was to restore the Jewish people to their homeland, permanently, in the latter days, which would point to the fact that the return of our coming King was quickly approaching.

Remember God's other promise, the one He made to Abraham, "Those that bless you will be blessed, and those that curse you will be cursed." So, following the Holocaust, it suddenly became fashionable to become a friend of Israel, and many did not want to be seen as their enemy, and therefore, God's enemy. There was growing sentiment that the Jewish people should, once again, have a land to call their own as God promised they would…forever.

But it was an uphill battle for those, as Harry Truman was, in favor of recognizing Israel as a nation once again. Many in his administration tried to talk him out of it saying, "Why should we upset the Muslim world for the sake of a few Jews?" History tells us that Truman was a godly man, with a strong Christian upbringing, and he knew it was not only the right thing to do but also, biblically correct.

Even the name of this new nation was hotly contested. Some wanted to call it Palestine, others preferred Zion. But after much debate, it was decided that the name Israel was the right choice, biblically and otherwise. And so it was, God's promise that Abraham would be the "father of a great nation," a nation which ultimately would be named after his grandson, Jacob (who God called Israel), finally came to be a reality once again in 1948.

One interesting side note to all of this, of course, is the fact that the Book of Revelation does not address the returning of Israel to their homeland as a sign of things to come. The messages to the seven churches (or should I say "assemblies") are not to Christians in Israel. Those are all Greek cities. That should serve as just another reminder that John's revelations were not meant to be seen only as forward-looking, chronological, or sequential. These churches were from the first hundred years following the death and resurrection of Jesus Christ, most scholars believe. So again, many times, prophecies have more than one application and fulfillment.

This would, of course, add some weight to the theory that Day Five and Day Six (the last two thousand years) are, in the bigger picture, the Last Days. I tend to look at both theories as credible, with the Day Five/Day Six theory being the "long view" of end-time events, and the birth of Israel as a nation again, in 1948, as the "shorter" or more current view. Either way, it means we are living in the "last days." I have no doubt about that.

So, we should always keep in mind that some things which are thought to be relevant to the "end times" may not always be pointing to future events. It seems clear that the seven letters to the seven "assemblies" (as we talked about before) have two applications. One is regarding those first-century "gatherings of the summoned", in particular. And the other, I believe, has implications towards the condition of Christian "congregations" that will be on the earth in the days leading up to the days of trouble, just before the return of Christ. Think of these messages as a "head's up."

BTW…if you have not read a book called "The Harbinger" by Rabbi Jonathan Cahn (especially if you are an American), I highly recommend you do so. The warnings from God of "impending judgment if we do not return to the Lord" are getting louder and more frequent.

I believe that regardless of which starting point we choose to embrace, it is reasonable to assume that the Lord's return is approaching quickly and that the events the Lord pointed to, in His Olivet Discourse, have already begun to occur, in line with His and other prophecies.

One thing is clear, at least in my mind, the Bride needs to get ready!!!

GOD WILL HELP HER WHEN THE MORNING DAWNS
[PSALM 46: 5]

CHAPTER NINETEEN

"AS IN THE DAYS OF NOAH..."

Now, let's look at the second question posed by the disciples in Matthew 24:3. I would say it is another "sixty-four-million-dollar question," which means this tiny little verse has added up to one hundred and twenty-eight million dollars-worth of questions. And why not? These questions loom large in helping us to come to the right conclusions as to how end-time events will unfold.

> *"And what will be the sign of Your coming, and of the end of the age?" [Matthew 24:3 NASB]*

The first thing that leaps out to me is the fact that the disciple who asked the questions said, "sign of Your coming," not "signs of Your coming." It would be reasonable to assume, I believe, that there might be more than one critical sign pointing to His promised return. The fact that the word "sign" was singular and not plural caused me to remember how Jesus answered the Pharisees in Matthew 12 when they asked for a sign. Here is what He said to them:

> ***Then some of the scribes and Pharisees said to Him, "Teacher, we want to see a sign from You." But He answered and said to them, "An evil and adulterous generation craves for a sign; and yet no sign will be given to it but the sign of Jonah the prophet; for just as Jonah was three days and three nights in the belly of the sea monster, so will the Son of Man be three days and three nights in the heart of the earth. [Matthew 12:38-40]***

Now, I would agree that what the Lord said to the Pharisees was not meant to refer to the last days, but rather to His death and resurrection. However, in line with the theory that the final days began with His death and resurrection (Day 5/Day6), His answer might seem to add weight to what He said later in Matthew 24…a single sign will take center stage when the time of His return is drawing near.

One could make the case that Jesus pointed to Jonah as a prophetic picture of what was to come regarding His crucifixion and resurrection and, as we all know now, what He said came true, quite precisely. Should that not give us more confidence that when referring to His return to Earth a second time, whatever He would point to as a sign of His coming should not be taken lightly. You can "take it to the bank," as they say. His words are "good as gold."

The story of Jonah was understood to be a sign, prophetically, confirming that Jesus was the Promised One, the Messiah. And His death and resurrection were intended to be enough to remove all doubt (of course, to some, it did not). If that happened exactly as He said (and it did), should we not take the parable about the fig tree bearing fruit again as a sign that summer (or His return) seriously? With that in mind, let's take a look at some comments He made later in the Matthew 24:

> *For the coming of the Son of Man will be just like the days of Noah. For as in those days before the flood they were eating and drinking, marrying and giving in marriage, until the day that Noah entered the ark, and they did not understand until the flood came and took them all away; so will the coming of the Son of Man be. Then there will be two men in the field; one will be taken, and one will be left. Two women will be grinding at the mill; one will be taken, and one will be left. [Matthew 24:37-41 NASB*

As a writer, myself, I could not overlook the fact that His comments about the "days of Noah," and the illustrations about "two men in the field" and "two women grinding at the mill" were lumped together. I know I talked about this briefly earlier, but I want to comment a little further as to why I think this is significant. And, yes, I will be happy to do that at the end of this chapter. But, let's talk about Noah and his descendants first.

What were the most memorable aspects of "the world as we know it" regarding the days of Noah?

1) The sons of God (commonly believed the fallen angels who, along with Satan, rebelled against God) found the daughters of men to be beautiful, took some as wives and had children with them.

2) The world became exceedingly evil to the point that God said, "I will wipe mankind off the face of the earth...I regret that I made them."

3) Noah found favor with God and was called to build an ark to allow for him and his family to survive the flood and repopulate the earth.

4) Those who were alive at the time, yet rejected Noah's warnings, were removed, "wiped off the face of the earth" (as God put it). But Noah and his family were protected and preserved through it all. In other words, they remained here on Earth, "left behind" by God, to repopulate the earth and carry on.

So, the days had become exceedingly evil to the point that God took action causing a great flood to cover the earth and kill every single human being except for eight people (the number of new beginnings). They were Noah, his wife, his three sons, and their wives. They were chosen, by God it says, because "Noah was pure in all his generations." I believe that to mean that his bloodline, at least up to and including Noah, had not been corrupted by the seed of the serpent, as so many others in those days had been. He was worthy to be the one through whom the Messiah was yet to come, many generations later. That is not to say that Noah was without sin. No one is sinless, as the Apostle Paul reminded us in Romans 3. But, the bloodline was still pure, not corrupted by the enemy. And that is very important.

Now, here in Matthew 24, Jesus is telling the disciples that the world will be very much like the days of Noah when He returns a second time. The days will be exceedingly evil, not just evil (sin has always been present), but greatly so, and increasing all the more as the day of His return approaches. Do you feel like we are living in times where it seems the world has become exceedingly evil? I do. Just in my lifetime, I contend that it has become much worse.

In the last one hundred years, we have seen two world wars, the likes of which the world had never seen before. It is estimated that over 17 million people died as a result of World War I, and as you might expect with the bombs being dropped on Hiroshima and Nagasaki, the death toll for World War II was far worse, coming in at around 60 million people. And may God help us, should there be a World War III. With the increase of nuclear weapons these days, I suspect the number could be astronomical…probably in the billions of deaths. In fact, the Bible does predict a time when one-third of the population of Planet Earth will be wiped out in one day. Right now, that would be over 2 billion people. That sounds like nuclear war to me.

Plus, in the last 100 years, we have seen the Holocaust, which resulted in over 6 million Jews being killed by Hitler and his Nazi regime. And, just in the US since 1973, when the Roe vs. Wade decision was made by the US Supreme Court, over 60 million innocent babies have been terminated while they were still in their mother's womb, which I consider the greatest human tragedy of all time. And, if we were to look at the number of abortions performed worldwide, my guess is it might be at least double that.

We have also seen not only a dramatic rise in homosexuality in the world, but even a "stamp of approval" as governments around the world have moved to make it not only "accepted," but go a step further and make it legal for gay couples to marry. Let me just say, here and now; I am no man's (or woman's) judge. But I believe according to God's Word, marriage was intended to be a covenant, a life-long relationship between one man and one woman. We are taught that marriage is to resemble the relationship between Christ (the Bridegroom) and His redeemed ones who have been washed in His blood (the Bride).

For me, that signifies that there is more to marriage than just an earthly relationship. It is meant to be a spiritual joining, as well. The Bible says, "The two shall become one," and that is meant to be more than merely in the physical sense, I am sure. So, as with the seven-day week, God established patterns for us to follow, all meant for our good, not our harm. I believe since it takes a man and a woman to make a baby, that should be "the icing on the cake," confirming that this is how He intended it to be.

Then, we have the terrorist attacks, of which 9-11-2001 was the worst we have witnessed so far, the horrific school shootings, family members killing each other, and the dramatic increase in police officers killed in the line of duty.

If all of these things are not reason enough to suspect that the order God created out of chaos, which we talked about in Chapter One, has now turned back towards chaos, Lord help us. I don't know what it would take, then, to get our attention. But, if the Bible is true, I have every reason to believe we are going to find out one day soon. God will not be mocked, and at some point, all wickedness will be punished.

But, before we move on, there is one more part of the Noah story I feel the need to elaborate on because I believe it will answer one of the biggest questions looming in the minds of many reading this book, not to mention millions of other folks around the world who study the Bible, as well. If, indeed, the Great Flood was God's way of removing evil from the world and starting all over with eight righteous people, why is there still evil in the world today? Great question. I will give you my personal view on this, and I won't even charge you anything extra. You are welcome!!

According to biblical history, Noah had three sons, Shem, Ham, and Japheth, and they were all born before the flood. All three were obvious married, also, before the flood because the Bible says Noah's three sons and their wives were saved, as well. Now, we have every reason to believe that Noah's three sons were not corrupted by the seed of the serpent. But, what about their three wives?

We have good reason to believe that Shem's wife was not corrupted because it was through Shem's descendants that the Messiah would come. That negates any chance of her being the bad seed. But there is one incident recorded in the Bible that gives us a strong indication of how the "seed of the serpent" may have survived beyond the flood. Let's look at another passage of Scripture from the Noah story:

> *Now the sons of Noah who came out of the ark were Shem and Ham and Japheth; and Ham was the father of Canaan...Then Noah began farming and planted a vineyard. He drank of the wine and became drunk and uncovered himself inside his tent. Ham, the father of Canaan, saw the nakedness of his father and told his two brothers outside. But Shem and Japheth took a garment and laid it upon both their shoulders and walked backward and covered the nakedness of their father; and their faces were turned away so that they did not see their father's nakedness.*
>
> *When Noah awoke from his wine, he knew what his youngest son had done to him. So he said, "Cursed be Canaan; servant of servants He shall be to his brothers." He also said, "Blessed be the LORD, the God of Shem; and let Canaan be his servant. "May God enlarge Japheth and let him dwell in the tents of Shem; and let Canaan be his servant." [Genesis 18-27 NASB]*

That is a lengthy passage, I know, but I believe it is crucial to our discussion, here, because not only has the pure bloodline of Christ, the seed of the woman, survived, I suggest that this story tells us how the seed of the serpent was able to survive beyond the flood, as well. Though it is not the only theory out there, I believe it makes good sense to consider the possibility that Ham's wife came from corrupted ancestors. Hence, the giants lived on.

Plus, in the very first sentence of the above passage, it mentions all three of Noah's sons by name, but only mentions one grandson by name. Canaan, the son of Ham. We have all heard of the Canaanites, I presume. They were enemies of God's people. Remember when Joshua and Caleb were sent to spy out the Promised Land? They got as far as Canaan and came back and said, "There are giants in the land." Well, what do you know? The Nephilim, the sons of the seed of the serpent, are yet alive and now living in the land of Canaan, the land of Ham's son.

We should also take note that Nimrod, of Babylon, was a descendant of Ham, as well. He was the son of Cush, one of Ham's other sons. Through Ham's sons came the nations of Ethiopia and Babylon (Cush), Egypt (Mizaim), Libya (Put) and of course, Canaan. Most of the enemies of God Almighty and His people came through Ham. Keep that in mind. It is my guess that the Antichrist will, too.

So, Noah drinks some of his own wine one night, goes back to his tent, takes off his clothes and falls asleep. And it is Ham who finds him in the morning. But Ham does something he should not have done. He looks upon his father's nakedness. Now to some, this might not seem like a big deal. After all, they are both males, right? But the Scriptures are clear about "honoring your father," and a son should do nothing to dishonor him. Noah believed Ham had dishonored him by looking upon his nakedness. It was thought to be equivalent with telling others about your father's sin. That is referred to as "uncovering your father's nakedness." I think you get the picture. We should always honor our parents, no matter what. It's right there in the Ten Commandments, but you already know that, I'm sure.

The other two boys grabbed a blanket and walked in backwards, with their faces turned away from Noah and laid it over him. They did not dishonor their father. Noah cursed Ham and his descendants for what he had done. He said Canaan would become the servant Shem and Japheth, a "servant of servants," it says.

It is also interesting to note that all through the Old Testament, we hear of giants. Abraham ran into some. As I mentioned, Joshua and Caleb saw them, when they were spying out the Promised Land. And that, of course, led to Israel sinning against God because they chose to go around the land of Canaan, instead of trusting in God and taking the land He promised them.

We hear of tribes such as the Canaanites, the Rephaim, the Amorites, the Anakim, and of course, Israel's nemesis, the Philistines (remember Goliath?). All of these were considered to be tribes that had very large men among them, men the patriarchs referred to in their writings as giants or "the watchers." I know we don't talk about these things much in church circles, but they are frequently mentioned in the

Scriptures. So, I don't think it is something we should sweep under the rug (a giant would make a pretty big "rug bump," just sayin').

So, why do we need to talk about such things? Well, many believe (and I am among them) that in the last days we will see evidence, once again, of the return of "the seed of the serpent." Many believe that this is part of not only what Jesus was referring to when He spoke of the days of Noah, but I believe it is a factor as to why the world is becoming, once again, exceedingly evil. I believe, to some degree, the seed of the serpent is "alive and well" in the earth today. I also believe we have only seen "the tip of the iceberg" with regards to their reappearance on the world stage as we move towards those final days of trouble.

So yeah, when Jesus said that before His second coming, the world would once again be like the days of Noah. I do not think he was talking about a horrific flood or a great big boat. I think it was more of a spiritual reference, a prophecy regarding the state of the world in the final days. Wickedness will be on the rise again…and it will again rise to the level where God Almighty will choose to intervene.

And lastly, I wanted to elaborate on what I hinted at earlier, the two men in the field and the two women at the grinding mill. This final portion of this passage first jumped out at me when I was writing my second book, "The Red Letter Parables." I was quite intrigued by the fact that they are lumped together with His comment that, prior to His return to earth, the world will be like the days of Noah. And immediately after that, He gives us two examples of situations, where "one person will be taken, one will be left…" Why was it important for Jesus to bring that up at the same time?

Many people see these two examples as evidence of an "early departure plan" for the church and, in some ways, I would agree that it seems like a reasonable conclusion. But, the word "rapture" has also been said to be a "catching away." Now, it is important to recall that the words "catching away" would generally have a negative connotation. The Greek word for "catching away" would be "harpazo," and that can be interpreted to mean "to seize; or carry off by force." Think of it as more like a kidnapping, than a rescuing. Oh my, now that does not sound at all like what I think about when I think of "the rapture."

I have even heard some Bible teachers and preachers refer to Noah and the Ark as "the first rapture." If, by rapture, they mean "catching away," or "carried off by force," Noah and his family are not a good fit. They were the ones who were allowed to remain and repopulate the Earth. It was the wicked ones who were "snatched away."

So, that raises a gigantic question in my mind. If Jesus chose to talk about these two men and two women (and in each case, one was taken, and one was left), immediately after saying the final days leading up to His return would be like the days of Noah, then who are we led to believe will remain, and who are we led to think will be "taken?" Is it possible that some "wishful thinking" may have led us to a flawed conclusion?

I think a strong case can be made that it is God's people, the ones who have put their trust in Christ (the ultimate ark by which we are saved) who will remain (be "left behind") on the earth long after the wicked ones have been removed. That is my story, and I'm sticking to it.

BLESSED IS THE ONE WHO PERSEVERES UNDER TRIAL
[JAMES 1:12]

CHAPTER TWENTY

"TELL US WHEN…"

So, there we have it. There are two major questions that will lead us through this fact-finding mission to help us come to a better understanding of end-time events. When will these things happen? And, what will be the sign (or signs) of His coming?

> *Jesus came out from the temple and was going away when His disciples came up to point out the temple buildings to Him. And He said to them, "Do you not see all these things? Truly I say to you, not one stone here will be left upon another, which will not be torn down." As He was sitting on the Mount of Olives, the disciples came to Him privately, saying, "Tell us, when will these things happen, and what will be the sign of Your coming, and of the end of the age?" [Matthew 24:1-3 NASB]*

He starts Matthew 24 with a prophecy that only took about forty years to be fulfilled…the destruction of the Temple by the Romans in 70 AD. Maybe that was His way of showing the disciples, rather quickly, that the things He says will happen, will indeed happen, just as He said. Maybe He was giving them a good reason to pay close attention to the rest of the things He said, as well. Either way, I think it worked.

But it does not take Him long to start speaking of things to come, things much farther down the line. Let's move to the next section of Matthew 24, which the Lord chose to compare to a period during a woman's pregnancy when the day of delivery is drawing near, but the fullness of time has not yet come.

THE BEGINNING OF BIRTH PANGS

And Jesus answered and said to them, "See to it that no one misleads you. For many will come in My name, saying, 'I am the Christ,' and will mislead many. You will be hearing of wars and rumors of wars. See that you are not frightened, for those things must take place, but that is not yet the end. For nation will rise against nation, and kingdom against kingdom, and in various places, there will be famines and earthquakes. But all these things are merely the beginning of birth pangs." [Matthew 24:4-8 NASB]

The first thing that Jesus mentions, here, is the rise of false prophets, apparently bent on "misleading" His people. He wants them (and us) to always be on the lookout for them. But, when we see a rise in not only the number of false prophets, but the magnitude of their lies and deception as well, we should take note that the coming of the Lord is not far off.

The second thing the Lord mentions during his statements about the birth pangs is, "wars and rumors of wars." Once again, you will hear people say, "Oh, there have been wars forever, and religion is usually the cause of them, not the solution." While it is true that peoples and nations have fought since the beginning of time, I believe the Lord, again, is speaking of a time when the number and the magnitude of the wars will reach record levels.

It was only about one hundred years ago that World War I was fought, killing 17 million people. At no time in history had there ever been a war that was far-reaching enough to be called a "world war," and never before had there been that many people killed in one collective conflict. Again, notice the breadth of the fighting and the magnitude of it, not to mention the casualties. This war broke new ground, sad as that is to say.

And, it wasn't long (the birth pangs were starting to get closer together) until World War II came along. And once again, it exceeded

War I in size and magnitude, and the death toll set another record, over 60 million people died during this one. The birth pangs were not only getting closer together; they were getting stronger.

And lastly, from this passage, we see the Lord pointing to things like famines and earthquakes. Once again, these are also things that have been with us forever. But, we have to look at the frequency and the breadth of these things, as well as the sheer magnitude of their destructive force, if we are to understand the direction things are headed. In the Twitter world, it is called "trending." And the concept of war and natural disasters, as well, are not "trending" in a positive direction, that's for sure.

Let's take a look at some statistics on world hunger and the frequency and strength of earthquakes globally, and see if we see an undeniable spike, as we have with the outbreak of wars and, I believe, the rise in the number of false prophets active in the world today:

World Hunger: While over the last few decades the number of people globally who were considered under-nourished has been steadily dropping, since 1950, based on percentages. But the world population has nearly tripled from 2.5 billion to around 7 billion people. That negates any good news we received from the smaller percentages. The bottom line is more people are under-nourished today, in real numbers, than at any time in history. It is fair to say that, today, world hunger is at epic proportions, with over 800 million people around the world who are starving or severely under-nourished, as of 2017. May God have mercy (and may we be willing to help!!).

Earthquakes: While the statistics on earthquakes is a little harder to nail down, with so many organizations (all with different agendas) making their numbers public, it seems quite clear that for earthquakes measuring 6.0 or greater, the numbers stayed fairly flat from 1900 until 2000. But since then, they have spiked greatly, with as many as five times as many "killer quakes" being reported in some years, over the numbers from the previous century. And, of course, some people like to blame the increases on everything from "global warming" to "Planet X" entering our solar system. But, these scientists never point to this spike in seismologic activity as being an indicator that the return of Christ is near. I wonder why?

At this point in our study, I want to take time to talk about a few things that are not specifically mentioned in Matthew 24. They, however, may very well fall into the same period we are talking about, a time before the seven years of tribulation get rolling. We are just not told, from Scripture, how long "the beginning of the birth pangs" will be manifesting themselves.

Let me stress, here and now, that my views on when these things will take place are educated guesses. Neither I, or others, can say exactly when these things will take place, or whether some of them already have. We can only speculate, based on the information given to us, through Scripture and comparing that with world events and the like. So again, while using Matthew 24 as a template for when these things will happen sequentially, I will do my best to drop the other key end-time events into the timeline where they most likely fit best and, hopefully, help us to see things more clearly.

I believe this would be a good time to talk about the three sets of judgments (seven in each) talked about in Revelation that does not seem to have any set time attached to them...the Seven Seals, the Seven Trumpets, and the Seven Bowls (sometimes called vials). Will these things happen before the seven years of tribulation, during them, or after? Lots of folks have detailed theories and explanations, but honestly, I believe only God knows for sure.

However, I do want to give you my take on these horrific events, and I will be the first to tell you, these are my own opinions which I have come to after many years of listening to many other people state their ideas. Then, through study and prayer, I have done my best to try to sort things out as best I could.

So here we go. Feel free to put on your skeptic's glasses. I always try to read this kind of stuff with a discerning eye. Then, as I let it sink in, I trust the Lord to help me find my way to the truth. After all, He is the way, the truth, and the life. He knows far better than I.

Let me begin, then, with a general "rule of thumb" that many teachers and preachers use to gauge the timing of these events. They believe that the Seven Seals are the longest judgments (in duration), followed by the Seven Trumpets (which are shorter in duration), and lastly, the Seven Bowls, which mostly all experts believe are very short in duration and come at the end of the seven years of tribulation. They are often referred to by many as "the Wrath of God" which, in the final days, will be poured out on His enemies.

THE SEVEN SEALS

The seal judgments start off in Revelation Six, with the first four seals being described as four horsemen on different color horses. It is important to note that a similar vision of different colored horses was prophesied by Zechariah in Chapter Six, with both John and Zechariah seeing horses of four different colors, red (or chestnut), white, black and pale horses. Now in Zechariah, the horses and chariots were described as "the four spirits of heaven, going forth after standing before the Lord of the earth. That is important, I think. Keep these four spirits in mind.

Oh, by the way, why are these judgments called seals? Well, back in those days, scrolls would be kept closed by a seal, as would an envelope, or a letter sent by someone in authority, like a king. The seal was a drop of hot wax that the VIP would mark, using what is called a signet ring. He would make an impression in the wax to verify it was from (or at least approved) by him. Often, there was only one seal on a document. On this scroll, there were seven (there is that number again). And we are told that no one in Heaven was worthy to remove the seals but the Lamb of God, Jesus Christ.

If I am being honest, when I read Zechariah 6, it makes me think about the fact that if you have a scroll and it has seven seals on it, can you open the scroll after just removing one seal, or two, or three? I would say "No." Then, when I read about the four spirits, going forth from heaven, I ask myself, "Could it mean that the first four seals are speaking of these same four spirits going forth, to see when the appropriate time might be to release the trumpet judgments?" Once again, no one knows for sure.

Maybe there are not three sets of judgments, but only the two... the trumpets and the bowls. The removing of the seals could be just revealing the preparations for what is to come. If we read the description of the opening of the first four seals closely, each rider is either given authority, or power to remove peace, or a sword and permission to kill. But, no real action is taken by these four living creatures. They appear to be only preparing and assessing when the time is right for the judgments to begin. Food for thought.

But for our discussion here, I will stick to John's version in Revelation Six, and look at how others have interpreted the opening of these seals...for comparison sake.

Seal #1: The first horse and rider were white. And the rider was given a crown and he had a bow, but no arrows. That is interesting. No arrows, yet, he seems to be capable of conquering. What could this mean? Well, many would point to the color white and suggest it means, "religious in nature." OK, that might explain the bow with no arrows. He does not need weapons to bring people under his authority. But, what kind of religious person wears a crown? The best example I have been able to find is our old friend Charlemagne, who was crowned emperor of the Holy Roman Empire in 800 AD. Yes, Jesus was back in Heaven at that time, so could this be the first seal? I believe a strong case could be made that it is. However, some believe that the seals will all be opened during the seven years of tribulation, and after the followers of Christ have been snatched away. I do not. I believe the four riders are four spirits from heaven sent to look over the whole earth and perceive when the time is right for the judgements to be released. So, I believe the first seal refers to a false "religious spirit" being released upon the earth.

Seal #2: The second horse and rider are red, and we are told that to him, authority was given to "take peace from the earth," that men would slay one another...and a great sword was given to him. Well, I did not need bible scholars to tell me what the color red might signify. Red is the color of "communism." We know that Russia is called "Red," as is China...both are Communist countries. Iran's flag also has red in it, along with white and green. That might suggest that they are aligned with Russia and China (red), religious in nature (white), and also Islamic (the color of Islam is green). And let's not leave out Turkey, whose flag is also red. Iran and Turkey are also Islamic, religious, and said to be part of the group of nations pointed to in Ezekiel Thirty-Eight, ones that will align and come against Israel in the battle of Armageddon, right before Christ returns victoriously.

But for the sake of our discussion, I would suggest that the second seal could be referring to the birth of Communism in the mid-1800s, the spirit of communism...which could be referred to as the triumph of the human spirit, relying on itself to figure things out if you will. It is people pulling together "in community," to take care of themselves and each other. That is a good example of what communism is at its core, people trying to solve their own problems. No God is needed here...it is humanism in its purest form.

Seal #3: The third horse and rider are black, and the rider is holding a pair of scales saying, "A quart of wheat for a denarius, three quarts of barley for a denarius...but do not damage the oil and the wine." That sounds like some sort of economic collapse. I have heard some folks point to the Great Depression of 1929. That would fit the model, but I doubt something that would be mostly considered "an American event" would be included in the Bible as something as important as the third seal. But, if we look at another part of the puzzle, most of us know that the US Dollar is the currency that all international trade uses as the "reserve currency," which means all countries buy and sell in US Dollars. Now, if we look at the change in the value of the US Dollar, from 1950 until 2017, it has declined by over 90%. What you could buy with one US Dollar in 1950, would now cost $10.17. Meanwhile, the average wage has only tripled in the same timeframe. That sounds to me to be a lot like "a quart of wheat costing a denarius" and "three quarts of barley costing a denarius."

In other words, people, who in 1950 would not be considered poor, would be very poor today, especially if they did not have a job that kept up with the rate of inflation. Result...many more hungry people in the world. So, yes, I see the third seal as pointing to hyper-inflation. If the trend continues, eventually the world economy will collapse when the US Dollar officially hits zero in value. This third spirit, I believe, is ready to bring financial doom, when the time is right.

Seal #4: The fourth and final horse in Revelation Chapter Six is described as pale, ashen, or dappled in some translations. The fourth seal may be the hardest to nail down, timewise, but there are a couple of hints. First, in the original Greek, the world for pale is "chloros," which is green, as in chloroform. And, as I mentioned earlier, green is widely accepted as the color of Islam. And the rise of Islam, starting in the 1980s, would be a good fit for the "sword" part of the fourth seal. And the fourth seal has the name "Death" and that is what I think the fourth spirit is all about...death. And, for the famine and pestilence part, we have the devalued dollar, and the Greek word for pestilence used here is "thanatos," which could be interpreted as disease or plague. One could point to the dramatic rise in deaths resulting from cancer as a possible part of the puzzle, here. But, let me point back to the portion of Matthew 24 we are talking about. In verse 7-8 of this chapter, Jesus says the following words, and they seem to "fit like a hand in a glove," if you ask me:

For nation will rise against nation, and kingdom against kingdom, and in various places, there will be famines and earthquakes. But all these things are merely the beginning of birth pangs. [Matthew 24:7-8 NASB]

In that one short passage, our Lord mentions "nations rising against nations" (death by sword...i.e....weapons), famine (world hunger,) and earthquakes (which are certainly on the rise). And I will throw in pestilence (disease or plagues), which seems to go hand-in-hand with famine. In third world countries, hunger and disease are almost inseparable.

So, as best I can ascertain, I would place the first four seals as being opened by the Lamb in Heaven, before the start of the seven years of great trouble on the earth. We will deal with the final three seals a bit later, at a place I believe they fit best.

THE SEVEN TRUMPETS

Ah yes, the trumpet judgments, the most popular of the judgments (if there is such a thing). Once again, I believe that some of the trumpet judgments may occur before the beginning of the seven years of tribulation. But, to kick this off, I want to highlight three passages, first:

Then the angel took the censer and filled it with the fire of the altar and threw it to the earth; and there followed peals

of thunder and sounds and flashes of lightning and an earthquake. [Revelation 8:5 NASB]

And the temple of God which is in heaven was opened; and the ark of His covenant appeared in His temple, and there were flashes of lightning and sounds and peals of thunder and an earthquake and a great hailstorm. [Revelation 11:19 NASB]

And there were flashes of lightning and sounds and peals of thunder; and there was a great earthquake, such as there had not been since man came to be upon the earth, so great an earthquake was it, and so mighty. [Revelation 16:18 NASB]

No, your eyes are not playing tricks on you, and no, I did not just make you read the same passage three times (like some diabolical authors' joke on their readers). The first passage is from the Seventh Seal. The second one is from the Seventh Trumpet. And the last one is from the Seventh Bowl judgment. Does that sound like three different events to you? It does not, to me. It sounds like three different accounts of the same event that occurs at the very end of the seven-year tribulation period.

Like many others have noticed (I am not that smart to figure this out all by myself), the seals, trumpets and bowl judgments all seem to end at the same time. They end when the Lord returns in victory, to pour His wrath upon His enemies, and claim His Bride for all eternity. For me, this adds weight to the theory that the seals are the longest in duration, the trumpets are shorter, and the bowl judgments are very short and are poured out quickly. For me, that is what seems to make scriptural sense, when we take the Bible as a whole, and at face value. I believe the Bible speaks for itself, through the Helper, the Holy Spirit, if we let it. And, as best I can, that is my goal.

So, what about the other six trumpet blasts, you ask? For that, I am going to break my own rule for this book, just for a moment, and borrow from a man I have great respect for, Irvin Baxter Jr. of Endtime Ministries and the show, "End of the Age." He has done an incredible amount of research on the Seven Trumpets, and I would love to share his conclusions with you. I will share his findings briefly, here, but I really would encourage you to go to his website and view the whole video on the Seven Trumpets, it is incredible!! So here are his summations:

Trumpet #1: He is convinced this is World War I. Reverend Baxter points to a "scorched-earth policy" used by the Russians in WWI. Here is a quote from Wikipedia: *"Napoleon's army arrived in a virtually abandoned Moscow, which was a tattered starving shell of its former self that was largely due to the use of scorched-earth tactics by retreating Russians."* That sounds like a logical fit to me.

Trumpet #2: Reverend Baxter believes that World War II coincides with the second trumpet. The thing that got his attention on this one was the fact that his research showed that one-third of all the ships in the world were destroyed during WWII, just as it says would happen in Revelation Eight (again, the video goes into a lot more detail than I am here). That is a fact that is hard to ignore.

Trumpet #3: This, according to Reverend Baxter, is where he first began to pursue his "trumpets timeline" because this trumpet is, by far, the most convincing, and it is the first explanation he stumbled on first. Did you know that the Russian word "Chernobyl," in English, means "Wormwood?" I did not. But, it is true. Revelation says, "A third of the waters became wormwood, and many died from the waters because they were made bitter." And we know that many died because the water supply became tainted from the radioactive fallout from the explosion at the Chernobyl nuclear plant. Now, that seems to be more than just a coincidence. That is very specific, is it not?

Trumpet #4: This is from the New York Times in April of 1991: *"**Saddam Hussein's** troops set off an inferno in Kuwait ...the Greater Burgan oil fields continued to obliterate the sun and the flames and lit* up the desert horizon." During Operation Desert Storm, in Feb. 1991, Hussein set fire to 605 of 732 of Kuwait's oil wells, and they burned out of control for ten months. This is what Reverend Baxter points to, as the connecting dot for the fourth trumpet. And it fits in quite nicely with passages on the fourth trumpet in Revelation Eight. Again, some speculation is being done here, but these are some thought-provoking points being made by Reverend Baxter, are there not?

And just as with the Seven Seals, after the fourth trumpet, there is a break in the action. Here is what it says in Revelation 8:

"Woe, woe, woe to those who dwell on the earth, because of the remaining blasts of the trumpet of the three angels who are about to sound!" [Revelation 8:13 NASB]

Let me try to sum up, then, if I may. In the portion of this chapter where Jesus talks about the birth pangs, we see "the pot beginning to boil," so to speak. False prophets are cropping up like weeds. Wars are getting bigger, with far greater casualties and maybe even more frequency. Earthquakes and natural disasters seem to be increasing in both frequency and magnitude, each and every year, and famine and disease are all at record rates.

My friends, to the best of my ability to discern, with the Lord's help, I believe we are right smack-dab in the middle of the birth pangs. But, in the not too distant future, things are about to get much worse for those who remain on the earth (which is one great big question I hope to answer...who will remain on the earth, once the seven years of tribulation begin?)

So, what's next? Well, if the passage above is any indication, there are "three woes" coming swiftly, each marked by the sounding of another trumpet blast.

THE FIFTH TRUMPET

Then the fifth angel sounded, and I saw a star from heaven which had fallen to the earth; and the key of the bottomless pit was given to him. He opened the bottomless pit, and smoke went up out of the pit, like the smoke of a great furnace; and the sun and the air were darkened by the smoke of the pit. [Revelation 9:1-2 NASB]

Many prophecy experts view "a star from heaven who had fallen to the earth" as a giant asteroid that could hit the earth, causing catastrophic events to take places, such as tsunamis, earthquakes, volcanoes and staggering amounts of human casualties. While I do admit that the possibility of something like that being part of the unfolding of end-time events, I hesitate to go as far as suggesting it will be part of the fulfillment of the fifth trumpet judgments for one reason. The reference to a "star falling from heaven" also lines up with a prophecy from Isaiah that was describing Lucifer's fall. The prophecy refers to Lucifer as "the morning star" who, because of his pride, fell from grace with God Almighty and would be cast down to the earth. But more on that, when we talk about the appearance of the Antichrist on the earth. But, it is the second part of the passage above that is an even greater disqualifier, in my mind.

It says, **"...the key of the bottomless pit was given to him. He opened the bottomless pit...and the sun and the air were darkened by the smoke of the pit."** If we are talking about a huge asteroid, I don't think it would make sense to say the key to the bottomless pit was given to him, or that he opened it. So, it seems there may be other explanations that make more sense, here, and what do you know? There are more than a couple of other options out there.

They have as king over them, the angel of the abyss; his name in Hebrew is Abaddon, and in the Greek, he has the name Apollyon. [Revelation 9:11 NASB]

I don't know how much you followed the events around Operation Desert Storm when the US defended Kuwait against attacks by Saddam Hussein and the Iraqi forces and the events that followed. But, many prophecy experts were digging deep into the subject to see what, if anything, might add more pieces to the end-time puzzle. The most amazing thing that was found was that Saddam when he was in his mother's womb, was said to be very hard on his mother. So much so, she named him Saddam, which means "destroyer," because she felt fortunate to survive the pregnancy. Does anyone want to guess what the Apollyon means? Bingo...it means "destroyer." And we heard earlier about the oil wells that he set on fire during that war, and how the sun was darkened, and the air was filled with smoke and ash from these incredible fires that burned for many weeks. So, it should not surprise us that some believe that the Gulf War is thought, by some, to possibly be the fifth trumpet judgment. But, although that was an incredibly devastating event, I am not sure it meets the criteria.

But there is another possible scenario, one that is happening right now, that could check all the boxes in the not-too-distant future. Have you heard of CERN, otherwise known as the Large Hadron Collider, the largest and most powerful "particle super-collider" ever constructed. It is a circular tunnel, on the border of France and Switzerland (near Geneva), that is seventeen miles wide and as deep as five hundred feet below the surface, at some points (it is in a mountainous area). This super-collider has been operating for a few years now and is primarily intended to gather research from smashing atoms at high velocity and sort of "see what happens." By their own admission, they have already identified something they call "the God Particle" (aka Higgs boson), which they describe as "the particles that give mass to matter." It has also been described as the glue that holds the universe together. But, ok, what is the prophetic connection?

According to CERN's own website, they are hoping to "open the door to other dimensions." And one high-ranking official is quoted as saying, "If we are successful, and open the door, we are not exactly sure what may come out, or how one would go about getting it to go back through the door." Trust me, when I say that I am not the only one who's ears perked up when they said, "we are trying to open the door to other dimensions." Does that sound like a possible "bottomless pit" hidden deep below the earth's surface to you? It does to me. And if that is true, there is nothing on the other side of that door that we want to see released into our dimension.

You may, or may not realize, that going all the way back to the Tower of Babel, some have been trying to open the door to other dimensions (and may I suggest "spiritual dimensions"), and it never ends well. And, of course, we have talked about the Nephilim and the other tribes of giants that found in the Old Testament, right? Well, pardon me for thinking that the people behind CERN may truly be trying to open a door that we would be better off keeping solidly shut. They could be providing a way for the enemies of God to facilitate a major assault into our world. This time, the bad seed may not manifest themselves as giants, but it does talk about a bottomless pit being opened. And, only the Lord knows what could come up from there. After all, the Lord supposedly preached to the fallen angels who were imprisoned in Sheol. Maybe they are the ones who will be released. Either way, it will not bring peace on Earth, I presume.

And, I am sure that is precisely what Satan has in mind...chaos. But, before we move on, I want to take a quick look at the last part of the description of the fifth trumpet judgments, if we can. I think there is something here that we should not just gloss over. It is something that we have talked about, but this just cements it, if you ask me:

Then out of the smoke came locusts upon the earth, and power was given them, as the scorpions of the earth have power. They were told not to hurt the grass of the earth, nor any green thing, nor any tree, but only the men who do not have the seal of God on their foreheads. [Revelation 9:3-4 NASB]

Take note of the fact that it says they were told (the locusts and scorpions) to not hurt the grass, nor any green thing, but only the men who DO NOT have the seal of God on their foreheads. This is just another comforting confirmation that our amazing God, Creator of all things, is more than able to punish some, while at the same time, leave others and other things untouched.

For those who believe that, for Christians, going through the seven years of tribulation would be subjecting the redeemed of the Lord to experience God's wrath, this should put that thought to rest. God will not pour His wrath out upon those that are His. In this passage, it talks about the Lord sealing "for protection" the ones who are faithful to Him. But, more on that a little later, when the smoke really hits the fan.

The first woe is past; behold, two woes are still coming after these things. [Revelation 9:12 NASB]

WHO CAN STAND BEFORE HIS INDIGNATION?
[NAHUM 1:6]

CHAPTER TWENTY-ONE

THE FORK IN THE ROAD

Moving beyond the birth pangs, we will find that in the very first sentence of our next passage, the Lord uses the word "tribulation." Now, I am no C. S. Lewis or Frederick Buechner, but I take that to mean that things have just gone from bad to worse. But before we plow ahead in Matthew 24, there are two more stepping stones that we must address...war and peace. No, not the book. However, before we see the fulfillment of verse 9, where Jesus says, "Then they will deliver you to tribulation," I firmly believe another great war must occur first, followed by a very special peace agreement.

THE SIXTH TRUMPET

Then the sixth angel sounded, and I heard a voice from the four horns of the golden altar which is before God, one saying to the sixth angel who had the trumpet, "Release the four angels who are bound at the great river Euphrates." And the four angels, who had been prepared for the hour and day and month and year, were released so that they would kill a third of mankind. [Revelation 9:13-15 NASB]

Almost all prophecy experts believe that the next big event on the prophetic timeline (barring an early departure of the believers in Christ, which some believe could come any day now), is likely to be a horrific war that would kill one-third of the people on the planet. At today's numbers, that would be roughly two billion people. The death toll would be about thirty-three times worse than World War II, which killed around 60 million people.

Some might call it World War III; others might choose to call it the war of Gog and Magog, or the Psalm 83 War. But, for the sake of clarity, I will refer to it as the Euphrates River War because, in the passage above, it states that this war will start in the area around the Euphrates River. And we should take note of that, because, there is a war being waged right now against ISIS that got its start in the area around the Euphrates River. Many nations are already involved... the United States, Great Britain, France, Russia, Turkey, Iran, and of course, the Islamic groups such as ISIS, Al-Qaeda, and the Taliban.

Meanwhile, around the borders of Israel, there are frequent skirmishes between Israel and the Palestinians, with the help of Hezbollah and Hamas. Some believe the battles being fought in the Middle East, right now, are the start of World War III. But, for them to fulfill the prophecy of the sixth trumpet, it will have to get a lot worse. Most people believe it will take a nuclear war to reach the point where two billion people die.

A FIRM COVENANT WITH THE MANY

"Seventy weeks have been decreed for your people [Israel] and your holy city [Jerusalem], to finish the transgression, to make an end of sin (when Christ returns)...and the people of the prince who is to come (which was Rome) will destroy the city and the sanctuary (in 70 AD)... even to the end there will be war (the sixth trumpet)... And he will make a firm covenant with the many for one week..." [Daniel 9:24,26-27]

Most scholars and those who know their Bibles from cover to cover agree, this "firm covenant with the many" will mark the beginning of the final seven years before the Lord returns at the sound of the seventh and last trumpet. These same experts agree that the "prince who is to come," the one of whom Daniel says, "he will make" that firm covenant, will be the Antichrist. It is important to remember that he will be at that table signing that peace agreement, according to the prophet Daniel, which many believe suggests that he is alive on the earth today (if we are truly living in the last generation).

So, after a war breaks out that results in one-third of world's population being killed, those who survive decide there needs to be global governance in place, an overriding authority to prevent something like this from ever happening again. However, this will not be a new idea. After World War I, the League of Nations was formed in 1920. Less than twenty years later, there was the Holocaust, and then Pearl Harbor, followed by World War II, a very costly war being fought on opposite sides of the world at the same time.

And, of course, at one end of the world, Hitler and Nazi Germany were defeated. On the other end, that part of the war ended with the United States dropping two atom bombs on Japan, one on Hiroshima and the other on Nagasaki. All the fighting came to an end in 1945. And around that time, the nations of the world formed the United Nations, again, primarily to stop another World War before it starts.

Then, within three years, on May 14th, 1948, the United Nations voted to give Israel the right, once again, to be a sovereign, independent nation. But within days, Israel's Islamic neighbors came together and attacked them, with the hopes of snuffing it out before it could even get settled in.

So, while those efforts to produce "world peace" have failed to produce lasting harmony among the nations, there will be another "covenant with the many," as Daniel called it, including a plan for Israel and the Palestinians to peacefully co-exist "for one week" (Bible-speak for seven years). This peace plan will include a "sharing agreement" for the Temple Mount which will lead to another miraculous development that will serve as solid confirmation that the final seven years before the return of Christ has begun. And that is what I want to talk about next.

THE CONFIRMATION

Then there was given me a measuring rod like a staff; and someone said, "Get up and measure the temple of God and the altar, and those who worship in it. Leave out the court which is outside the temple and do not measure it, for it has been given to the nations; [Revelation 11:1-2 NASB]

This portion of Revelation 11, of course, speaks of the preparations for the building of the Third Temple on the Temple Mount in Jerusalem. The first Temple, built by Solomon, was of course destroyed by Nebuchadnezzar and the Babylonians in 586 BC. The second Temple, which came into the picture following the return of the Jews from their seventy-year exile in Babylon, was later destroyed, as Jesus prophesied, by the Romans in 70 AD. But here, the Lord is revealing that a Temple will be built one last time.

It is important to note that in this passage, the Lord says not to measure the outer court, "for that has been given to the nations" (other translations say "to the Gentiles"). I believe this points to the fact that the peace agreement will include a "sharing arrangement" of the Temple Mount, so the Muslims can still worship there, and so the Jews will be able to worship freely there, as well. Many of the Jews feel that the building of this third and final Temple will begin in the not too distant future…and believe it or not, preparations to do so are already well underway.

Recent news reports have said that an organization called the Temple Institute has already been getting everything ready, so that when the agreement comes, and the permission to build is granted, there will be very little delay. All the utensils, furniture and fixtures have been made to very precise biblical specifications. And even now, if you go to their website, you can take a "virtual tour" of the new temple. They have even been breeding cows in such a way as to bring forth "a red heifer," which will be needed for the temple sacrifices to begin. And just recently, the Temple Institute has announced that they have produced one heifer that has passed all the biblical tests. That was not easy to do. It took many generations to bring forth one pure enough to meet the requirements. So, they are prepared now, in that way, as well. That gives hope, at least in the hearts and minds of the Jewish faithful who have been waiting for two thousand years for this prophecy to come to fruition, that the day of fulfillment appears very near.

One more piece of news regarding the imminent rebuilding of the temple. It has been reported that Israel has approved the funding of a project to build a high-speed rail system from the airport in Tel Aviv to the area of the Temple Mount in Jerusalem. This will be designed to accommodate the millions of Jews who will be traveling there frequently, to meet their requirements to go to the Temple three times a year. If you have been to Jerusalem lately, you would know that you land in Tel Aviv, and then you have about a ninety-minute bus ride to Jerusalem. This train would get visitors there in around twenty minutes. The Jews are serious about this, folks. They believe the time to get ready is now, and so do I.

My wife is not quite the prophecy geek that I am (although she does enjoy hearing about these things, especially the ones connected to the future of Israel since she traveled there in 2016). But she often tells me (when I get jazzed up about one prophecy update or another), "When you see them building the Third Temple, let me know. Then, I will know the seven years of tribulation has come." That is why I called this portion of the chapter "The Confirmation."

So, to all of you who may be reading this…my friends, my family and many others who just thought this book looked interesting (thank you…btw), when we hear of a peace agreement being signed between the Palestinians and Israel, it would be easy to say, "There have been other peace agreements, but they never last. How do we know that this is the one that Daniel prophesied about?" Good point. But, in the words of my lovely wife, Lauri Lee, "When you see them building the Third Temple, let me know." That will be confirmation for her, and I could not agree more. It is something you do not want to be unaware of when it happens. It is a big deal…a very important "fork in the road," if you will.

As we believers have talked about for many, many years, there will come a moment in time, for Christians, when the faithful followers of Christ will be resurrected (or changed in the twinkling of an eye) and "meet Him in the air." The question we all would love to know the answer to is, "When?" Some folks believe it will be before the seven years of great trouble. Others are convinced it will be at the sound of the seventh trumpet, which happens at the end of the tribulation period.

According to Daniel, the signing of a peace agreement that allows for a sharing arrangement of the Temple Mount is that "point of no return." Once you see those things materialize, the final seven years have begun. Certainly, for those who believe in the reliability of Scripture, there should be no doubt, at that point. The Bible says it, I believe it, and that settles it.

Here is what troubles me the most, however, regarding this coming, and all-important "fork in the road." Those who have spent their whole life (at least their Christian life) believing that the Lord promised to come and "catch them away" before things get bad, many of them will be crushed with disappointment. It could be compared to a bride being left standing at the altar on her wedding day. We are, after all, referred to as the Bride of Christ, are we not?

Some will think their faith was misplaced. Others will think they have been lied to by their pastors and other believers. And, there will be many others who feel like they are lost at sea, with no shore or rescue boats in sight. Some have suggested that this traumatic type of disappointment could lead to the great "falling away" that the Apostle Paul pointed to...the one that he said would come right before the Antichrist is revealed.

That is one of the main reasons I wrote this book. I want to challenge everyone who reads these words, to not take anything for granted. Get into God's Word, do a deep dive and get as much information as you can to help you make the best decision possible. Go back and look at what other Christians believed, years ago. Then, ask yourself if it is possible that some of those early church influences could have twisted the truth just enough to nudge us, as believers in Christ, to put our hope in something that is not entirely biblical. Now, I am not saying anyone would do that intentionally. But our enemy is very clever and uniquely deceptive. As I said many times, here, sometimes the truth and the lies are very hard to tell one from the other. That is all the more reason we need to be passionate students of the Word of God, and fervently and frequently given to prayer to allow the Holy Spirit to shine His light on the truth.

The return of Christ is something that, hopefully, none of us want to be wrong about. The cost is too high. I have often said, "If the Lord wants to come and take us to Heaven before the tribulation period starts, that works for me. I'm ready!! But I am also going to be prepared to go through it and allow Him to use me however He sees fit." I have always loved the statement, "If the Lord has brought you to it, He will see you through it."

I often think back to the prayer that Jesus taught His disciples to pray, during the Sermon on the Mount. He said, "Thy kingdom come, Thy will be done on Earth, as it is in Heaven." As a Catholic, I prayed that prayer more times than I can remember. But back then, it was just words that I had memorized. Now, since I gave my heart to the Lord and begun studying the Bible intently, those words have taken on real meaning in my life. I truly want His will to be done in my life, and the world around us. I wouldn't want it to unfold any other way because I truly believe His way is best…no matter what.

Yes, I have my opinions and my personal beliefs about these things. It is a subject I enjoy studying. But, I will never "put all my eggs" into the one basket called "my beliefs." I prefer to hold on to the possibility that my conclusions may be wrong because as we talked about earlier, the perfect has not come yet, and the partial has not been done away with. So, it is fair to suggest that the best we can do is learn all we can and ask the Lord to lead us according to His will. Remember, when God called Abraham, He did not tell Him where He was leading him. He just said…"Go..I will be with you." And in faith, Abraham did.

SIDENOTE: If you were inclined to skip over "Parenthetical Pause #2: "Lost in Translation," you may feel the need to go back and review those Scriptures (and there were a lot) that I included and commented on there. It is at this point in my timeline that they become quite important. We have come to that "proverbial fork in the road." As I said, this is precisely where, in my estimation, the road to deception splits off from the road to sound biblical interpretation.

Now, I am not suggesting that I have "the one true understanding of the end times," or that correctly knowing when Christ will return is a "salvation issue." It is not. Our salvation is based on Christ, and His blood, and nothing else…period. But, having the wrong view of these matters could certainly make things more difficult for those who believe they saw their "blessed hope" of an early departure fail to materialize. It would be wise to, at least, consider and prepare for a "Plan B."

Having said that, I am not going to claim to know which road is ultimately right, or wrong. I believe our Father in Heaven is the only one who knows the timing of these things. What I am bringing to you in this book are my conclusions, based on forty years of walking with Christ and studying God's Word. You may agree or disagree, that part is up to you to decide. We are called to "study to show ourselves approved." And, that is what I have applied myself to do here.

What you believe is up to you, and I respect that!! I would only ask you to seriously consider what we have talked about in this book. If we, as Christians today, believe that the human soul is immortal, and at the moment of our death, we go to be with the Lord; and if those beliefs can be traced back to the early Catholic Church fathers and their fascination with the writings of Socrates and Plato…and not based on sound biblical reasoning…we could have false hope. Besides, if there is no "human soul" that is separate from the body (flesh) and the spirit (breath), as I believe Genesis 2:7 teaches, what part of our existence would be "alive" and "present with the Lord? I believe that our breath (spirit) goes back to the One who gave it. But is our breath "alive," apart from the body? I do not believe the Bible teaches that.

If what the writer of Hebrews taught us, that the patriarchs of the Old Testament were seen as righteous by God because of their faith, but "did not receive what was promised because God had something better for us…that apart from us (who would come later), they would not be made perfect," why should we expect to receive our promise before anyone else?

And, if those who have died are merely asleep (not in the physical sense) and awaiting their resurrection at the sound of the last trumpet, as I believe the Bible clearly teaches, then what justification is there for an early departure of the saints. If no one who has experienced death before us (which leaves out Enoch and Elijah) is presently in Heaven with the Lord (except for the handful of possible exceptions that the Bible hints at…the twenty-four elders come to mind), does it make sense that God would take us up before all the others who are yet to die? I would say, "No." That would not seem to be in line with God's nature, as He has displayed it in the past.

So, yes, I believe that at the time of the "firm covenant with the many," the greatest play ever written will begin its final and climactic act, and God will want his star actors on the stage, giving the greatest performances of their lives, albeit their final performances. Glory to God!!

Let's move on, now, into the next part of the timeline Jesus unveiled in Matthew 24:

> *"Then they will deliver you to tribulation, and will kill you, and you will be hated by all nations because of My name. At that time many will fall away and will betray one another and hate one another. Many false prophets will arise and will mislead many. Because lawlessness is increased, most people's love will grow cold. But the one who endures to the end, he will be saved. This gospel of the kingdom shall be preached in the whole world as a testimony to all the nations, and then the end will come." [Matthew 24:9-14 NASB]*

In the first sentence, here, Jesus is proclaiming the beginning of the seven years of tribulation. So, who is the "they" He speaks of that will deliver those who are yet alive at the time to tribulation? I would point to the peace agreement and a certain prince who was at the table, signing his name to that agreement. He is the "seed of the serpent" we know as the Antichrist. I believe it is him and his followers who will be behind it all. Quietly, at first.

I heard a story many years ago that you may have heard, too. If you are sitting by a tranquil lake and you see some ducks float by, you may believe they are calmly floating around with little or no effort being exerted. Meanwhile, underneath the water, their little legs are paddling like crazy. I believe that is how it will be with the rise of the Antichrist during the first three and a half years of the tribulation period. He will be quietly and peacefully acquiring strength and authority, getting ready to pounce when the time is right. I am reminded of the words of the Apostle Paul, who said:

While they are saying, "Peace and safety," then destruction will come upon them suddenly like labor pains upon a woman with child, and they will not escape. But you, brethren, are not in darkness, that the day would overtake you like a thief; [1 Thessalonians 5:3 NASB]

In this passage, Paul says those who are "the powers that be" will be saying, "Peace and safety," but like a thief in the night, the birth pangs will be over and the real labor pains will be kicking in. But he also says that we (as believers in Christ) are not in darkness and should not be surprised by this thief when he comes. That sounds more like "the elect" will be around to witness the thief's arrival...not "out of the picture."

So, what else will be happening during this so-called "time of peace and safety," while the Antichrist, portraying himself as a man of peace (thanks to the peace agreement he signed), is gaining influence and popularity with people all over the world?

Strangely enough, the next thing Jesus mentions is a great "falling away." And I presume that means a falling away from faith in Christ. What on Earth could cause such a thing at such a critical time?

THE APOSTASY

Now we request you, brethren, with regard to the coming of our Lord Jesus Christ and our gathering together to Him...Let no one in any way deceive you, for it will not come unless the apostasy comes first...and the man of lawlessness is revealed [2 Thessalonians 2:1,3 NASB]

The Christians in Thessalonica were quite worried that maybe they had missed the Lord's return. Of course, they had not. In this passage we see Paul giving them two clear-cut signs to be on the lookout for. Two things that must happen BEFORE the return of our Lord and our gathering unto Him. A great apostasy must occur, and the Antichrist must be revealed. And by "revealed," I believe Paul is pointing to his "coming-out party," when the Abomination of Desolation appears in the Temple and declares "equality with God." We will be talking more about that in the next chapter.

So, what about this great apostasy? What causes so many to lose hope? Some would say that because of their fear in those days, their faith waned. Some would suggest that out of fear of being sought out and killed by the Antichrist and his followers, maybe they will be afraid to stand up for the Lord. And yes, I would think there is some truth to all of that.

But I would also go back to the fact that there will be millions of Christians around the world who might be emotionally and spiritually wounded because the Lord did not come and take them home before all the trouble started, as they believed He would. That is a biggie, if you ask me. I can only imagine how it would feel for those folks to see the Third Temple being built and the Antichrist quietly gaining power, and the Lord has not yet come to save them. That would be a heartbreaker, to say the least, would it not?

LAWLESSNESS ON THE RISE

We remember that Jesus told us that, prior to His return to the earth, it would be "as in the days of Noah." I would have to say that this period of time sure sounds like that. People who do wrong go unpunished, while those who do not are persecuted for not "following along with the others." Many will "love evil and hate good," It will be a really bad time to be a good person, especially one who loves and seeks after God.

PERSECUTION INCREASES

We are living in a day and age where we hear of Christians around the world being persecuted for their faith in Jesus Christ. In the times yet to come, it is going to get a lot worse. And that leads me to ask a critical question, if all the Christians were taken home to be with the Lord before the seven years of trouble start, who is "left behind" to be persecuted? I believe many Christians will still be alive and serving the Lord as best they can in those days if for no other reason, this one seems to be quite fitting:

The Law came in so that the transgression would increase; but where sin increased, grace abounded all the more [Romans 5:20 NASB]

I believe God will have His people present and active when it all goes down, not to be defeated, but rather they will be equipped and empowered to be victorious!! Jesus said, "Greater things than I have done, you will do in My name." I, for one, can't wait!!

THE GOSPEL PREACHED WORLDWIDE

This gospel of the kingdom shall be preached in the whole world as a testimony to all the nations, and then the end will come. [Matthew 24:14 NASB]

Those who believe in an "early departure" refer to this verse all the time, suggesting that the Gospel must be preached to the whole world, and then and only then can the rapture come. Some believe that this prophecy has been fulfilled, thanks to television, the internet and, of course, the missionary work of thousands of those committed to fulfilling the Great Commission. Therefore, they would say there no longer is any reason why the Lord could not come back today…this very moment, in fact.

But, based on the chronology that the Lord has provided in Matthew 24, I would make the case that He said, "the Gospel shall be preached in the whole world, as a testimony to all the nations, and then the end will come." I would think that He may also have been referring to a day when a godly alternative will need to be preached to all the nations aligning themselves under the banner of this new, emerging world leader. There will certainly need to be "light shining in the midst of the darkness."

I believe people will still have a choice at that time. After all, if my conclusions are right, the "door to the ark will not have been closed yet." The Holy Spirit will still be present on the Earth, and people of every nation and tongue will still be able to fall on their faces and declare "Jesus as Lord," and be saved. Many also believe that this will be a time of great revival. And it will likely be a time of great miracles being performed by the believers who are alive in those days. That would be hard to do, I believe, without the Holy Spirit being present.

Then, Jesus says, "the end will come," and we are reminded:

"But the one who endures to the end, he will be saved."
[Matthew 24:13]

"FEAR NOT FOR I AM WITH YOU..."
[ISAIAH 41:10]

CHAPTER TWENTY-TWO

THE MAN OF SIN REVEALED

"Therefore, when you see the ABOMINATION OF DESOLATION WHICH WAS SPOKEN OF THROUGH DANIEL THE PROPHET, STANDING IN THE HOLY PLACE (LET THE READER UNDERSTAND), then those who are in Judea must flee to the mountains. Whoever is on the housetop must not go down to get the things out that are in his house. Whoever is in the field must not turn back to get his cloak. But woe to those who are pregnant and to those who are nursing babies in those days! But pray that your flight will not be in the winter, or on a Sabbath." [Matthew 24:15-20 NASB]

One of the best parts of being an author, I must confess, is how much you learn in doing all the research necessary for a book like this (and for this one, in particular, I have probably done at least ten times more research than I did for my first two books, combined...but I enjoyed every minute of it). And, if you have been following along since the beginning of this book (and didn't jump ahead to Part Three to cut to the chase...you know who you are...lol), you know how much I like it when I get to talk about prophecies that have more than one fulfillment. Well, in getting ready to write this chapter, I struck gold. The prophecies regarding an "abomination that makes desolate" (that is what "abomination of desolation" means), have not two fulfillments, but three. One for each of the temples of the Lord. Once again, we see that God confirms his plans by "two or three witnesses."

EARTHLY EMPIRES REVEALED

But, to get a fuller grasp of how these examples of desecrating the Temple fit in with the bigger historical picture, and how they point to another end-time fulfillment, we need to look at Daniel Chapter 2. It is there that the prophet lays out the five great empires that will rise upon the earth, leading up to the divine kingdom yet to come:

> *"You, O king, were looking and behold, there was a single great statue; that statue...The head of that statue was made of fine gold, its breast and its arms of silver, its belly and its thighs of bronze, its legs of iron, its feet partly of iron and partly of clay. [Daniel 2:31-33 NASB]*

Daniel went on to interpret this dream, so we do not have to guess as to which kingdoms he was speaking of. Babylon was the "gold head." Medo-Persia was the "arms of silver". Greece was the "belly and thighs of bronze," Rome was the "legs of iron," And the feet were a mixture of iron and clay. So, that would be some sort of blending of Rome (iron) and a religious empire (clay). Imagine that. We should not be surprised. Let's look at how this dream connects to the destruction of the first two temples.

The first of the "abominations that make desolate" occurred in 586 BC, when Zedekiah was the King of Judah. He was appointed by Nebuchadnezzar of Babylon, who besieged Jerusalem, destroyed Solomon's Temple, and took most of the Jews captive. But, a remnant of Jews chose to stay behind (and possibly die), and Zedekiah was hand-picked to be their babysitter or ummm...their overseer, yet who was under Nebuchadnezzar's authority. Here is how this was recorded in 2 Chronicles 36:

> *Zedekiah was twenty-one years old when he became king, and he reigned eleven years in Jerusalem. He did evil in the sight of the Lord his God; he did not humble himself before Jeremiah the prophet who spoke for the Lord... Furthermore, all the officials of the priests and the people were very unfaithful following all the abominations of the nations; and they defiled the house of the Lord which He had sanctified in Jerusalem. All the articles of the house*

of God, great and small, and the treasures of the house of the Lord, and the treasures of the king and of his officers, he brought them all to Babylon. Then they burned the house of God and broke down the wall of Jerusalem...and burned all its fortified buildings with fire and destroyed all its valuable articles. [2 Chronicles 36:11,12,14,18,19 NASB]

And, so it was that the first Temple of the Lord was "made desolate," due to the sins of not only the people but the "officers of the priests," as well (government corruption). How does that saying go, "Absolute power corrupts, absolutely?" It sure did back in those days, both in Israel and Judah.

Around 400 years later, in 167 BC, after the Jews were miraculously delivered from their exile in Babylon (with the help of Cyrus, Darius, and Artaxerxes of Persia), and they were able to rebuild the city and the Temple of God, the Jews saw the Temple desecrated again. This time it was at the hands of the Greeks, and a man named Antiochus Epiphanes (the name means "god manifest"...how ironic). Since this happened after the writings of the Old Testament were completed and Christ had not come yet, we do not have the benefit of Scriptures to document this. But, the historical writings of the day certainly do.

Not unlike, the Babylonians, the Greeks robbed the Temple treasures, set up idolatrous abominations in the Temple, and persecuted the Jews. That would be the second time the Temple of the Lord was "made desolate" and replaced with abominations that were displeasing in the sight of God. And, as we all know, the Greeks fell to the Romans, who finished the job by destroying the Temple in 70AD, just as Jesus said would happen. Once again, it was the sin and wickedness of the people and their unwillingness to repent, plus the fact that the Jews rejected the Messiah when He came, that caused judgment to come. This time, their exile lasted two thousand years (Day 5/Day 6), until 1948, when Israel became a nation again.

There is one other thing we should take note of, regarding these desecrations. In the future, we do not know for sure if the Abomination of Desolation that Jesus was speaking of implied that it would be the Antichrist, himself, personally standing in the Temple and claiming equality with God. Many believe the false prophet will put an abominable image (a statue, an image...maybe even a hologram of himself) on the altar that will make his claims for him. The Greeks sacrificed a pig (deemed unclean according to Temple practices) on the altar of God to "add insult to injury." So, the man of sin may or may not physically stand in the Temple to make his claim. He might be fearful that the fire of God would come down and consume him on the spot if he did (that has happened before...see 2 Kings 1:12-16). We will just have to wait and see how this unfolds.

Isn't it interesting that, just as we talked about in Chapter Ten, "Greco-Roman Wrestling," the influence of the Greek culture persisted long after their empire had fallen? Of course, the Greek language was the dominant language in those days, and they were also known for their art and philosophy. Even the Apostle Paul felt it was important to point out the fact that, through Christ, there was "no longer any distinction between Jew and Greek" (he didn't even mention the Romans, who controlled Jerusalem in those days). And that was long after the Greek empire had been defeated. I see Paul's comment as partially referring to the two main languages of the day, Hebrew and Greek, as well. The Old Testament was primarily penned in Hebrew. The New Testament was penned in Greek or Aramaic, a Greek dialect.

So, we should not be surprised that the religious hierarchies that sprung up shortly after Christ's death and resurrection leaned heavily on the Greeks. There was the love of their architecture, the paintings, the statues and, of course, much of their concepts regarding spiritual things lived on, as well. None of these things were especially pleasing in the eyes of God Almighty.

All we have to do is look at how Protestant churches seemed to run as far from these things as they could. The reformers wanted no part of ornate buildings (paid for by the indulgences that Luther was upset about), the statues and paintings (that elevated men and women to almost God-like status, before and after their death), or any of the other extravagant trappings of early man-made religions. These things were believed to be in the same ballpark as the golden calf that Aaron formed while Moses was on the mountain. Anything that could become an object of worship, other than God, was considered an abomination. Believe it or not, even the image of the cross was troublesome to some, which is why many Bible-believing churches, nowadays, do not have a cross in the sanctuary. They do not want to encourage the worship of anything, except God and/or Christ alone.

Once again, I want to remind the readers that I do not share these things to point a finger at anyone's faith or beliefs. Whatever way people choose to worship, it is between them and their God (even if it is wrong…we have been given free will), so I respect their right to choose. But hopefully, we can learn from these things. Our enemy is very clever. The Bible says he can even transform himself into "an angel of light." I believe that means Satan can use things that appear to be good, maybe even godly, to deceive us. We have to be diligent and not leave the door open to the false teachings that Jesus said would surely come into our midst, not even a crack.

I am only choosing to share the historical and religious happenings I share in this book because I see them as foundational to some of my conclusions regarding end-time philosophies. I want the reader to understand how I came to my conclusions, not just see them as something shiny, new or different, but rather have a solid grasp on the things I based them on.

Again, thank you for bearing with me. Some of these things are hard to share because as I said, many of my friends, relatives, and acquaintances might take issue with what I am suggesting here. If I have offended you, please forgive me, I had no intention to hurt or accuse. I hope I have made that clear. My only intention was to shed light on some key points of this extremely important debate that, in my opinion, seem to have been left in the shadows for far too long.

The "rule of large numbers" teaches us that the more information we have available to us, when faced with tough questions, the better chance we have of coming up with the right answer. I fear that many people, nowadays, are basing their conclusions regarding these things (if they consider them at all) on very little information, and largely based on the conclusions of others. They have not thoroughly studied the Scriptures for themselves…and that can be dangerous.

And that brings us back to the subject at hand, yet another fulfillment of the prophecies concerning the Abomination of

Desolation, which may be coming soon, maybe sooner than we think. And when it does manifest itself again, it will be for the same reason as before. There will be many sins, or abominations, taking place among us (even in our churches) and there will be an unwillingness to repent (despite repeated warnings and calls to do just that). Humanity will indeed leave the door open to deception, again (or should I say... still). And once again, the Lord will allow an evil dictator to appear on the stage who desires to be considered "equal with God." And when that day comes, the "thief in the night" will have officially appeared. At that point, it will be "No more, Mr. Nice-guy." Things are going to get real ugly, real fast.

Let's look at what Daniel said about this, since I believe Jesus was pointing to Daniel's prophecies when He made his comments regarding this future event:

> **Forces from him will arise, desecrate the sanctuary fortress, and do away with the regular sacrifice. And they will set up the abomination of desolation...By smooth words, he will turn to godlessness those who act wickedly toward the covenant, but the people who know their God will display strength and take action. Those who have insight among the people will give understanding to the many; [Daniel 11:31-33 NASB]**

So, this adds weight to the thought that the Antichrist will rise to power during tranquil times, and with smooth words, not by military power or might. He will be quietly, and without bringing much attention to himself, acquiring influence, wealth and power during the first three and a half years of the seven-year peace agreement. But, make no mistake about it, a day will come when his tune will change, once he has the strength, the power, and the support of many nations worldwide, to thwart any challenges from those who may resist his enticing offers to join him and be "on the winning side."

As you might be able to guess, this will be a time in the world (and I believe we already see the beginnings of it) where globalism will become fashionable. Nations will buy into the idea that a powerful global authority would be a good thing. They will believe it would help to offset the threat of war, and even help to facilitate the sharing of the world's resources more evenly, so that there are not "the haves and the have-nots," as we see in the world today. And, for the most part, national borders or sovereignty will mean very little. The overriding authority of "global governance" will have real teeth in those days.

In this passage above from Matthew 24, the one at the top of this chapter, Jesus makes it very clear that those who are in Judea need to flee to the mountains, if you are on the housetop, do not go back in the house, and if you are in the field, do not stop to get your coat. It will be time to run and run fast or pay the price. But run from what…or whom? Who is this "man of lawlessness?" From where will he come, and from where will he get his power?

THE TRINITY OF SATAN

"How you have fallen from heaven, O star of the morning, son of the dawn! You have been cut down to the earth… you said in your heart, 'I will ascend to heaven; I will raise my throne above the stars of God, I will ascend above the heights of the clouds; I will make myself like the Most High. "Nevertheless, you will be thrust down to Sheol, to the recesses of the pit. [Isaiah 14:12-15 NASB]

A number of times, we have talked about how God's archenemy, the devil, likes to try to copy the things of God in an effort to deceive many. So, to better understand who the Antichrist is, we need to understand the history of the spirit of rebellion from which he came to be. The first manifestation of the devil on Earth was, of course, the serpent in the Garden of Eden. So, is Satan truly a serpent who could talk? No, he chose to manifest himself as one to deceive Adam and Eve, and it worked.

Satan's origin is found in the passage above. He was an angel of the Lord before the universe was created. But he was not just any angel, was he? His name was Lucifer, and he was said to be the most beautiful of all the angels (which contributed to his pride and eventual fall). In fact, here we see Isaiah referring to him as the "star of the morning." The prophecy talks about how this star has fallen (into rebellion) and will be cast down to the earth, even Sheol.

Hey, wait a second, where else have we read about a star that will fall to the earth? When we read about the Fifth Trumpet, the Apostle John wrote this, *"I saw a star from heaven which had fallen to the earth and the key of the bottomless pit was given to him." [Revelation 9:1 NASB]* Now, some have referred this star falling to Earth as an asteroid that kills many in the last days. And that could happen, as well. But, as I said earlier, I do not believe the "key of the bottomless pit" will be given to an asteroid that fell to the earth. I believe what John saw was a prophetic confirmation of what Isaiah had seen many years earlier.

> *And the dragon stood on the sand of the seashore. Then I saw a beast coming up out of the sea, having ten horns and seven heads, and on his horns were ten diadems, and on his heads were blasphemous names. And the beast which I saw was like a leopard, and his feet were like those of a bear, and his mouth like the mouth of a lion. And the dragon gave him his power and his throne and great authority. [Revelation 13:1-2 NASB]*

Here, we get to see two members of the trinity of Satan in one passage. The serpent is now referred to as a dragon (another one of his manifestations), and he is standing on a seashore. Then, up out of the water comes a beast and on his head were blasphemous names. I believe this was Satan's attempt to copy "the Word became flesh and dwelt among us," like the Son of God who had come down to Earth. And as with Jesus, this beast will only do and say the things which the dragon leads him to do and say. He is the devil's "point man" on Earth.

> *"Then I saw another beast coming up out of the earth, and he had two horns like a lamb, and he spoke as a dragon. He exercises all the authority of the first beast in his presence. And he makes the earth and those who dwell in it to worship the first beast, whose fatal wound was healed." [Revelation 13:11-12 NASB]*

The third member of the three-person Godhead is, of course, the Holy Spirit. He is the force that empowers us, as it did those who were faithful to God in the past and Christ, Himself, to do God's will. When we yield to Him, He speaks through us, and He enables us to do signs and wonders in His name. Satan has one, also, through whom his rebellious spirit can become the driving force and enabler of the first beast. This second beast is…the False Prophet. He is the leader of a religious organization, only this one will not be taking its marching orders from the God of the Bible, unfortunately. Quite the contrary, as we shall see.

So who, exactly, does this false prophet draw his power from? You got it, the dragon (or as it refers to him in Revelation 20, *"the dragon, the serpent of old, who is the devil and Satan…"*). So, we see that Satan (who is the dragon), the Antichrist (the first beast), and the False Prophet (the second beast) are merely a cheap imitation of the Father, the Son, and the Holy Spirit. Nice try, Lucifer. But, cheap imitations are never as good as the genuine article. Those who know what to look for can spot them immediately. As Jesus said, "Let him who has eyes see, and those who have ears, hear."

But there will be some other huge developments, not mentioned in Matthew 24, that we should talk about, at this point. Let's start with something we first hear about in Revelation 14 and is revealed in greater detail in Revelation 17-18. It is a subject that has garnered much debate among Christians and Bible scholars for centuries. Here's hoping there is room for one more take on this great mystery. Mine, of course. I have been itching to talk about this for about forty years!!

MYSTERY BABYLON

Probably no other part of the end-time revelations have intrigued me as much, or so early in my Christian walk (mostly because of my Catholic upbringing) as those found in Revelation 17 and 18, the ones regarding Mystery Babylon.

If you remember back when we looked at Daniel Chapter 12, I talked about how it seemed to jump right out at me that "the restrainer" was Michael the Archangel, largely based on what we read in Revelation 12 and Daniel 12. Both passages seem to be talking about the same person…one who restrains the evil one from coming down to Earth and bring great trouble upon the world, and its people.

Well, my first impressions of Mystery Babylon were no different. Upon my first reading of these two chapters, similarities between this Mystery Babylon and my recollections of the Catholic Church were popping up like weeds. She (churches are often referred to as "her" or "she" in the Bible) wore purple and scarlet (colors often associated with harlotry). Priests often wore purple and scarlet robes, strike one. She drank from a golden cup of abominations (of course, this immediately reminded me of "transubstantiation," the Catholic belief that during communion, after the Priest prays over the cup and the wafers, they actually become the body and the blood of Christ...not just symbolically or for remembrance as Jesus taught), strike two. But, here was the clincher for me:

"Here is the mind which has wisdom. The seven heads are seven mountains on which the woman sits," [Revelation 17:9 NASB]

The city of Rome has long been referred to as "the city of seven hills," for the seven mountains on which it sits. And, to my knowledge, no one has ever said that of the original city of Babylon, or New York City (another city that is thought by some to be Mystery Babylon). So, for me to assume that Mystery Babylon, in the last days, would be centered in Rome, that was not much of a stretch. But, the passage went on to say that the seven mountains also represented seven kings. It is not unusual, of course, for a prophecy to point to more than one thing, as I said many times. But how does that tie in, I wondered?

We need to jump backward a bit, to Revelation 13 (to another "parenthetical chapter," more evidence that the Book of Revelation cannot be taken as sequential or chronological). Most scholars agree that this first beast from Revelation 13 is an empire (one-world government) controlled by the Antichrist. It says that it came up out of the sea, and in Revelation 17, we learn that "the many seas on which the harlot sits are many nations, peoples, and tongues." So, this will be a political empire made up of a group of ten nations and seven kings, and it will be brought into power by "the people," not unlike Hitler, who was greatly loved by the people, at first.

Then, in Revelation 13, we read of a second beast, but this one seems to have the horns of a lamb, and not perceived to be as fierce as the first beast. But, he speaks like a dragon (Satan), which can be quite deadly. This second beast is thought to be religious in nature. It will be a powerful organization, from which the "one-world church" will come and it is led by someone referred to as "the false prophet." And, to make this more troubling, the second beast seems to get its authority from the first beast. When the government controls the church, as we saw with the Church of England, it usually does not end well.

Do you remember when we talked about the first seal that was opened? We saw a white horse and rider. And, the rider had a bow, but no arrows. So I believe this second beast is one and the same as the white horse and rider. This beast will not need weapons to control the masses. I believe the first beast, here, and the second beast, are latter-day manifestations of the Holy Roman Empire, which officially came to power in 800 AD, and controlled much of Europe and Great Britain, with Charlemagne being crowned as it's emperor. But, it was the pope and the church of Rome that helped consolidate the empire's power.

So, I believe that Mystery Babylon will be the revival of the Holy Roman Empire (which was more political, than religious), and its primary leader will be the Antichrist, who will gain gather his political strength with the help of the religious wing of this revived empire, which will be centered in Rome and will be led by the false prophet. I believe it will be the false prophet's compassionate and gentle nature, that will cause him to be loved by many nations and tongues, worldwide, who will willingly throw their support behind the Antichrist (not realizing he is an enemy of God). We know that, at first, he will quietly be acquiring power and influence around the world. But, as we see in Revelation 17 and 18, the sins and abominations of the woman in purple and scarlet will catch up with her, and the Antichrist will destroy her, as he will anyone else that he considers to be a threat.

As we move on to the next "heavily-debated subject", I think it is worth noting that the enemy gets things rolling at the beginning of the final three and a half years, by raising up two key players, the

Antichrist and the False Prophet, who will work in concert to spread the serpent's wickedness across the entire globe. Is this another one of those "copy-cat moves" by the enemy meant to deceive many, or even preempt what God has in store, for this period? I would say, "Yes."

In the great spiritual chess match that I like to call "the seed war," the Lord will respond with two key players of His own. They will be working together, as well, to counteract the works of the beast and his unholy alliance with Rome, by bringing forth a message of repentance and impending judgment to those who reject God's offer of mercy and redemption.

THE TWO WITNESSES

And I will grant authority to my two witnesses, and they will prophesy for twelve hundred and sixty days, clothed in sackcloth. These have the power to shut up the sky, so that rain will not fall during the days of their prophesying; and they have power over the waters to turn them into blood, and to strike the earth with every plague, as often as they desire. When they have finished their testimony, the beast that comes up out of the abyss will make war with them and overcome them and kill them. [Revelation 11:3, 6-7 NASB]

Although we can never know for sure, since the Lord does not provide us with concrete predictions regarding the timing or sequence of all these end-time events, I believe it is safe to conclude that the unveiling of the Antichrist, the Abomination of Desolation, and the appearing of God's "Two Witnesses" happen closely to one another.

In Revelation Chapter 11:1-2, the Lord instructs John, in this vision, to measure the Temple of God, all except the outer court (which is reserved for the Gentiles…this points to the "sharing agreement" of the Temple Mount that will be part of the seven-year peace agreement). And it says that the holy city will be "tread under foot" (or under the authority of the forces of Antichrist) for forty-two months, or three and a half years.

This, as we discovered earlier, is the official declaration that the final half of the tribulation period has begun. So, the Third Temple will have been built during the first three and half years, the Temple sacrifices will have been restored, as well, and the Temple Mount will be shared by the Jews and the Gentiles. But, according to Scripture, the Antichrist will make an announcement (at the middle of the seven years) that the sacrifices in the Temple will be no longer permitted. Some believe this is likely to be outrage from the voices of "animal rights activists" who will see the reinstitution of the sacrifices as "animal cruelty." Oh yes, the Antichrist will seem very "politically-correct," yet behind the mask, he will be as evil as the day is long.

At this point, it is "Game On." The Antichrist has been revealed, the Temple sacrifices have been stopped and this "man of sin" will declare himself to be equal with God. And, what is the very next thing we read about in Revelation 11, the appearance of the "Two Witnesses," who will be commissioned to prophesy against the wickedness in the world and call for repentance. These two men will have great powers, as well. They can stop the rain (as Elijah did), they can bring about plagues (as Moses did), and even turn the waters to blood (which was part of the judgment associated with the second trumpet.

But, who are these two men or, are they even men? Some might say that they are angelic beings. Once again, this is hard to say for sure. Some say they are the spirits of Elijah and Moses (for the reasons mentioned above). Some say they are the spirits of Enoch and Elijah because they are the only two people in Scripture that never tasted physical death. If we recall, Jesus referred to John the Baptist as the "Elijah who was to come." (Elijah 11:14). So, we can see that Jesus was suggesting that the spirit of Elijah (or someone else) could manifest itself in another human being, if God so chooses.

For that reason, I believe the two witnesses will be two human beings, endowed with special powers from on High. And it says, in Hebrews that "it is appointed for men to die once after this comes judgment." So, it would make sense that Enoch and Elijah would be the ones to reappear…and die a physical death (which, of course, happens to these two witnesses). But, as for me, I tend to think that they are more likely to be the embodiment of Moses and Elijah, for two reasons:

The first, as we talked about, is the fact that they had power over the rain, and the power to strike the earth with plagues. Elijah had power over the rain, and Moses had the power to bring about plagues. So, it seems fitting that since these two powers are specifically given to these two witnesses, and mentioned here in Revelation 11, that they might be the ones.

But secondly, if we look at the following passage from Matthew 17, a good argument could be made that there is a second confirmation of their identity:

> ***Six days later Jesus took with Him Peter and James and John, his brother, and led them up on a high mountain... and He was transfigured before them... and behold, Moses and Elijah appeared to them, talking with Him. Peter said to Jesus, "Lord...if You wish, I will make three tabernacles here, one for You, and one for Moses, and one for Elijah." [Matthew 17:1-4 NASB]***

When I ponder why these two appeared to Jesus at this time, and how Peter wanted to erect three tabernacles (tents), one for each of them, it adds weight to the argument for Moses and Elijah, I believe. After all, when the Lord returns, He will come to "tabernacle (reside) among us." So, Peter must have been on to something, although his timing was not right. It seemed Peter had a knack for often "being in the right church, but the wrong pew," as they say. This seemed to be another example of that.

And to this day, the Feast of Tabernacles is celebrated by the Jews as the seventh and final feast of the year. And it is all about "looking forward" to when the Lord comes and tabernacles with His people forever more.

One more thing, regarding the often-debated timing of the appearance of the Two Witnesses. Some say it will be during the first three and a half years of the time of trouble. Others believe it will be during the second half, once the Antichrist is revealed. But, many have seen a connection between the things we read in prophecy, specifically ones that include a timespan of three and a half years, twelve hundred and sixty days, or forty-two months. The ones assigned that amount of time, in Scripture, all seem to happen during the second half of the tribulation period, and I believe this is the key point for us, as well.

As we know all too well, when these Two Witnesses appear, it is not the end. There is much more to be done by the Lord, before He comes to take His people home, about "forty-two-months-worth."

Coincidence? I tend to think not.

"THESE THINGS MUST HAPPEN FIRST..."
[LUKE 21:9]

CHAPTER TWENTY-THREE

THE GREATEST TRIBULATION

"For then there will be a great tribulation, such as has not occurred since the beginning of the world until now, nor ever will. Unless those days had been cut short, no life would have been saved; but for the sake of the elect those days will be cut short. Then if anyone says to you, 'Behold, here is the Christ,' or 'There He is,' do not believe him." [Matthew 24:21-23 NASB]

If I were writing the above passage (not suggesting I am a better writer than Matthew or Jesus...shut my mouth!!), I might have been inclined to write, "For then there will be the greatest tribulation the world has ever known," since Jesus was saying that the pain and suffering will be reaching levels never experienced before. The Lord certainly is not saying "great tribulation" in the same way I might say "that was a great football game," or that "Amazing Grace" is a great song. No, he is saying the amount and extent of suffering will be exceedingly great (as in "really bad"). Now, that might be obvious, and I get that. But I wonder, sometimes, because we have heard about it so many times (or maybe because we don't think we will be around then) if we might be tempted to minimize the full implications of the phrase, "the Great Tribulation."

Think about the worst thing you have ever seen in your lifetime. Multiply it by a thousand. And that might not even be enough. Things are going to get BAD!! When was the last time you heard men crying out for rocks to fall on them and kill them? It will be beyond anything we have seen or can imagine.

Since we believe the Antichrist will be "in full bloom" by the mid-point of the "final week of Daniel's seventy weeks," we should be looking for a few key developments that will indicate there are only three and a half years left before we see the King of Kings coming in the clouds and every eye will see Him. We have already talked about the Abomination of Desolation and the halting of the Temple sacrifices. And we pointed to the arrival of the "Two Witnesses" who will be revealed by the Lord to stand and prophesy against the two "chosen ones" of God's archrival, Satan (they are, of course, the Antichrist and the False Prophet). Once these things happen, you can start marking off days on your calendar. There will be only forty-two months left for the Antichrist to reign supreme on the earth. His days will be numbered, to say the least. But there are a few other key happenings that will further confirm the times at hand. Let's look at a few of them:

THE 144,000

I want to start off this section with two parallel passages. I think is critical that we understand this. Otherwise, I believe our fears would consume us:

> *"Do not harm the earth or the sea or the trees until we have sealed the bond-servants of our God on their foreheads." And I heard the number of those who were sealed, one hundred and forty-four thousand sealed from every tribe of the sons of Israel: [Revelation 7:3-4 NASB]*

These, of course, were the Jews who were being sealed, twelve thousand from each of the twelve tribes of Israel. That is the most common interpretation, and I tend to agree with it.

> *After these things I looked, and behold, a great multitude which no one could count, from every nation an all tribes and peoples and tongues, standing before the throne and before the Lamb, clothed in white robes, and they cry*

out with a loud voice, saying, "Salvation to our God who sits on the throne, and to the Lamb." [Revelation 7:9-10 NASB]

Here, we see "a great multitude" from among the nations who came, it says, "out of great tribulation" (Revelation 7:14). They have made their robes white (by professing their faith in Christ) and loved not their own life, even in the face of death. In return for their faith, they will hunger no more, thirst no more, and every tear will be wiped from their eyes.

They are the ones, as I see it, who are "the dead in Christ" who will be raised first (or changed in the twinkling of an eye) at the sound of the seventh trumpet, and those who have remained alive throughout the seven years of trouble. And remember, since the Book of Revelation is not sequential, we do not really know exactly when this takes place. I am convinced that this is another view the "gathering of the elect" that we read about in Matthew 24:31, which of course, takes place when the final trumpet sounds at the end of the tribulation period.

But, if we back up a bit to Revelation 6, the fifth seal (and fifth spirit to be released) dealt with martyrdom and was speaking of the ones who would die for His namesake, crying out for justice. But when did they cry out? It's hard to say. Without a clear reference to the timing of these events, it leads to much speculation.

As I mentioned earlier, the Seven Seals could be looked at as preparations being made for the hardships and judgements to come. Remember, as I said, if a scroll has seven scrolls, you cannot fully open it until all seven seals have been removed. So, I am not convinced that the Seven Seals are seven judgements, separate from the trumpets and bowls. John was being shown a number of visions and we are not sure the timing of them. Plus, there does seem to be some overlap occurring in some of his visions.

It gets quite difficult to tell, sometimes, when it seems that similar events are mentioned more than once (like the 144,000 or the reappearance of Babylon, for instance) if those are separate events, or just two different views of the same event. Hence, we see great variations of how and when these things will take place.

I tend to think of the seals more as preparations of the terrible things that would be coming in the final days and years before our Lord returns to claim His bride (such as false prophets, war, financial collapse, martyrdom, etc.). These are all things that will likely happen during the seven years of tribulation, or even the years leading up to them. Here's what it said about the fifth seal in Revelation 6:

"How long, O Lord, holy and true, will You refrain from judging and avenging our blood on those who dwell on the earth?" And there was given to each of them a white robe; and they were told that they should rest for a little while longer, until the number of their fellow servants and their brethren who were to be killed even as they had been, would be completed also. [Revelation 6: 10-11 NASB]

This passage leads to two questions in my mind:

1) Are these martyrs killed during the tribulation period? We do not know. It really does not specify. As we know, many Christians have been martyred for their faith already, and the final seven years have not yet begun. So, are these the martyrs this passage is pointing to? Could be.

2) Are these martyrs in heaven already? Again, I am not sure. We have to remember that this is a vision, and in the vision that John sees, these martyred ones are told that they will have to wait a little while longer, until the rest of the brethren who will die for their faith in Christ join them. But where? From everything else we have talked about, I believe they will be waiting, along with the rest of us who have passed away by then, in the grave. Again, the vision is not clear about the timing or the place. Since this passage is part of the Seven Seals, again, it could just be looking forward to things yet to come.

So, not unlike what we read in Hebrews 11, where the patriarchs of old died, gaining recognition for their faith, yet did not receive the promise...it sounds to me, again, that there is going to be one great big "resurrection party" following the blowing of the seventh trumpet, and that all the saints will be gathered together at that time. In other words, these martyrs are being told, "Have no fear...justice is indeed coming...just not quite yet!!"

It is amazing when you think about it. It reminds me of the Parable of the Workers (Matthew 20), where those who came to work early got paid the same as those who were hired later in the day. The ones who showed up early did not think it was fair, but the landowner did. The workers were made a promise, as we are with the Lord, and nothing was said regarding some getting paid more than others, based on when they started working. That is not the nature of God. Our reward, in the end, will be more than enough no matter when we started working on His behalf. Praise be to Him alone.

Moving on, let's think about this excerpt from the Matthew 24 passage above:

Unless those days had been cut short, no life would have been saved; but for the sake of the elect those days will be cut short. [Matthew 24:22 NASB

What could be so bad that the Lord would feel the need to step in and cut the time short, to avoid a catastrophe that would snuff out all human life before some who are destined for redemption could be saved? Some might say, "nuclear war," others might say "pestilence and plagues," and no doubt, those could both destroy all humanity rather quickly, should the Lord not intervene. But I can think of one other way this could happen…and it seems to coincide with another biblical event that the Lord said will happen before His return to Earth…starvation.

THE MARK OF THE BEAST

And I saw another angel ascending from the rising of the sun, having the seal of the living God; and he cried out with a loud voice to the four angels to whom it was granted to harm the earth and the sea, ³ saying, "Do not harm the earth or the sea or the trees until we have sealed the bond-servants of our God on their foreheads." [Revelation 7:2-3 NASB]

One of the things that often gets overlooked, when people talk about the Mark of the Beast, is the fact that the Lord sends forth His angel first, bearing "the seal of the living God." He is instructed to "seal the bond-servants of our God on their foreheads." Isn't it nice to know that those of us who are set apart for Him, will be protected with the seal of God on our foreheads before the fiery arrows start flying? I know that I, for one, am overjoyed to know we will be protected in those days, should we still be among the living.

Then, as Satan loves to do, after God marks those that are His, he plays "copycat" again and does some marking of his own:

And he causes all, the small and the great, and the rich and the poor, and the free men and the slaves, to be given a mark on their right hand or on their forehead, and he provides that no one will be able to buy or to sell, except the one who has the mark, either the name of the beast or the number of his name. [Revelation 13:16-17 NASB]

So, let's review what is happening here in Chapter 13. It starts with a beast coming up out of the sea and standing on the seashore. Now, for the record, it is widely accepted by most biblical scholars that the word "beast" often refers to a kingdom or empire, not a person. This first beast, as we talked about earlier, is said to have ten horns and seven heads. Many believe this refers to a ten-nation alliance which very likely be the revival of the Holy Roman Empire (or as we are more likely to hear today…the New World Order or the One-World Government). And the seven heads would represent the seven leaders of these ten nations that make up the global alliance that will get its power from Rome.

The second beast in this chapter comes up from the earth, having two horns like a lamb and speaking as a dragon. I believe as many others do that the second beast is some religious entity from which the false prophet will come (One-World Church). And this false prophet will be aligned with the first beast and help him to convince the masses to come under his authority.

This second beast will have been given great authority by the evil one (Satan) to be able to work many signs and wonders, even call down fire from heaven. And he will call for anyone who does not worship the beast to be killed, which will strike fear in the hearts of men and women all over the world. And it is that fear, I believe, that leads so many to willingly accept his mark, thusly signing their own eternal death warrant.

The mark given out by this second beast allows people to buy and sell goods, food, and services. Without this mark, you will not be able to buy or sell anything. This will be the "cashless society" that so many are talking about these days (one-world money system). It will be trumpeted as a good thing. Many believe it would help to greatly reduce crime because no one would be carrying any money or have money in their homes or businesses. We are already seeing early attempts at this with things like Apple Pay and other electronic payment applications. Some suggest there could be a microchip, smaller than a grain of rice, implanted in the bodies of people (maybe even in babies when they are born) that would make it so you would not have to carry a purse, wallet or credit cards. Just wave your hand over a sensing device (like we see now with barcodes), and the payment is made. I, for one, do not believe a microchip would the Mark of the Beast. But I do believe it could be a step in that direction because people would become less opposed to taking "the mark" if they have already been indoctrinated into buying and selling electronically, without using cash.

But yes, of course, there is a huge downside to this. What if an individual does not want to be part of this system? What if parents refuse to allow their babies to be implanted with the chip, or assigned the mark at birth? I would not have wanted that, with our children. They could be squeezed out of existence. They will not be able to buy food, clothing, gas, or anything else, for that matter. They would eventually starve to death, that is unless the Antichrist's militia gets to them first and puts them out of their misery. This doesn't sound like a very pretty picture being painted for the redeemed of the Lord who might still be alive in those days. Maybe the "early departure plan" is not such a bad thing to hope for, right?

As Jesus said, "Fear not, I will be with you, even to the end of the age," and at this point, take note, the end of the age has not yet come. But we will not be alone. God will be with us. His angels will be surrounding us, and He will protect and provide for us, as He always has. Nothing bad can ever happen to us, apart from His will, of course. Did He not provide "manna from heaven," when the Jews were crossing the desert from Egypt, on their way to the Promised Land? Of course, He did, and I have no doubt that He will provide for His chosen ones, once again, in the day of trouble.

Yes, I believe many saints will be persecuted and even die during these terrible days. But as we saw, however, numerous times in Part One of this book, God only allows bad things to happen to those that are His when it is for the greater good of His overall mission...the final harvest. And oh...what a great harvest it will be!! I do believe there will be a great revival during the final seven years as many who are unbelievers turn to the Lord, cry out to God for mercy and help. And I believe He will hear their cries and answer them. But again, I think without the presence of the Holy Spirit in the world, working through God's anointed ones, that would not be possible (or should I say, "God's preferred method of operation," since we know that with God, all things are possible).

So here we are, at the end of the seven years, and there remains one more noteworthy event to take place, one that we can be sure that no one will miss. It will not be shrouded in secrecy, trust me. And, it would be a shame not to mention it because it gives us such great hope...for every eye shall see Him:

For just as the lightning comes from the east and flashes even to the west, so will the coming of the Son of Man be. [Matthew 24:27 NASB]

"THY KINGDOM COME, THEY WILL BE DONE..."
[MATTHEW 6:10]

CHAPTER TWENTY-FOUR

"AFTER THE TRIBULATION..."

One of the best arguments for an "early departure" is the idea that, as it says in 1 Thessalonians, "God has not destined us for wrath," and I would agree with that, but I look at it a little differently. I would like to make two points regarding this issue. First, if it is true that we, as believers, will remain on the earth during the seven years of tribulation, I believe God will protect us and provide a way for us to pass safely through the storm, as He did with Noah. Remember what Jesus prayed in John 17:15, *"I do not ask You (Father) to take them out of the world, but to keep them from the evil one.* And as we talked about a few times here, God is able to preserve those that are His while He, at the same time, punishing those who have rejected His grace and mercy.

And secondly, I believe (as many others do) that the seven years of trouble are not God's wrath, but Satan's wrath. They will begin when Michael the Archangel (the restrainer) steps aside and allows Satan and his minions to be cast down to the earth, "having great wrath... knowing that he has only a short time" (Revelation 12:12), causing wickedness to rise to levels never seen before. And the evil one was also given the ability to "make war with the saints" (Revelation 13:7). So, I would say there needs to be saints who are still present on the earth, for him to make war with, right? That is why I say that I believe the tribulation period is "the wrath of Satan," not "the wrath of God." The Bible says definitively that it is the beast who will make war with the saints, not God Almighty.

But up next, we are about to see "the wrath of God" being poured out upon the earth, when our Lord returns, riding His white horse to victory over His enemies, once and for all eternity:

For the wrath of God is revealed from heaven against all ungodliness and unrighteousness of men who suppress the truth in unrighteousness, because that which is known about God is evident within them; for God made it evident to them. [Romans 1:18-19 NASB]

Isn't it interesting that the Apostle Paul writes here, "that which is known about God is evident within them?" He is talking about unbelievers there. He is saying that even though they reject the truth, deep in their hearts, they know it. They have just suppressed it to the point that they can neither see it or hear it, and that is very sad.

And, it is at this point that the third and final woe, "the wrath of God," is about to be poured out upon the world. And those who will suffer it, they are without excuse. They knew the truth but rejected it. For remember, it was said that the Gospel of Jesus Christ had to preached to the whole world before He could return.

THE SEVENTH DAY BEGINS

By this time, the sixth day will have ended, and the seventh day begun. I spoke earlier, just briefly, about "the great and terrible day of the Lord." How is it, we might ask, that it is both great and terrible? My response is, "It depends on who you ask." If you ask one of the redeemed, it will be great. I mean REALLY GREAT!!! But, if you ask those who reject God's mercy and grace, "terrible" might not be a strong enough word.

Once again, as I look at these things at "face value," I understand that the seventh day will last a thousand years. That is one long day!! So, even if it took the Lord thirty days to wipe out His enemies (which I doubt) and reclaim the kingdoms of this world, finally restoring them as the kingdoms of our God, that part will not last long. And since none of us know exactly how these things will unfold, remember in Daniel 12, there was three different numbers relating to the second half of tbe seven years...1260 days...1290 days...and 1335 days. Maybe that points to a slight "time gap" between the official end of Day Six and the start of Day Seven. And again, maybe not? What we do know for sure, however, is that what will remain is a great and glorious day for the people of God, and the rejoicing will never end!!

For those who like quibbling over the details, some do disagree as to when the sixth day officially ends, and the seventh day begins. Who is right? Got me. The Jews believe the Sabbath begins and ends at sunset. We believe each new day begins at midnight. Six of one, half a dozen of the other. What matters is, when darkness falls, it will not be long until a new day dawns. I tend to see the sixth day ending when "Satan's wrath" ends, and "God's wrath begins." So, how does the Lord Jesus introduce the coming of these days in Matthew 24? Let's see:

> ***"But immediately after the tribulation of those days the sun will be darkened, and the moon will not give its light, and the stars will fall from the sky, and the powers of the heavens will be shaken. [Matthew 24:29 NASB]***

The Lord starts this passage with the phrase, "immediately after the tribulation those days." Now, while I would agree that He is referring to the seven years of tribulation being over, I also think there might be "a nod and a wink" to the idea that the first six days have ended, and the "day of rest" is about to begin." And, what marks the beginning of this period that comes after the tribulation? The sun is darkened, the moon does not give its light, stars fall from the sky (notice this is different from "the star that fell from Heaven") and the heavens will be shaken.

> *I looked when He broke the sixth seal, and there was a great earthquake; and the sun became black as sackcloth made of hair, and the whole moon became like blood; and the stars of the sky fell to the earth, as a fig tree casts its unripe figs when shaken by a great wind. [Revelation 6:12-13 NASB]*

Well, what do you know, that is almost exactly how John saw the sixth seal being broken. Sun darkened, moon turned to blood, stars falling from the sky and the heavens being shaken like a fig tree, shaken by a great wind.

So, if we connect the dots, here, there will be a time of great wrath upon the unbelievers of this wicked world. They will continue to refuse to accept the "free gift of God," the salvation of their souls. They will cling to their right to not believe, even in the face of eternal damnation. I think that might be where we got the phrase, "Pride comes before the fall." In this case, it most certainly will. This time of even greater wrath is also known as the "seven bowl (or vial) judgments" that we read about in Revelation 16 (and remember, it seems to be a logical conclusion that the seventh seal, the seventh trumpet and the seventh bowl judgement all happen right around the same time...since they all bring thunder, lightning, hail, and a great earthquake). But I want to mention one more thing that happens at this moment in time, as we pass from Day Six into Day Seven:

But for those who may still be struggling with the idea that God's wrath will be poured out at the beginning of the Day Seven (at the very end of Day Six) rest assured, God's judgments are swift and thorough. So, whether we prefer to think of His wrath as coming "before the strike of midnight," or just after, it will not matter much. It is coming, and it will not last very long. In fact, we might be given a hint as to just how long it will last, in the very next passage, which talks about sounding of the seventh trumpet:

And the temple of God which is in heaven was opened; and the ark of His covenant appeared in His temple, and there were flashes of lightning and sounds and peals of thunder and an earthquake and a great hailstorm. [Revelation 11:19 NASB]

Hmmm...that's interesting. It says that this is when "the temple of God in heaven was opened." And this appears when John sees his vision of the seventh trumpet, at the end of the seven years of tribulation. So, silly me, my mind is thinking, "Was the temple of God not opened before that? I mean, if the departed saints are all in Heaven before this time, why was the temple not opened? Jesus did say, 'I go to prepare a place for you, that where I am you may be also (John 14). If that place was ready for the saints to come as far back as the time of the resurrection (as many believe), wouldn't you think the temple of God in heaven would be open for them to commune with their God? I would think so. Enquiring minds want to know!! Up next... breaking of the seventh and final seal ...Heaven falls silent:

> ***When the Lamb broke the seventh seal, there was silence in heaven for about half an hour. And I saw the seven angels who stand before God, and seven trumpets were given to them... And the seven angels who had the seven trumpets prepared themselves to sound them. [Revelation 8:1-2, 6 NASB]***

So, we see here that John talks about how, in his vision, ***"there was silence in heaven, for about half an hour."*** Now, can we assume that would be a literal thirty minutes? I would say, "No." In Scripture, things often have a literal meaning and a figurative one. I do not know if this silence refers to the amount of time it took for the Lord to destroy His enemies (again...it is not really clear), or maybe to John, this part of his vision seemed to take about half an hour (my understanding of Heaven does not include the passing of time, as here on Earth). Who can say for sure? Just as we have seen many times, we will never in this lifetime fully understand all of the tiny details...some things are left to faith. We just need to trust God and believe He is in complete control, no matter what happens. For the sake of our discussion, here, let's just say there appeared to be (at least in John's perception of things) a small and temporary period of silence in Heaven. One might call it, "the calm before the storm."

For instance, when we read about the opening of the seventh seal, it clearly refers to the moment that the seven angels were given the seven trumpets, and they prepared themselves to sound them. And even that can be a little confusing, because did we not already talk about the blowing of six of the trumpets? Why are we now talking about the seven trumpets getting ready to blow? I can only go back to the fact that the Book of Revelation is not sequential. John received, in pieces, these visions of what would happen. They were not meant to be "time or order specific." It is a little bit like watching an episode from the TV show, "Lost." Sometimes they were leaping forward in time, at other times they leaped backwards in time, and at other times they were showing what was happening in the present. But for the viewer (I will raise my hand), at times it was a bit confusing. Just sayin'...call me old fashioned, but I prefer a story that unfolds sequentially. Sure... all that hoppin' around may be creative and edgy. But is it necessary?

God chose to reveal things a little differently, and that is fine by me. If we think about the letters to the seven churches, they were all lumped together in John's vision. But what is the timing of these letters? When were these messages delivered to the respective churches? Was it back then, around the time of John's writing of the Book of Revelation? Most assume that, as I do. But we really do not know. Were they all to be delivered at roughly the same time, or were they to be delivered over many months, or even years? Scripture does not say. We just know they seemed to be speaking to specific congregations, back in the first or second century (John wrote Revelation near the end of the first century). And apparently, we are led to believe those same messages would be relevant to those of us who follow Christ as the day of His return draws near (I certainly hope I am part of those who most closely relate to the Church at Philadelphia...the Lord seemed to have a soft spot for them!!).

I think we have to look at all of the visions recorded in the Book of Revelation that way, especially the ones which seem to be set in Heaven. God is not bound by our earthly limitations of time. He reveals what He chooses to reveal, whenever He chooses to reveal it. It does not mean it will occur in a certain order or timeframe. If something is revealed in Revelation 12, I think it would be wrong to insist that it happens after the things we see in Revelation 11. That is why they are called "parenthetical chapters." We have to be careful, then, when we look at matters regarding future biblical events, to not jump to conclusions regarding the order or timing of these things. We are on a "need to know basis," and I am just fine with not knowing all the details. When we see these things happening, we will know what time it is.

And that brings us to the second occurrence in this part of the Lord's words, from Matthew 24, the ones dealing with the time he referred to as being, "after the tribulation of those days."

And then the sign of the Son of Man will appear in the sky, and then all the tribes of the earth will mourn, and they will see the SON OF MAN COMING ON THE CLOUDS OF

THE SKY WITH POWER AND GREAT GLORY. [Matthew 24:30 NASB]

The Lord continues, after talking about the darkening of the sun and moon, and heavens being shaken, by saying, "And then the sign of the Son of Man will appear in the sky…" and, "they will see the Son of Man coming in the clouds of the sky with power and great glory." It does not seem likely to me, when we put the pieces all together, that He will "appear in the sky" before the seven years of great trouble and His coming "with power and great glory." It all seems to be one continuous event, not separate events. I cannot envision Him appearing in the sky (apparently not yet in power and glory), calling His people home, and then disappearing back into the clouds only to return seven years later in power and great glory. That would be three trips to Earth, not two, if you ask me…and I see no biblical support for that.

So, after many years of studying, praying and seeking God's to allow me to better understand His ways, I am led to believe with all my heart that His coming will happen at the end of the seven years of tribulation, not before them. But, I say again, for those who see these things differently, I love and respect you as co-laborers of the Gospel of Christ. These are not "salvation issues" we are talking about here. We just disagree about what time the train is going to come and take us home. Meanwhile, what matters is…we all know that train is coming…so "be ye ready."

THE FIRST RESURRECTION

As I researched these things for this book, and during my years of listening and reading how others perceived the "hows and whens" of the catching away, one thing always struck me as peculiar. Those who believe in an "early departure" rely heavily on the words of the Apostle Paul and his writings in 1st and 2nd Thessalonians. And when I read the passages they often point to, I can understand how that might lead to that conclusion. But this same Paul, in the same letters to the Thessalonians, seemed to say things that appear very contrary to that conclusion, as well:

> **But we do not want you to be uninformed, brethren, about those who are asleep, so that you will not grieve as do the**

> *rest who have no hope. For if we believe that Jesus died and rose again, even so, God will bring with Him those who have fallen asleep in Jesus. For this, we say to you by the word of the Lord, that we who are alive and remain until the coming of the Lord, will not precede those who have fallen asleep. [1 Thessalonians 4:13-15 NASB]*

First, we see Paul talking about those who have "fallen asleep.". He does not say, "I do not want you to be uninformed about those who have died and are cheering us on from Heaven with the Lord." He is saying that one day, when the Lord returns for us, God will bring back to Heaven with Jesus, those who have fallen asleep in the Lord, and those who remain alive in Christ at this time, as well. It would be hard for me to conclude from Paul's words that all of the believers in Christ, those dead and yet alive, had already checked out seven years earlier. And, it would be hard to imagine that there are yet Christians who are washed in His blood and still alive at this time if all the redeemed were taken home before the tribulation period started. Think about it, if all the believers who are alive suddenly disappear when the seven years begin, any Christians alive after that would have to be saved during those seven years. Anyone already saved will have caught the first plane out.

Of course, those who are awaiting that early departure believe there will be people saved after the rapture happens. I do, too. But, I do not believe that could happen if the Holy Spirit were no longer present on the earth. It is the Holy Spirit that convicts us and leads us to repentance. We are not able to do that by ourselves. The Bible teaches that no one can come to the Lord unless the Father draws them (John 6:44). And, how does He draw them? By the power of the Holy Spirit, of course, and the Lord chose that the Holy Spirit would reside in and operate through us, His people. So, not unlike those who believe in a pre-trib rapture, I agree that if we are gone from the earth, so is the Holy Spirit. How then, are those who are "left behind" to be saved? It all gets a bit too confusing for me. I believe God intends for His people to be present and active at this most crucial point in human history. I believe He wants us to display His glory in the midst of the greatest darkness…and emerge victorious in Christ.

THE SEVENTH TRUMPET

So, getting back to what we were talking about, whether we are asleep and awaiting our resurrection, or yet alive and awaiting the moment we are changed in the twinkling of an eye, it is at His coming, at the sounding of the seventh trumpet, that we take on the incorruptible and become "like Him." Here is how Paul explained it:

For the Lord Himself will descend from heaven with a shout, with the voice of the archangel and with the trumpet of God, and the dead in Christ will rise first. Then we who are alive and remain will be caught up together with them in the clouds to meet the Lord in the air, and so we shall always be with the Lord. Therefore comfort one another with these words. [1 Thessalonians 4:16-18 NASB]

I know I am comforted by these words. Hopefully, you are, as well. What a glorious day that will be. Paul writes that He will descend with a shout (nothing secret about that), and THEN, we will be caught up with them (the dead in Christ) and meet Him in the air (raptured… taken by force…Satan will not be able to stop Him) so we shall always be with the Lord. Hallelujah. Come, Lord Jesus!!!

Here's how our Lord Jesus described it, in Matthew 24:

And He will send forth His angels with a great trumpet and they will gather together His elect from the four winds, from one end of the sky to the other." [Matthew 24:31 NASB]

Yes, and Amen!! The elect will be gathered together, those who are asleep, and those who are yet alive. And, I believe that final trumpet will sound after the wrath of God has been poured out and His enemies are defeated, not before. I tend to think His wrath is what will come "as a thief in the night," and you don't sound a trumpet to announce the arrival of a thief. Robbers comes in silence, and under cover of darkness. But not our Lord. In a moment, everything will all change. Every eye will see Him, for it says, **"all the tribes of the earth will** *mourn, and they will see the Son of Man coming on the clouds of the sky..."*

But before moving on, I want to point out one more amazing prophetic fulfillment that the sounding of the seventh trumpet brings about. Remember when we were talking about the Seven Feasts of Israel? Well, let's look at the passage where God announces the Feast of Trumpets. I believe a great mystery is revealed, here, for "those who have eyes to see."

> *Again the LORD SPOKE TO MOSES, SAYING, "Speak to the sons of Israel, saying, 'In the seventh month on the first of the month you shall have a rest, a reminder by blowing of trumpets, a holy convocation. You shall not do any laborious work, but you shall present an offering by fire to the LORD.'" [LEVITICUS 23:23-25 NASB]*

Isn't it interesting that the Lord decreed that the Feast of Trumpets would fall on "the first day of the seventh month?" Have we not been talking about how the seventh trumpet would sound at the beginning of the seventh day (the day of rest)? So here, the Lord confirms that on the first day of the seventh month (prophetically pointing to the beginning of the seventh thousand-year period since creation, I believe), when the trumpet sounds, He says "you shall have a rest... you shall not do any laborious work..." That is why I believe we will be gathered to Him after His wrath has been poured out. The seventh trumpet ushers in "a time of rest." Is that amazing, or what? None of this is happenchance...it is all by design from the hands of the Great Designer.

Ok, so God's wrath has been poured out, His enemies defeated, and the redeemed are gathered unto Him in the clouds. What happens next? I am so glad you asked. I was growing tired of sounding like "a prophet of doom." There are some miraculous things about to happen, and I would not want to miss them for the world.

THE MILLENNIAL KINGDOM

Then I saw an angel coming down from heaven, holding the key of the abyss and a great chain in his hand. And

> *he laid hold of the dragon, the serpent of old, who is the devil and Satan, and bound him for a thousand years;* [Revelation 20:1-2 NASB]

Besides the fact that our Lord, Savior and King Jesus will once again "dwell among us," here on Earth, there is one other major change that will make "the great and terrible day of the Lord" exceedingly great. His enemies will be defeated and the chief adversary of God, Satan, along with those who followed him in his rebellion, they will be bound (or we can say imprisoned) for almost the entire one thousand years that Christ will reign here on Earth.

There will be one brief period of time, however, near the end of the thousand-year reign, where Satan will be released again. But that is to test those who did not live before the coming of the Lord. These are the ones who will be born during the thousand years following Christ's return. Yes, there will be children born then, and they must be given a chance to freely accept God's offer of salvation or reject it, just as we were given that chance. No one will be able to see the New Heaven and New Earth without having had the chance to reject or accept God's mercy and grace. No one will inherit entrance into the eternal Kingdom of God, other than through displaying faith in Jesus Christ as their Lord, Savior, and King over all of creation.

> *"In that day there will be no light; the luminaries will dwindle. For it will be a unique day which is known to the Lord, neither day nor night, but it will come about that at evening time there will be light. And in that day living waters will flow out of Jerusalem, half of them toward the eastern sea and the other half toward the western sea; it will be in summer as well as in winter."* [Zechariah 14:6-8 NASB]

There are three things included in this passage of which we should take note. Included, here, are three important confirmations of who He is. And it prompts me to reiterate what I have said since the beginning of this book, "What God has done in the past, regarding His people, is what He will continue to do in the future, He is God, and He changes not:

1) We know that Jesus is "the light of the world." But, in the millennial kingdom, there will be no lights in the sky. It says, "the luminaries (sun, moon, and stars) will dwindle." He will truly be the light of the world. Not, just spiritually speaking, but He will physically be the light source. It says, ***"it will come about that at evening time there will be light."*** If the luminaries have gone dark, it can only be the light of the Lord that lights the world in those days.

2) We know from when Jesus met the Samaritan woman at the well, that He is the source of "living water." Here, it says that ***"living waters will flow out of Jerusalem,"*** and from where else could they come, but from the Lord Himself.

3) And, of course, we know from the Parable of the Fig Tree, Jesus said that when we see the fig tree (Israel) bloom, we will now "summer is near." Well, my friends, when the Lord establishes His earthly kingdom…know this…summer has come!!!

But, let's not forget, the Scriptures are clear that at the end of this "day of rest," Satan will be released for a short period before being cast into the "lake of fire" for all eternity. But if all the enemies of God are to die when God pours out His wrath, just before the seventh trumpet sounds and "the elect" are gathered unto Him, why would Satan again be released? Certainly, the redeemed will not be tested a second time, right?

I am so glad you asked that question. It is one I wondered about for many years. But the Bible does give us a helpful hint. It says that those who are part of the "first resurrection," they will not be subject to "the second death," which is eternal death, otherwise referred to as "eternal separation from God" (as opposed to "eternal life with God" in His eternal Kingdom). So, if there is a first resurrection, then, there must be a…you got it!!

THE SECOND RESURRECTION

As we discussed earlier, there will be some people who are born, and even die, during the thousand-year reign of Christ, here on Earth. We know that at the sound of the seventh trumpet, the dead in Christ shall rise first, and then those who are yet alive and in Christ, they will be changed from corruptible to incorruptible in the twinkling of an eye. But what about the dead who are not "in Christ," and how about those who are still alive, but have not accepted Christ as Lord and Savior? How do they fit into the millennial picture, or do they fit there at all? The Bible makes it quite clear that at the end of the thousand-year reign of Christ, there will be another resurrection, this one for those who have died in their sins, either before the thousand-year reign, or during it.

So, let's recap. The "first resurrection" (not counting Christ and those who were raised with Him, of course) is what happens at the seventh trumpet. It will be for the redeemed of the Lord, both those who have died and those who are yet alive at that time. But the dead who are not in Christ, they will continue to sleep for a little longer (I usually would say, "Lucky them," but this time, not so much!!)

However, most Christians and biblical scholars do agree on this point. Out of those who are alive at the time of the seventh trumpet, and are not "believers in Jesus Christ," some will survive and live on, even as Christ sets up His millennial kingdom here on Earth. And, of course, those who are resurrected, or changed at His coming, they will be alive and present (although with new bodies), as well. This will allow some unbelievers to be convicted, repent and seek the Lord in those days, since the Holy Spirit will still be present and active in His people, at that time. The Lord always prefers to work through His people, not apart from them.

Let's take a look at what the Lord revealed to the prophet Isaiah around twenty-seven hundred years ago in Israel. And, I believe that this prophecy was as much for us today, as it was back then. They were looking forward to a day when God would deliver them and establish His Kingdom here on Earth, as well, just as you and I are today:

> *"For behold, I create Jerusalem for rejoicing and her people for gladness. And there will no longer be heard in her, the voice of weeping and the sound of crying. No longer will there be in it an infant who lives but a few days, or an old man who does not live out his days; for*

the youth will die at the age of one hundred and the one who does not reach the age of one hundred will be thought accursed. They will build houses and inhabit them; they will also plant vineyards and eat their fruit...for as the lifetime of a tree, so will be the days of My people." [Isaiah 65:18-22 NASB]

This passage has been the subject of much debate, also, for a couple of reasons. First, in the verse preceding this passage it says, "I create new heavens and a new earth (v 17)," but we need to be careful in jumping to conclusions, there, because when the "new heavens and new earth" finally do come, there will be no more dying. That would be the eternal kingdom of God, which will be revealed following the thousand-year reign. So, I tend to think that Isaiah was seeing both, the new heavens and new earth, and the millennial kingdom since there will still be some being born and others dying at that time. He just may not have seen a distinction between the two. Let's face it, when studying prophecy, it is easy to misunderstand what the prophets saw, and mistakenly put things into separate boxes. Hence the phrase, "rightly dividing word of truth..." (2 Timothy 2:15).

Don't you wish there was a Google or Siri, primarily dedicated to the things of God? A place where we could get an instant download of the correct information of all things related to spiritual things and the afterlife? I know, I do. As I did my research for this book, I was constantly amazed at how many different theories there are out there on just about every aspect of end-time events. It seemed like I was like walking through a maze that had no way out, at times.

Secondly, in this passage, Isaiah is prompted to speak about "an infant who lives but a few days." That refers, I believe, to the types of childhood diseases that seem to be on the increase in recent generations (which I think also points to the fact that the day of His return is drawing near). He is saying, that when Christ returns, and Satan is bound for one thousand years, that will not happen any longer. And it says that young people will live to be (at least) one hundred years old. But, it does not say that no one will die. It only says that if a young person does die before the age of one hundred, he or she will be thought to be accursed (in sin).

And lastly, it says that a man's length of life will be similar to that of a tree and that they will not die "before their time." I believe that means that since Satan is bound and unable to tempt, he will not be able to cause some to "die before the fullness of their days" as many do now (thanks to crime, wars, and disease...all tools of Satan).

But, as we see in Scripture, Satan and his minions will be released near the end of the thousand year reign of Christ, for one more round of rebellion against God (and he will gather forces to go after Jerusalem again), and to tempt those who have not yet been tested. Those of us who were already set apart for eternal life will not need to be tested again. However, the devil's "last rebellion" will be short-lived. He and those who choose to follow him instead of Christ, like the tares in the parable, will be cast into the Lake of Fire. This is, as I mentioned earlier, "the second death."

TWO JUDGMENTS...OR JUST ONE??

This is, yet, another discrepancy that often arises among who study these things. The Bible mentions two coming judgments. The first is called, "the judgment of the sheep and the goats." The second is called, of course, "the white throne judgment." But here is question...will there be two distinct judgments, or are there just two different accounts of the same one. The first one was spoke of by Jesus, Himself, and the second one is recorded by the Apostle John, in the Book of Revelation. I believe a solid argument could be made for both conclusions. So, let me see if I can draw some distinctions from both passages and try to explain how I perceive the puzzle pieces falling into place, regarding this matter.

> *"But when the Son of Man comes in His glory, and all the angels with Him, then He will sit on His glorious throne. All the nations will be gathered before Him; and He will separate them from one another, as the shepherd separates the sheep from the goats; and He will put the sheep on His right, and the goats on the left." [Matthew 25:31-33 NASB]*

Here we have Jesus, coming in his glory, and His angels with Him. This sounds like it occurs before the New Heaven and New

Earth are revealed because it says, "all the nations will be gathered before Him," and there will still be goats (meaning there still will be unbelievers alive at this time). So, I believe this will happen at the end of the thousand-year reign. Here Jesus speaks of those who "fed Me and clothed Me," Those are the sheep, and they will be put on His right. And then there are those who did not feed Him and clothe, Him, even though He was hungry and naked." These are the goats and will be put on His left. Of course, He was speaking of the poor, hungry and naked among us. And, He was saying "if you did it to the least of them, you did it to Me."

So, this judgment seems to be based on good works. And those that did not "feed Him or clothe Him" were judged for their unwillingness to care for those that were hurting among them. They had rejected the Lord and His mercy (which brings forgiveness of sin), so they were judged by their lack of good works. They trusted in themselves, rather than God. Therefore, they will be told, "Depart from Me, into the fire prepared for the devil and his angels." The judgement of the sheep and the goats is one based on works, not faith in Christ. So, the goats will share in the punishment of the "great tormentor and seducer of mankind," and I believe that happens at the end of the thousand years, as well.

> *Then I saw a great white throne and Him who sat upon it, from whose presence earth and heaven fled away, and no place was found for them. And I saw the dead, the great and the small, standing before the throne, and books were opened; and another book was opened, which is the book of life; and the dead were judged from the things which were written in the books, according to their deeds. And the sea gave up the dead which were in it, and death and Hades gave up the dead which were in them; and they were judged, every one of them according to their deeds. Then death and Hades were thrown into the lake of fire. This is the second death, the lake of fire. And if anyone's name was not found written in the book of life, he was thrown into the lake of fire. [Revelation 20:11-15 NASB]*

In this judgment account, the Lord sitting on a white throne (we were not told the color of the throne in the words of Jesus from Matthew 25) and it says "the dead, great and small" were standing before Him. Then it talks about books (more than one). It says the dead were judged by what was in one of the books, according to their deeds (sounds like the judgment of the sheep and goats). Even the sea gave up its dead at that time. So, I believe when it speaks of "the dead" who were judged, it means those who have no hope or those who are not "in Christ." They will be judged by their deeds which will be recorded in a book. Then, they will be cast into the lake of fire along with the devil and His angels. This, it says "is the second death," which we talked about earlier.

Then, we hear about another book that will be opened, the Book of Life. It goes on to say, at the end of this passage, that "if anyone's name is not found written in the Book of Life, he (or she) will be thrown into the lake of fire. So, it sounds like everyone's name will be in one book or the other. The people found in this book will obviously NOT be judged according to their deeds. They will have accepted the gracious gift of forgiveness for their sins, purchased by the Lamb of God and His precious blood upon the Cross, two thousand years ago. These, of course, will be the redeemed, the elect, the forgiven ones in whom the Bible says, "the Lord sees no guile." All praise and honor to Him who died on our behalf, or we would be headed to that burning lake, along with the goats who rejected Him. But, thankfully, "His arm is not so short that it cannot save," the Bible says. Question is, which book is your name in?

So, as much as I have studied the two renderings of these judgments, and as much as I believe that both views of these judgments have some merit, I believe we are reading two different accounts of the same judgment, the white throne judgment at the end of the thousand-year reign. I believe that Jesus spoke of "the sheep and the goats" to highlight how the goats would be judged "according to their deeds," because they did not receive Christ and the forgiveness found in His blood. So, by their own works, they shall be judged. They had a choice, just as we did. They chose to trust in themselves and reject His grace and mercy, as sad as it is to say. It says in the Bible that, "the Father desired for all to come to repentance." Obviously, many will not.

Then, we hear about the sheep who was placed on the Lord's right, being judged by a different book, the Book of Life. These were not judged by their good deeds (or lack thereof), but rather by the good works of Jesus, as Savior of the world. They will be judged not by what they did, but rather by what He did on their behalf. All I can say is, if you have not been encouraged by the things we have talked about in this book up to this point, right about now, you should be. Especially if you have applied the blood of the Passover Lamb, Jesus Christ, to the doorposts of your heart. If you have not, what are you waiting for? No man is promised tomorrow. Sooner or later, for all of us, our time for making decisions will run out, and the door of the Ark will be closed.

But I want to touch very briefly on one more notable event, before talking about the new heaven and new earth. There is a great wedding coming soon, but when? You think Princess Diana's wedding was something? You will not want to miss this one.

THE MARRIAGE OF THE LAMB

Here is what it says about this blessed event. Read closely, my friends:

Let us rejoice and be glad and give the glory to Him, for the marriage of the Lamb has come and His bride has made herself ready." It was given to her to clothe herself in fine linen, bright and clean; for the fine linen is the righteous acts of the saints. Then he said to me, "Write, 'Blessed are those who are invited to the marriage supper of the Lamb.'" And he said to me, "These are true words of God." [Revelation 19:7-9 NASB]

Not unlike the words of Jesus, in Matthew 24, we are foretold of another glorious coming celebration, but we are not told when it will happen. Here, John sees a vision that proclaims, "His bride has made herself ready." According to Jewish tradition, while the bridegroom is away, "preparing a place" for him and his bride to dwell in, the bride readies herself for His return (she does not go with the groom at this time). He will then, at the appropriate time, come back and get her. She must get ready before he returns, not after he comes back for her. I believe that is how it will be with the Lord's return, as well. Then the very next thing recorded, two verses later in Revelation 19, is the coming of Christ upon His white horse, and it says He will "judge and wage war."

So once again, this passage above does not appear to be a vision of a great wedding feast happening in Heaven, specifically. It only speaks of the marriage of the Lamb. It appears to focus more on the fact that the bride is now ready for her groom to return. But a few verses later in verse 17, after the Lord judges and wages war, an angel cries out, "Come, assemble for the great supper of God."

I would tend to look at it in much the same way as we do with modern weddings. You have a marriage ceremony, where the groom officially takes his beloved bride, a joining that no man can put asunder. Then, a bit later, there is a wedding feast with much jubilation, great food and dancing for joy. The time for waiting and readying has passed. The Bridegroom has come...just as he promised He would.

THE NEW JERUSALEM

And at long last, we have arrived at our final destination, the New Heaven and New Earth. It is the culmination of all that we have talking about, the final stop on the Gospel Train if you will.

> *Then I saw a new heaven and a new earth; for the first heaven and the first earth passed away, and there is no longer any sea. And I saw the holy city, new Jerusalem, coming down out of heaven from God, made ready as a bride adorned for her husband. [Revelation 20:1-2 NASB]*

There are a couple of interesting points that leaped out at me, from these two short verses. I will tackle the second one first since we just talked about this in the previous section. It says here that the New Jerusalem, the holy city, will be "coming down out of heaven from God, made ready as a bride adorned for her husband." Let's be clear. It does not say, "the bride is coming down out of heaven." It says the New Jerusalem is coming down from heaven, adorned as a bride would be for her husband. Some people have concluded that this is more evidence that the redeemed of Christ will be in Heaven, awaiting this moment.

Once again, that is not what the Scriptures say. That would be a man-made conclusion. And, I am trying to avoid those like the plague, here. So, even in the last few chapters of the Bible, we are still talking about a bride being readied for her husband. The two have not been eternally joined yet (more evidence that these visions are not recorded sequentially). But that day is coming, I have no doubt. I have gotten my invitation, I have accepted and have already RSVP-ed. I am looking forward to it, to say the least. The good news is I will not have to shop for wedding clothes. They will be provided for me. Hallelujah.

But honestly, I was scratching my head a little bit when I read this statement, "there is no longer any sea." That seemed strange to me, why no sea? And when I told my wife about my discovery, she was not pleased. She loves to be by the ocean, and I suspect she thought there would be the best beach ever in Heaven. So, I had to do some digging into this puzzling news. Turns out, that many times in Scripture, the sea is connected with things that are not good. We just read about "the sea giving up her dead," and we know that the Antichrist is depicted as a beast coming up out of the sea. Plus, there are a few mentions in Scripture of this thing called Leviathan, which most people believe is some sort of sea monster (or another reptile-like manifestation of "you know who"). So, in our eternal home, there will be no sea. But there will be a river, however. It is called the River of Life.

And, that leads me to share one more eye-catching detail, this one from Revelation 22. I was amazed to read that on either side of the River of Life, there was a Tree if Life. That got me thinking, in the Garden of Eden, there were two trees mentioned, the Tree of Life and the Tree of the Knowledge of Good and Evil.

Here, in our eternal home, there is no longer any mention of the second tree. That is because it bore the fruit that produced sin and rebellion in mankind. That tree will no longer be needed in Heaven, now that all wickedness has been dealt with forever. And remember, after Adam and Eve ate of the fruit from the forbidden tree, they were forbidden to eat from the Tree of Life. That is because they chose the wrong path. They chose the path that leads to sin and death. Now that sin has been dealt with, those who remain with the Lord forever are welcome to eat of the fruit of the Tree of Life. Ooh, can you imagine how wonderful that will taste? My mouth is watering just thinking about it.

> *And He will wipe away every tear from their eyes; and there will no longer be any death; there will no longer be any mourning, or crying, or pain; the first things have passed away. And He who sits on the throne said, "Behold, I am making all things new." [Revelation 20:4-5 NASB]*

And at last, we behold the promises of God. Behold, all things are new. No more death or sickness. No more mourning, or crying, or pain. He will wipe away every tear from our eyes and "the first things" (the temporary world we live in and all the suffering that goes with it) will have passed away. It will be no more.

Welcome to the end of the End Times. Welcome to the eighth day, the day of new beginnings!!

Right now, in the back of my mind, I can hear MercyMe singing, "I Can Only Imagine."

But on that day, we will not be "imagining things." It will truly be our "forever home!!"

Hope 2 C Ya There!!!

"BEHOLD, I AM COMING QUICKLY"
[REVELATION 22:7]

FINAL THOUGHTS

NOT WHEN YOU THINK...

"Therefore, be on the alert, for you do not know which day your Lord is coming. But be sure of this, that if the head of the house had known at what time of the night the thief was coming, he would have been on the alert and would not have allowed his house to be broken into. For this reason, you also must be ready; for the Son of Man is coming at an hour when you do not think He will."
[Matthew 24:42-44 NASB]

First of all, let me thank you once again, for your interest in this book and for hanging with me as I took "the long way around the block." Hopefully, it was worth the time and effort. I so very much wanted to give you the full picture of how and why I have reached the conclusions that I have, so you would understand where I am coming from. As I said at the outset, "If you want to know what God will do, going forward, it helps to have a solid grasp on what He has done in the past."

And that can be hard, sometimes, because thousands of years have elapsed since the story first began to unfold and there have been countless interpretations by so many well-intentioned people that we sometimes tend to put man's interpretations on the same level as the Word of God, itself, and that is always a dangerous path to walk. That is why for our study, here, I wanted to take the Scriptures at face value, and stay away from the trap of "man's interpretations." As I said before, I believe the Bible is fully able to speak for itself, if we let it.

As we begin this final chapter, I found myself chuckling a bit when I realized that I was inclined to use Matthew 24:42-44 as the passage to begin my final explanations. That was not the plan from the beginning, but it just seemed right.t really captures the main thrust of what I want to say in this book. None of us know when the Lord will return. Even Jesus said that only the Father knows. So, we started off with the disciples asking Him to, "Tell us when these things will happen." And by the end of that same chapter, He had given them many things to be watching for. Yet, He does not give them any firm predictions regarding dates or times to help us zero in on when they will happen.

He just says, "The Son of Man is coming at an hour when you do not think He will." [Matthew 24:44 NASB]

So, after all we have talked about, it comes down to one clear answer...it's not when you think!!

If you are among those waiting for that "early departure," it's not when you think.

If you are persuaded that we are going to have to tough it out with the "late check-out" crowd...it's not when you think.

Here is what the Lord said in Luke 12:

But if that slave says in his heart, 'My master will be a long time in coming, and begins to beat the slaves, both men and women, and to eat and drink and get drunk; the master of that slave will come on a day when he does not expect him and at an hour he does not know..." [Luke 12:45-46 NASB]

It is more than possible that our Father in Heaven will choose a day or hour before I think He will come. So, I better be ready. The Lord could also come at a time beyond that which some are preparing for. And that would be a shame, as well. The risk, there, is one might be less concerned about "getting ready," if they believe they will be called home before the bad stuff starts happening.

So, with all of that in mind, here is my absolute favorite parable from our Lord Jesus. It is special to me for a number of reasons. One of which is that very early in my Christian walk, I became a fan of a young Christian singer, songwriter, and guitarist who was from Northeast Ohio, as I was. His name is Phil Keaggy. He had written and recorded a song called, "Sorry" (which is on YouTube, if you would like to hear it), based on the Parable of the Ten Virgins from Matthew 25. At that point, I was not familiar with the parable...but I loved the song and the message it conveyed. Just to refresh your memory, here is that amazing parable:

> *"Then the kingdom of heaven will be comparable to ten virgins, who took their lamps and went out to meet the bridegroom. Five of them were foolish, and five were prudent. For when the foolish took their lamps, they took no oil with them, but the prudent took oil in flasks along with their lamps. Now while the bridegroom was delaying, they all got drowsy and began to sleep. But at midnight there was a shout, 'Behold, the bridegroom! Come out to meet him.' Then all those virgins rose and trimmed their lamps. The foolish said to the prudent, 'Give us some of your oil, for our lamps are going out.' But the prudent answered, 'No, there will not be enough for us and you, too; go instead to the dealers and buy some for yourselves.' And while they were going away to make the purchase, the bridegroom came, and those who were ready went in with him to the wedding feast; and the door was shut. Later the other virgins also came, saying, 'Lord, Lord, open up for us.' But he answered, 'Truly I say to you, I do not know you.' Be on the alert then, for you do not know the day nor the hour. [Matthew 25:1-13 NASB]*

In this parable, it is interesting that at one point we read that "the bridegroom was delaying." Some were wondering what was taking him so long. They were not prepared to wait that long, and they were running out of oil for their lamps. Then we read that suddenly there was a shout, "Behold, the bridegroom!" I have always liked that about this parable. It addresses both those who think he may come sooner, or later than what our Father may have in mind. Both assumptions could prove to be troublesome. I believe it is far better to not put all our eggs in any one basket, and just make sure we are ready for whatever He brings our way.

One other word of encouragement I would like to share is that just as with the ten virgins in the parable, we need to have our eyes fixed steadily forward...looking ahead to...and anticipating His promised return. When God delivered the Jews from Egypt, as soon as they started encountering difficulties along the way, some of them turned their thoughts back to Egypt saying, "Maybe it wasn't so bad there. Why did we leave? We are out here in the middle of this desert and we may die here, as well. Oh, how I wish we had never left." Here is how the writer of the Book of Hebrews put it:

And indeed, if they had been thinking of that country from which they went out, they would have had opportunity to return. But as it is, they desire a better country, that is, a heavenly one. Therefore, God is not ashamed to be called their God; for He has prepared a city for them. [Hebrews 11:15-16 NASB]

Do not fear and have no doubt, as we learned in Part One, it is God's divine nature to "change not," and "to do that which He has promised to do." We should have to look no further than the birth, death, and resurrection of Jesus Christ to be assured of the fact that the God we serve is a "promise-keeper." He does not and cannot lie. It is not His nature to do so...thanks be to God!!

So, what have we learned in our time together? What does the Bible teach us regarding the nature of God, His eventual return to claim His beloved bride, and in addition, what should we expect to happen when we die? Since the number twelve usually deals with eternal things, here are my twelve conclusions that I am confident will get us safely to the Promised Land (the eternal one), with Christ's help, of course. I believe these are biblically-based and if nothing else, they provide an overview of how I believe things will unfold.

1) God creates order out of chaos. He did that at creation, and He will again as the world descends into chaos again. The

Bible talks about "the restoration of all things." What He said He will do, He will do.

2) God changes not. We often hear that "the best predictor of future behavior…is past behavior." I believe that applies to God, as well. After all, are we not made in His image?

3) The human soul, according to Genesis 2:7 is what results when the body and the breath (spirit) of God are combined. The body without breath is not a soul. The breath of God without a body is not a soul. There is no life where both are not present. Remember, it was the Greek philosophers who first came up with the concept of "an immortal soul" popular. And later, the early Catholic Church fathers embraced the idea. And today, many Protestants and evangelicals still believe there is a soul that is separate from the body and spirit. I believe that can lead us down a dangerous path. We need to ask ourselves this question, "If there is no soul, separate from the body and the breath God gave us, that lives beyond the grave, how can we go to be with the Lord immediately after our physical death? Remember, Daniel was told by the angel Gabriel that he would "enter into rest" (sleep), and then "rise at the end of the age" (not before). If there was a pre-tribulation resurrection of the dead, surely Daniel would be among them, would he not?

4) When we die, since there is no soul (a living being) without a body, our body enters a state of what Jesus and many others referred to as "sleep," where our body awaits its resurrection and life is again breathed into us. Those who die will have no sense of time, and King Solomon wrote, "The dead know nothing." It will be just like going to sleep at night and waking up in the morning. It will seem as if no time has passed. We will not know the difference either way. One moment we will be here…the next moment (as far as we know), we will be resurrected to be with Him where He is forever more. As we read in Hebrews 11:39, I think there will be one amazing "Resurrection Party" for all those who have put their faith in God. Think of a game of "Hide and

Seek" where at the end, someone yells, "All-ee…all-ee…in free!!" (see Romans 6:23)

5) Aside from the longer view, where there are 6000 years (six days) of work, followed by 1000 years (one day) of rest, with the last 2000 years (two days) being the "last two days before Christ returns," I believe "the last days" officially started when Israel became a nation again on May 14th, 1948. Jesus told us that the event would mark the beginning of the last generation. Most Bible experts believe that to be true, and I do, as well.

6) I believe there will be one more great war that will kill a large percentage of the population, worldwide. That will be followed by a peace agreement between Israel and the Palestinians (probably to prevent another war), which will allow the Jews to build the Third Temple and reinstate the Temple rituals and sacrifices (much of the preparations have already been made).

7) Three and a half years after the peace agreement is signed, the Antichrist will fully be revealed as the "man of sin," and he will abolish the Temple sacrifices and we will see the Abomination of Desolation standing in the Temple. At this point, the Antichrist will claim equality with God…and the second half of the tribulation period will have officially begun.

8) We will see the appearance of the "Two Witnesses," who will have great power to do signs and wonders and they will prophesy for three and a half years. Then, they will be killed, resurrected, and taken to Heaven three and a half days later.

9) We will also see the "Mark of the Beast" where no one without the mark will be able to buy or sell anything. And it is the accomplice of the Antichrist, the False Prophet, who will initiate this plan. But don't forget, before that happens, the Lord will send an angel to mark those who are His with the seal of God. And those who bear His mark will be protected and provided for, according to His will. Praise be to His name!!

10) There will be six trumpet judgements that will come upon the earth, and then the wrath of God will be poured out. Following that, the seventh trumpet will blow and the redeemed of the Lord will be gathered (or caught away... if you will) to "meet Him in the air." This will be "the first resurrection." At that time, His enemies will be defeated, and He will establish His Kingdom on Earth for one thousand years. Satan and his demons will be bound for most of that time.

11) Near the end of the thousand-year reign, Satan will be released for a short period to tempt those who have not been tempted or tested before. Then, all the dead who do not know Christ as Savior will be resurrected. It will be the moment when God judges all...Judgement Day, if you will. This will be "the second resurrection." Some will be put on the Lord's right, set apart for the eternal kingdom to come, and the rest will be put on His left and cast into the lake of fire with Satan and his fallen angels.

12) At that point, the New Heaven and New Earth will be revealed, the holy city called the "New Jerusalem," where God will finally see His peace (yir'eh shalim) established once and for all. And we shall be like Him...and with Him forevermore. Praise be to God who is worthy of all praise, honor, and glory forever and ever. Amen.

It is my honest and sincere hope, my friends, that I at least have given you some things to think about. I know that some of my conclusions are different from what you have been taught, or believe, but that is just fine. My goal was not to change anyone's mind, but rather give the reader something to think and pray about. Ultimately, my burden is, just as the Bible says of God, that no one would perish and that all would be saved. Now, of course, I also realize that there are some who will reject His grace and mercy no matter what. I just do not want that to be you...or me...or anyone else for that matter.

So, my goal was to put my thoughts down on paper for two reasons:

1) To point those who will read this book towards putting their faith in Christ as their Savior, if they have not done so already. The price for the sins of all mankind was paid by Jesus at the Cross. But it is up to each of us to choose (free will) to accept or reject the gift of redemption.

2) To help to make sure you have all the information available to make the best decisions along the way so that, if nothing else, you will be ready to meet the Bridegroom, whenever the Father sends Him back to us….and with that in mind, I have prepared a three-step plan to help you make sure you are ready.

BE YE READY

BE YE READY…in body and spirit to go home to be with the Lord, whenever the Lord calls your name (as the Lord said, "It could be tonight that your soul is required of you.") Or, should you still be alive at the time of His return, whenever the trumpet sounds for His angels to "gather the elect," I pray He finds you (and me) ready. This is the easy part because we do not need to pack bags, buy airline tickets or show up at the airport two hours early (only to find out the flight has been delayed by two hours). We merely need to call on the name of Jesus, be willing (to the best of our ability) to turn from our sinful ways (we all have them) and follow Him. The Bible says, "Today is the acceptable day of salvation" and that we should "Call on the Lord while we may be saved." In other words, whether your heart is going to stop beating today (who knows), or should you hear that final trumpet sound and the door to the Ark begins to close, this is one boat you do not want to miss.

He is ready and waiting for you, right now, to sincerely and honestly call His name. Just say, *"Lord Jesus, I realize now that I am a sinner in need of redemption and I realize that You are the only name by which we can be saved. I am asking you today, Lord, forgive me of my sins and be gracious to me by welcoming me into Your Kingdom. Fill me with Your Holy Spirit, so that You can lead me in the way I should go, from this day forward. Thank you, Lord. I pray these things in Your name, Amen.*

BE YE READY...as it says in 2 Peter 4, "in season and out of season" to share the Good News of Jesus Christ with whoever that Lord puts in your path. The Bible is clear that we are to be His witnesses, "as we have freely received, so shall we freely give" to whoever asks. No, you do not have to be a theologian or a Bible scholar to share your faith. The Lord will give you the words when they are needed. And, in fact, many say the best way to share the Gospel with others requires no words at all. All you need to do is *"walk in a manner worthy of His calling"* and *"Let your light shine before men in such a way that they may see your good works..."* The Lord will do the rest.

And lastly, BE YE READY...to face whatever it is the Lord wills for you to face with love, grace, and humility. His grace is always sufficient. If he chooses to call you home before the days of great tribulation, so be it. Consider it a blessing. But, should His plan require you to live on, into the days of great trouble, make sure you have *"put on the full armor of God,"* as Paul wrote to the Ephesians 6. Just as we talked about with the "Ten Virgins," I would not want to be one of the ones who were anxiously awaiting the Bridegroom's return but failed to prepare by "having enough oil for my lamp" and hear these words... *"Truly I say to you, I do not know you." [Matthew 25:12 NASB]*

The Lord does, however, provide us with a prescription for avoiding that terrible outcome:

"Be on the alert then, for you do not know the day nor the hour." [Matthew 25:13 NASB]

As I mentioned at the beginning of this book, I do not consider myself to be a disciple of the "early departure" theory, or a loyalist of the "late check-out" theory, specifically. I like to think of myself as a believer in what I call "the natural order theory." By that I mean, God will unveil all things, as He always has, according to His divine nature. He is not bound by time or space, and nothing is impossible to Him. So yes, He could call us home before the storm clouds roll in and it starts to rain, or He could provide us with a boat to safely carry us through the storm as He did with Noah and his family. I could try to choose my preference, and live my life according to that, but what good would that do? I prefer to do, just as I always have done with everything in my life since surrendering to Christ and becoming "captive to Him" in 1979...as the song says, I will put my hope and trust "In Christ Alone."

When the disciples asked the Lord to teach them to pray, He told them to pray like this:

"Your kingdom come, Your will be done on Earth as it is in Heaven." [Matthew 6:10 NASB]

I opened this book with a quote from Charles Spurgeon, and I would like to end this book the same way:

"If thou art now broken in pieces by a little adversity, what will become of thee in the day when all the tempests of God shall be let loose on your soul? If thou hast run with the footmen, and they have wearied thee, what wilt thou do in the swellings of Jordan? If thou canst not endure the open grave, how canst thou endure the trump of the archangel and the terrific thunders of the last great day? If thy burning house is too much for thee, what wilt thou do in a burning world? If thunder and lightning alarm thee, what wilt thou do when the world is in a blaze, and when all the thunders of God leave their hiding-place, and rush pealing through the world? If mere trials distress thee and grieve thee, oh, what wilt thou do when all the hurricanes of divine vengeance shall sweep across the earth and shake its very pillars, till they reel and reel again? Yes, friends, I would have you, as often as you are tried and troubled, see how you bear it—whether your faith then stance and whether you could see God's right hand, even when it is wrapped in clouds, whether you can discover the silver lining to the black clouds of tribulation." [Charles Spurgeon]

Therefore, be ye also ready: for in such an hour as ye think not the Son of man cometh. [Matthew 24:44 KJV]

"BE YE ALSO READY..."
[MATTHEW 24]

ABOUT THE AUTHOR

I was born, raised and currently live in Northeast Ohio (USA) with my lovely wife, Lauri Lee, and our mini-goldendoodle, Shiloh. Lauri Lee and I have four children and eight grandchildren, at least so far. This is my third book and there are plans to write many more, should the Lord allow. My first book, "Unlocking Creation," dealt with how God revealed aspects of His divine nature in the marvelous things He made. The second one, "The Red Letter Parables," takes a look at not only the forty most-loved parables of our Lord Jesus but the "storyteller," Himself, to see what could be learned about God's nature, as revealed through His only-begotten Son. And that led to this third book, which digs into how God's nature is revealed in one of my favorite subjects, Bible prophecy, and the End Times. I have been telling people for quite some time, "This is the book I have been itching to write for nearly forty years." And, I am so glad that God has brought me to this place where I have finally accomplished it.

On another front, for more than fifty years, music has been the primary release for my creativity, as a musician, singer, and songwriter. I have written and recorded well over two hundred songs in various genres; from Pop and Rock, Modern Country and, of course, Contemporary Christian and Worship music. I am still involved in the worship ministry at our local church, which I enjoy very much. I have often said, "Giving back to God what God gave to me is a great blessing."

But now, God has nudged me to do a different kind of writing, The Lord has led me to share what I have learned over the last thirty-nine years, as a Christian, by writing books that help others come to know Christ better, as well. And I can only hope that your life and your walk with Him is somehow enriched by the reading of them.

Thank you so much for coming along on this ride. God's blessings to you and yours!!

Bob Palumbo

Let's keep the conversation going:

WEBSITE: www.bobpalumbo.com
EMAIL: unlockingcreation@gmail.com
TWITTER: @bobsbooktalk
BLOG: unlockingcreation.wordpress.com

Made in the USA
Columbia, SC
12 January 2021